MULT

Max Haines was bo   t
the age of eighteen,   ed
by a sensational trial taking place in Halifax. Although
twelve witnesses swore they saw the accused drag a
woman down a street shortly before her death, the man
was acquitted.

Max began researching murders from around the
world, past and present, as a hobby. His Crime
Flashback column made its debut in *The Toronto Sun* in
1972, and since then he has researched over fifteen
hundred cases of infamous murders, crimes and scams.

Today, Crime Flashback appears weekly in *The
Toronto Sun* and is syndicated in over forty newspapers
across Canada, reaching an estimated weekly audience
of over three million. The column is also syndicated in
Latin America and is translated into French, Spanish
and Chinese.

Along the way he has written best-selling books on
the subject, including *The Collected Works of Max
Haines, Vol. 1*, which is considered by many to be one
of the finest collections of non-fiction crime stories
ever produced in Canada.

A member of Crime Writers of Canada, Max resides
in Etobicoke, Ontario, with his wife Marilyn.

MAX HAINES

MULTIPLE
Murderers
II

A SIGNET BOOK

NEW AMERICAN LIBRARY

Published in Canada by
Penguin Books Canada Limited, Toronto, Ontario

SIGNET
Published by the Penguin Group
Penguin Books Canada Ltd, 10 Alcorn Avenue, Toronto, Ontario, Canada
M4V 3B2
Penguin Books Ltd, 27 Wrights Lane, London W8 5TZ, England
Penguin Books USA Inc., 375 Hudson Street, New York, New York 10014,
U.S.A.
Penguin Books Australia Ltd, Ringwood, Victoria, Australia
Penguin Books (NZ) Ltd, 182-190 Wairau Road, Auckland 10,
New Zealand

Penguin Books Ltd, Registered Offices: Harmondsworth,
Middlesex, England

First published by the Toronto Sun Publishing Corporation, 1995

Published in Signet by Penguin Books Canada Ltd., 1996

1 3 5 7 9 10 8 6 4 2
Copyright © Max Haines, 1995
All rights reserved

Manufactured in Canada

Canadian Cataloguing in Publication Data

Haines, Max
Multiple murderers II

ISBN 0-451-18950-7

I. Murderers. 2. Murder. 3. Criminals. 4. Serial murderers.
5. Serial murders. I. Title.

HV6515.H35 1996   364.1'523   C95-933116-6

BOOKS ARE AVAILABLE AT QUANTITY DISCOUNTS WHEN USED TO
PROMOTE PRODUCTS OR SERVICES. FOR INFORMATION PLEASE WRITE TO
MARKETING DIVISION, PENGUIN BOOKS CANADA LTD, 10 ALCORN AVENUE,
TORONTO, ONTARIO, CANADA M4V 3B2

ACKNOWLEDGEMENTS

Many individuals and organizations contributed greatly to the writing of this book. I am particularly indebted to the Ontario Provincial Police, Quebec Provincial Police, Scotland Yard and the Federal Bureau of Investigation for their cooperation.

Citizens of Lucan, Ont., Schenectady, N.Y. and Bovingdon, England gave freely of information concerning the sensational crimes which took place in their communities.

Individuals who have contributed time and effort to this book are Tisa Arro, Susan Dugas, Catherine Flannery, Jillian Goddard, Jann Haringa, Bob Johnson, Julie Kirsch, Joe Marino, Anna Morrone, Katherine Webb Nelson, Kevin Tait, Glenna Tapscott, Joyce Wagler and Barbara White.

This book would not have been possible without the dedication of co-editors Glenn Garnett and Maureen Hudes.

A woman named Marilyn helped too.

CONTENTS

MULTIPLE
Murderers
II

Frank Alexander

The organ music could be heard long into the night. No one complained. After all, the Alexanders were otherwise a quiet, respected family who kept pretty much to themselves. No one knew they were as nutty as fruitcakes.

Harold Alexander was a stonemason who had moved with his family from Hamburg, Germany to Santa Cruz, the capital of Tenerife in the Spanish Canary Islands. Harold, 39, was a handsome man who had managed to eke out a living back in Germany. He had moved his family to Santa Cruz when his wife, Dagmar, received a small inheritance.

Once on the island, the Alexanders sought employment. Sabine and Petra, 15-year-old twins, obtained positions as maids at the home of Dr. Walter Trenkler. A native of Germany, Trenkler thought himself fortunate to have two beautiful young German girls as members of his household. It bothered the doctor somewhat that the girls, whom he knew to be deeply religious, never really became friends with any members of his family. They kept strictly to themselves.

The twins' brother, Frank, 16, worked for a shipping firm. The slender, good-looking boy was introverted to the extreme. While he appeared happy enough to colleagues, no one at the shipping firm got to know him well. He was, however, very attentive to his close-knit family.

Dagmar, Harold and a third daughter, Marina, 18, were not employed. The Alexander family would gather at their flat at 37 Calle Jesus Nazareno at every opportunity. On such occasions the drapes would be closed and organ music could be heard far into the night.

The music stopped on the afternoon of December 16, 1970. That was the day Harold Alexander and his son Frank showed up at the residence of Trenkler and asked to see Sabine. The doctor gulped, but summoned his young employee. As the astonished doctor gaped at father and son, soaked from head to foot with brownish caked blood, Sabine entered the room. Her father's first words were, "Frank and I have just finished killing your mother and your sisters."

Trenkler thought he might have misunderstood, but there was no misunderstanding Sabine's reply, "Oh, that's wonderful, father." Then the 15-year-old girl ran to her father and embraced him. As an afterthought, Harold, peering over his daughter's shoulder, addressed the dumbfounded doctor, "My wife and my other daughters; we have killed them. It was the hour of killing."

Trenkler dashed to the other room and called police, although he had a lingering thought: The Alexander family must have met with an accident. His only other theory was that he was dreaming.

When police arrived, Dr. Trenkler briefed them on the strange conversation which had just taken place. He didn't have to point out father and son, who stood before them caked in blood.

Harold Alexander explained to police that he hadn't actually killed his wife and two daughters. He was busy playing the organ at the time. It was the Prophet, better known as his son, Frank, who had actually carried out the sacrifices. Harold explained that the Prophet had declared The Hour of the Great Killing was at hand. Glory to the Prophet and all his holiness. Harold treated the police as if they were stupid creatures from another planet. It was all so simple. The Prophet had ordered the killings.

Police sent a car to 37 Calle Jesus Nazareno. Harold Alexander had told the truth all right. The police who broke down the door of the Alexanders' flat were physically ill and had to leave the premises. No wonder.

Marina's and Petra's naked bodies were in the living room, hacked beyond recognition. Their sex organs had been slashed away. Blood covered the room from floor to ceiling. The victims' clothing, as well as food and broken furniture, were strewn across the floor. Several bloodied knives and a saw were also found nearby. Even the organ keys were covered with blood. Strips of the girls' skin were tacked up on the walls.

The bedroom held additional horrors. Dagmar's body was mutilated. To add to the grisly scene, the murderer had removed her heart, fastened it with a cord and tacked it up on a wall.

Autopsies were performed on all three victims. Despite the horrendous condition of the bodies, the medical examiner was able to ascertain that, in all three cases, death had been caused by repeated blows to the head with a heavy wooden coat hanger found at the scene. Of all the items in the flat, only the coat hanger bore traces of skin and hair.

Considering Harold's initial statement that his son had carried out the killings alone, it was puzzling how he did it in succession with one hanger. Only the two men in the flat at the time of the murders could answer that query.

Frank said his mother had looked at him in a suggestive manner. He realized immediately it was the hour of killing. He picked up the hanger and struck her several times over the head until she fell unconscious. What was Daddy doing? Why, playing the organ, of course. And what were his two sisters doing? Waiting, what else?

Frank proceeded to club first Marina and then Petra into unconsciousness. Daddy played on. When the three women lay dead, Daddy did stop playing long enough to help with the mutilations. And why had Frank the Prophet killed his mother and his sisters? Replying as if his interrogators were simpletons, Frank said, "The lust of the women had to be punished." Harold agreed with his son's account of the slaughter, always referring to Frank as the Prophet.

Sabine, the surviving daughter, was placed in a convent, where one of the nuns became her confidant. She told the nun her two sisters believed implicitly their brother Frank was a prophet with supreme power over them. The girls and their mother would have sat quietly awaiting death at the hands of the Prophet.

Under sympathetic expert questioning, the Prophet explained that back in Germany when he was very young, he and his father had had an incestuous relationship. That's when Daddy started calling him the Prophet. His sisters often crowded into bed with him as well. Frank was one mixed-up lad. He enjoyed sex with his family, who obeyed his every command. In time, the Prophet's demands and wishes were considered his divine right and were to be followed regardless of the consequences.

The family never learned Spanish and didn't attempt to mix with colleagues or neighbors. The clan would gather, draw the drapes, play the organ and do whatever they did under the auspices of the all powerful Prophet.

Psychiatrists had a field day with the surviving Alexanders. It was more or less agreed that Frank's subconscious and conscious were torn between the deep-rooted belief that he was a divine Prophet and the periodic realization that what he and his family were doing was wrong. The conflict became so strong it exploded into a single episode of violence.

Frank Alexander and his father, Harold, were judged unfit to stand trial. They were confined to a mental institution, where they remain to this day. Sabine Alexander stayed in the convent to which she was taken immediately after the murders of her mother and sisters.

Jeremy Bamber

Neville and June Bamber had the world by the tail. They lived in a large home known as White House Farm in Essex, England. Neville, who stood six-feet four-inches, was a former magistrate and wartime fighter pilot. He had inherited an estate well in excess of $2 million, which enabled him and June to settle down to the genteel life which farming affords those who don't have to make a living at it.

Although the Bambers had just about everything, there was one blessing which had been denied them. They were unable to have children. In 1957, after 12 years of trying, they decided to adopt a newborn baby girl. They christened the infant, Sheila. Three years later, the Bambers adopted a second child, a boy, Jeremy.

It would be pleasant to relate that the two darlings were a joy to their parents. Little imagination is required to picture them frolicking about the farm, being kind to the animals, and later attaining superior grades at school. That just didn't happen. From earliest childhood, Jeremy got his jollies from torturing the domestic animals on the farm. Sister Sheila proved to be a handful from an early age as well. The child wouldn't obey her parents and seemed to relish getting into trouble.

As the two youngsters were growing up, they were sent to the best schools, where they distinguished themselves by their atrocious behavior. Jeremy picked on younger, smaller boys, while Sheila was borderline unmanageable.

When Sheila was 17, she talked her parents into allowing her to move out on her own to London.

Generous Neville provided her with a $30,000 per year allowance to make ends meet. Nicely ensconced in a West End flat, the attractive Sheila soon obtained sporadic modelling jobs. She also married a boy from back home. In the following two years she had two miscarriages, gave birth to twins, Nicholas and Daniel, and divorced her husband.

Around this time, Sheila was heavily into marijuana and cocaine. As a result, she became paranoid, firmly believing that everyone in authority was her blood enemy. Sometimes she felt she was possessed by the devil. On more than one occasion, she ended up in St. Andrew's Hospital. Sheila was slowly going around the bend.

While sister Sheila was having her mental problems, Jeremy had turned into an obnoxious playboy. In 1984, Neville financed a cottage and farm for him at Goldhanger in an attempt to straighten him out. He had no way of knowing that his son had grown to hate him for no particular reason. But then again, Jeremy hated his entire family. He regarded his mother as a hindrance to his lifestyle and was jealous of Sheila and her $30,000 allowance. He considered the twins bothersome little monsters who seemed always to be underfoot. No, Jeremy didn't care for his family. His main aim in life was to eat, drink and party with members of the opposite sex. He pursued these pastimes whenever he could slip away from the farm, which was often.

Jeremy loved to visit the closest town, Colchester, for fun and games. He took a part-time job in one of the pubs in order to be near the action. Often he had two or three girls on the string at the same time, but particularly favored one married local beauty who was 12 years his senior and the mother of two children.

Sometimes Jeremy confided in his girlfriends, telling them that he would like to kill his parents. The method he would use would be simple enough. He would sedate them and then set the house on fire. Authorities would assume that Neville had dropped a cigarette. His two closest girlfriends told him to grow up and stop behaving like a child. Jeremy laughed.

In the wee hours of the morning of August 7, 1985, police received a call from Jeremy Bamber. He related that his sister had wiped out the entire family. Police rushed to White House Farm. They found Neville lying on the kitchen floor. He had been bludgeoned about the head and shot eight times in the head and neck. Sheila's six-year-old sons, Nicholas and Daniel, were found dead in their bed. Nicholas had been shot three times in the head, while Daniel had been shot five times in the back of the head while he slept. June Bamber's body was found beside her bed. She had apparently been sitting on the bed and had attempted to flee before she was shot seven times. Sheila lay dead in the same bed with a rifle and a bible at her side. It was tragically clear that mentally deranged Sheila had killed her family before taking her own life. In all, Sheila had discharged 23 shots in killing her entire family with the exception of Jeremy. Fortunately, he had been out of the house at the time and so had escaped her wrath.

A few days later, the distraught Jeremy attended his family's funeral, but he wasn't one to mourn for long. Within days he was partying in London. He also slipped over to Amsterdam to replenish his supply of cocaine and marijuana. None of these actions were brought to the attention of the police. It took London's famed tabloid reporters to point out the rather simple fact that Sheila had been shot twice, once in the brain and once in the throat. Either shot would have been fatal. Sheila couldn't have killed herself twice.

Police decided to take another look. When they discovered that Sheila had been shot once with a gun equipped with a silencer and once without a silencer, they knew for certain that she hadn't killed herself. Other evidence came to light. Although the floors of the rooms where the family had been slaughtered were splattered with blood, Sheila's bare feet had been blood-free. It would have been impossible for her to have dashed about the house killing her family without getting blood on her feet. It also was difficult to believe that Sheila, who stood about five-and-a-half-feet tall, could have bludgeoned her six-foot-four-inch father before shooting him.

Although the police were now actively pursuing the theory that Sheila was a victim rather than a killer, it was left to one of the Bambers' relatives to find a silencer in a downstairs pantry. Everyone agreed that Sheila couldn't have put it there after being shot.

During the weeks in which the newspapers featured the gory details of the multiple murders, two of Jeremy's girlfriends kept their guilty knowledge to themselves. Jeremy had confided in them his desire to have his family dead. Not only did he hate them all, but upon their deaths, he alone stood to inherit the family fortune. Finally, unable to live with themselves, the two girls got together and went to the police.

Jeremy was taken into custody and charged with the murders of his mother, father, sister and two nephews. Tried in London's Old Bailey, he was found guilty of all five charges. Jeremy was sentenced to a minimum of 25 years to life on each count.

Jeremy Bamber will be eligible for parole in 2011. At that time, he will be 50 years old and will have spent exactly half his life behind prison bars.

Clint Bankston

Most murderers are not very clever. On occasion, more by luck than design, they manage to avoid detection. Sometimes, as if they want to be apprehended, they kill again.

This is the story of one such teenager who took innocent lives and, in the end, left a trail a cub scout could follow.

Clint Bankston was only 16 years old, but he was an adult in every sense of the word. He was attending school in Athens, Georgia, when the senseless murders took place.

It all began on Saturday, April 25, 1988. Neighbors of Rachel and William Sutton couldn't understand why the elderly couple didn't answer their phone. When they knocked on the Suttons' door, they received no response. The neighbors had good reason to be concerned. You see, Rachel was 78 years old, while William had seen 82 summers come and go. Both were employed as professors at the University of Georgia.

Police were notified. It was necessary for them to gain access to the home through a window. The sight which greeted the officers was not a pleasant one. William's body was lying on the hall floor beside the door to the dining room. He was draped over a laundry bag which held the body of his wife.

The crime scene was strange in many ways. A dining room rug had been thrown over the Suttons' bodies by the killer, who had attempted to clean up blood with a sponge mop which was found in the kitchen. It was impossible to ascertain if anything had been taken from the house. William's wallet was found intact in his pants pocket.

The couple's two vehicles, a Buick and a Chevrolet, were still in their garage. In the trunk of the Chevy, investigators found bloodstained clothing and a bloody dishpan. The trunk of the Buick contained blood-stained rugs and women's clothing, as well as a butcher knife, which proved to be one of the murder weapons.

An autopsy indicated Rachel Sutton had been stabbed six times, while William had been stabbed 11 times with the butcher knife. In addition, the killer had stabbed William twice with a decorative African spear which had been on display in the dining room.

What type of human predator had descended on this inoffensive elderly couple and snuffed out their lives for no apparent reason? The Suttons had no known enemies. Members of the academic community were interrogated without result. During the investigation, it was learned that the Suttons owned a dozen properties in and around Athens. Tenants were questioned, but it appeared no one had any reason to cause the Suttons harm, let alone kill them. Despite the array of clues and fingerprints recovered from the crime scene, police could not come up with the identity of the murderer.

Four months passed. On August 15, 1988, the killer struck again. Ann Morris left her home in Athens to visit a friend, Sally Nathanson. When friends of both women couldn't reach them by phone, police were dispatched to Sally's residence. On the lawn near the front door lay the body of 63-year-old Ann Morris. Inside, police found the bodies of Sally Nathanson and her daughter, Helen.

In reconstructing the crime, investigators felt the intruder had killed Sally first, then barged into the dining room where Helen was eating breakfast. Detectives found food on the dining room table, partially eaten. Both women had been sexually assaulted. Male hair and semen were found on both bodies. Ann Morris had no doubt arrived at the front door just as the killer was exiting the residence. All three women had been killed with what police felt was a small axe or hatchet.

Each of the three victims had owned an automobile. Only two were parked in the driveway. Sally Nathanson's 1984 Dodge Diplomat was missing. The Dodge's licence number was immediately issued to all police, who felt they would find the car abandoned. Surely the killer would rid himself of the incriminating Dodge within minutes of making good his escape.

It didn't work out that way.

Officer Kirk Graham couldn't believe his good fortune as he drove past a Moreland Ave. home in East Athens. There, in the driveway, was Sally Nathanson's Dodge Diplomat. Officer Graham notified homicide of his find and proceeded to knock on the front door of the house beside the wanted vehicle. Sixteen-year-old Clint Bankston answered the door. He handed over the keys of the Dodge to Officer Graham. Clint claimed a friend, Chris Ward, had loaned him the vehicle.

A few hours later, Clint changed his story. He told his interrogators he had found the car abandoned. When keys to Sally Nathanson's home were found in his shirt pocket, Clint lost his composure, but still contended his friend Chris Ward had committed the crimes. Clint admitted he had been in the Nathanson home with Ward. To gain favor with detectives, he led them to a wooded area, where they recovered a blood-spattered hatchet, a pair of women's slippers and a bloody man's shirt.

Once Clint felt police believed his friend Ward was responsible for the three murders which had taken place in the Nathanson home, he broached the subject of the Sutton murders. He also attributed these two murders to the mysterious Chris Ward.

Detectives felt it was time to pick up Ward. That task proved to be a difficult one. Clint led police to his friend's house. No Chris Ward lived there. Three more times, the accused killer led authorities on wild goose chases to locate Ward. After a week of searching, it was apparent Ward was a figment of Clint's imagination. In time he confessed to a psychiatrist that Chris was a fictional character he invented to take the blame for the five murders.

Meanwhile, police had built a formidable case against their suspect. Fingerprints taken from the Sutton and Nathanson homes proved to be Clint's. It was his hair that was found on the bodies of Sally and Helen Nathanson. Of course, all of this incriminating evidence was only matched to Clint after he was located, which might never have happened had he not been dull enough to park his victim's automobile in the driveway of his own home.

Clint Bankston was found guilty of multiple murder and received five sentences of life imprisonment.

As I said at the outset, most murderers are not very clever.

Beck & Fernandez

Nineteen-forty-seven was not a good year for Martha Beck. Her husband had just divorced her and to make matters worse, she lost her job as a nurse at a home for crippled children in Pensacola, Florida. Fate had left her with two children; one sired by her former husband and the other the result of a tryst with a bus driver.

Martha had been willing to marry the bus driver, but unfortunately he had an aversion to settling down, particularly with Martha. You might call it an absolute phobia, because the bus driver took a step which assured him that no marriage could take place. Rather than marry Martha, he committed suicide.

You see, Martha was not a raving beauty. She was of average height, but that is about all that was average about her. Tipping the scales at 203 lb., Martha had an array of chins and extra slabs of blubber that she wasn't even using. She was inclined to wear bright red lipstick, and overindulged her ample face with layers of rouge, which gave her an overstuffed, ghostlike appearance.

Martha had those normal urges which ladies sometimes have and longed for the company of a man. Facing the fact that she was not a cutie she joined a lonely hearts club. Before long she received a letter, which read:

Dear Martha,
I hope you will allow me the liberty of addressing you by your Christian name. To tell the truth, I don't quite know how to begin this letter to you, because I must confess, this is the first letter of this sort that I have ever written.

Would you like to know a little about me? I am 31 and I've been told I'm not a bad looking fellow. I am in the importing business from Spain, my mother country. I live alone here in this apartment, which is much too large for a bachelor, but I hope some day to share it with a wife.

Why did I choose you for my debut friendship letter? Because you are a nurse, and therefore I know you have a full heart with a great capacity for comfort and love.

Your friend,
Raymond Fernandez

Martha didn't know it, but Raymond Fernandez was having a busy year as well. He was a swindler and killer who worked the lonely hearts clubs. Once Raymond met, seduced, and got his hands on a lady's available funds, he disappeared leaving the poor women dabbling at their bloodshot eyes with the corner of a handkerchief. When absolutely necessary, he killed his victims.

Raymond had just returned from Spain where he had gone vacationing with a Jane Thompson. Jane unfortunately, didn't come back to the U.S. It seems she met with a car accident in La Linea, Spain. Fernandez had all the documentation concerning her death. He even had her last will and testament. Naturally it left the contents of her apartment to none other than Raymond Fernandez.

At Raymond's invitation, Martha went to visit him in New York. Raymond, always frugal, had moved right into the late Jane Thompson's apartment. My, my, what a surprise Raymond had when he threw open his front door and there stood the overstuffed, over-rouged, over-lipsticked Martha. Raymond gulped and said, "Come on in."

Fernandez was repulsed at the sight of Martha, but she thought he was an absolute heartbreaker. She fell madly in love with Raymond at that very first meeting. Not one to let grass grow under her bed, she let Raymond have his way with her the very first time they laid eyes on each other. Raymond, in his experienced way, checked out Martha's assets, and all things considered, decided to give Martha what they used to call the cold shoulder. Martha would have none of it. In desperation, Raymond decided to tell her the truth, namely, that she was falling for a con artist and killer. You can imagine his surprise when Martha professed undying love for him in spite of his wayward habits. She even went so far as to suggest that they should become a team. She would pose as his sister, and instill confidence into the ladies he proposed to fleece.

Raymond warmed up to the idea and the partnership was formed. From the very beginning the Spaniard and the fat lady were a perfect combination. Raymond would correspond with lonely ladies, mostly widows, through several lonely hearts clubs. Once contact was established, usually instigated by the ladies themselves, Raymond and Martha would show up at the mark's house. The unsuspecting victim would be impressed with Raymond and appreciate his honorable intentions of lugging his sister along with him. After they got their scheme rolling, the odd couple averaged one fleecing a month.

There was one fly in the ointment. Martha was almost driven crazy with jealousy. She couldn't stand the thought that her Raymond had to caress and make love to other women. Raymond assured her that it was just part of his chosen profession and that it meant nothing personal.

Business is business, as the saying goes, and the partnership continued on its merry way. One incident is worthy of note. Raymond and Martha had made contact with a 66-year-old widow, Janet Fay of Albany, New York. After Raymond had seduced her and gotten his hands on Mrs. Fay's life savings of $6,000, Martha wanted to leave her high and dry. It appeared to Martha that Ray was lingering a little too long after the money was safely in his hands.

In a jealous rage, Martha hit Mrs. Fay over the head with a hammer. Ray finished the job by strangling her with a scarf. Martha was later to state that she and Ray made love on the floor beside the body of their victim.

The following day Fernandez bought a trunk and placed the body of Mrs. Fay inside. He then managed to store the body at a friend's house for a few days. Raymond and Martha located a house for rent at 149th St., Ozone Park, Queen's and took it on a trial basis for one month. They dug a hole in the basement, placed Mrs. Fay's body inside, and cemented the floor over. They remained in the house for four days until the cement had dried. Then the odd couple moved out, informing the real estate agent that the house was unsuitable. In this way they effectively disposed of Mrs. Fay's body.

Out of sight out of mind — the strange pair went on their merry way. Six weeks later they made contact with a widow from the suburb of Grand Rapids, Michigan. Mrs. Delphine Downing had lost her husband two years previously. She was leading a lonely existence, raising her three-year-old daughter Rainelle by herself.

Soon Raymond and Martha visited Mrs. Downing at

her invitation. In his usual charming way, Raymond made friends with little Rainelle. Then following his regular script and drawing on his vast experience, he seduced the lonely Mrs. Downing. She became so enthralled with her lover and his large sister that she invited them both to move in with her and Rainelle. Raymond added to his role of lover and took on the extra responsibility of financial advisor. He and Mrs. Downing soon contemplated wedding bells. Raymond got busy converting her worldly assets to his name in anticipation of their impending marriage.

It appeared that Mrs. Downing could be the source of future concern for Raymond and Martha, so one fine day Raymond shot her in the head. Rainelle kept crying, and as a result made Martha nervous. Martha cured her nervousness by strangling the child. That same night Raymond dug a hole in the cellar. Here he placed the two bodies and poured cement into the hole. To relax after a hard evening's work, Raymond and Martha took in a movie.

The next morning, when neighbors couldn't get a satisfactory answer as to Mrs. Downing's whereabouts, they didn't hesitate to call the police. The authorities just couldn't believe that a woman who had lived in the same house for years would leave with her daughter, and not tell her future husband where she was going. They decided to search the house, and lo and behold they discovered that damp patch of cement in the basement.

Once the bodies of Mrs. Downing and Rainelle were uncovered, both Raymond and Martha poured out the whole horror story. They led police to the exact location in Queen's where the body of Mrs. Fay was buried under cement in the basement. As the house was now rented to new tenants, we can only speculate how they felt when informed that there was a body in their basement.

The authorities decided to extradite the pair from Michigan to New York State and charged them with murder. Michigan had abolished capital punishment while New York still retained the ultimate penalty.

Both were found guilty. On March 9, 1951, in the company of a Roman Catholic priest, Raymond was executed in the electric chair in Sing Sing Prison. Twelve minutes later Martha joined him.

The Bender Family

There have been some nasty families down through the years. I don't mean yours or mine, but those families who slayed together and stayed together.

One of the vilest little domesticated groups to kill together were the Benders of Kansas. Pop Bender was originally from Germany, and was around 60 years old when he settled in the Sunflower state. Ma Bender was a tough-looking doll about 10 years Pop's junior. The hard rock couple had two children. John Jr. was a strapping, dull 27-year-old, while daughter Kate was 25. Kate was a looker with an hourglass figure, who attracted members of the opposite sex like honey attracts bees.

In 1871, the Benders moved into a dilapidated house in Labette County, halfway between the small railroad crossroads of Thayer and the tiny town of Cherryvale. Old man Bender divided his 16 by 20-ft. home into two parts. One half was used as living quarters for the Bender clan, while the other half was used as a store and what could charitably be called a restaurant. The two sections were divided by a canvas partition.

Situated on the main road, and with Kate as a build-up attraction, the Bender establishment, despite its humble appearance, did a thriving business. During the daylight hours horsemen stopped for groceries. At dusk travellers stopped for a hotel meal, and were later put up on cots to spend the night.

If one was to believe rumors which circulated through the Kansas prairies, one would be forced to come to the conclusion that Kate did more for the tired strangers than wait on tables. Other than the oldest profession, Kate had another vocation, which to us unsuspecting souls appears to be diametrically opposite to her horizontal activities. Are you ready? She was a spiritualist who claimed to heal the ill. When thusly employed, she billed herself as Professor Miss Kate Bender. When the mood moved her, she also gave lectures on spiritualism.

From 1871 to 1873, using Kate and apparently good food as bait, the Bender family started killing people. Kate would seat the travellers with their backs to the canvas partition. Choosing only those who looked prosperous, Pop Bender and Junior would wait for an opportune moment to bring a sledgehammer down on the unsuspecting victim's head. The only thing left for the Bender family to do was slide the body under the canvas to effectively remove it from the public eating area and into the privacy of their living quarters. Here they would combine their talents to trap and rob the victims. Then the body would be dropped through a trap door in the floor into a pit. Later the family would pick a few quiet moments under the Kansas sky to plant the strangers in an adjoining pasture.

For almost two years this simple, diabolical little drama was enacted time and time again. Like most foolproof schemes, something happened to cramp the Benders' style. In the spring of 1873, Dr. William York was returning home from visiting his brother, a colonel in the army. His route took him past the Bender establishment. He had mentioned to his brother that he would be stopping over at the Bender place. When Doc York mounted his trusty steed for the trip, he waved goodbye to his brother. The doctor then rode into the sunset, never to be heard from again.

Well, folks, Col. York went looking for his brother

and ended up at — you guessed it — the Benders' friendly inn. The Bender group offered to look for the missing doctor. Remember, this all took place in 1873 when travelling was sometimes hindered by outlaws, not the least of whom was that well-known chap Jesse James. Anyway, Col. York was satisfied with the Benders and rode off to continue his search for his brother elsewhere.

The Benders figured that with guys like the colonel showing up, it was time to leave the scene. Neighbors first noticed that the house was deserted on May 5, 1873. Soon after, who should show up but Col. York, still looking for his lost brother. The colonel, accompanied by other men, discovered the murder pit under the trap door. It was encrusted with blood. The colonel stood looking out over the Benders' property and noticed several indentations in the pasture.

The men started to dig and ironically, the very first grave contained the body of Dr. York. The back of his head was crushed and his throat had been cut. In all, eight bodies were taken from the Benders' pasture, including that of a little girl who was unlucky enough to be travelling with her father. During the 18 months in which they operated, the family killed eight innocent people, averaging a victim every 10 weeks.

Later, men were to come forward with little tales of how angry Kate used to become when they chose not to sit at the table with their backs to the canvas. Their random choice of seating arrangements saved their lives.

Just like in the movies, a posse was formed to find the Benders. When members of the posse returned they were extremely grim and close mouthed. Later one of the Benders' wagons was found riddled with bullet holes which gave rise to the rumor that the posse had lynched the Bender family and decided not to talk about it.

You may choose to believe that the Benders got clean away. For 50 years off and on people believed they spotted members of the family. In 1899, the case again received a measure of notoriety when two women were extradited from Detroit in the belief that they were Kate and her mother. When they arrived in Kansas there was a great deal of difficulty in identifying the pair and they were eventually released.

If you're ever down Kansas way, you can drop into the Bender Museum in Cherryvale and see first-hand relics of the Bender clan and their crimes. You will notice a canvas partition dividing the room. While the gentle folks running the museum are hospitable enough, I might suggest that you don't sit with your back to the canvas.

Bickerstaff & Davis

Donna and Fred Bickerstaff were well aware that their 17-year-old daughter Teresa was a bad seed. She skipped school so often that her teachers gave up on her. During her last school year, she spent time in a drug rehab institution. Three years earlier she had run away from home and had hitchhiked to California, prostituting herself for drinks, drugs and rides. Yes, by the time she was 17, the slight, attractive teenager knew the ins and outs of existing by her wits.

The Bickerstaffs lived in an attractive home in rural Harrisville, Ohio, located about 40 miles from Cleveland, where Fred worked for Alcoa Aluminum. Besides Teresa, the Bickerstaffs had two other children; Fred Jr., 14, and Ken, 13. Unlike their wild reckless sister, the two boys were average teenagers.

When Teresa was around the house, there was usually some domestic disaster brewing. The latest turmoil resulted when she brought home a 21-year-old unemployed man from Cleveland. Fred and Donna disliked Eric Davis from the moment they laid eyes on him. The more they discouraged the budding romance, the more Teresa seemed attracted to Eric. On one occasion, Fred ordered the boy off his property and forbade him ever to return.

On August 28, 1980, Fred Bickerstaff's concern over his troubled daughter took a back seat to the major tragedy which befell his family. While Fred was at work, fire raged through his home. When the heat subsided, firemen found the bodies of 38-year-old Donna Bickerstaff and her two sons. They were told that Teresa had been home the night before when Fred Sr.

had left for work in Cleveland. Renewed efforts were made to locate Teresa's body, without success.

When neighbors informed police that the Bickerstaffs' second car, a Datsun, was nowhere to be seen, the search for Teresa took a more ominous turn. Detectives soon learned that the missing teenager was not your average daughter. They found out she was a drug abuser, part-time prostitute, and had previously run away from the parental nest.

Autopsies on the three bodies revealed that they had been shot with a .357 calibre Ruger. Donna and Ken had been shot in the head. In addition, Ken had been stabbed ten times in the chest. The shot to the head had killed Donna instantly, but Ken had survived two shots to the head and the multiple stab wounds for the few minutes it took for him to succumb to smoke inhalation. Fred Jr. had been shot in the shoulder, chest and head, as well as being stabbed once in the stomach.

To add to the evolving horror story, the state fire marshall's office informed investigating officers that the fire had been set by an arsonist who had used gasoline, evidence of which was found throughout the house. A $10,000 reward was offered for the apprehension of the killer or killers. Meanwhile, a nation-wide search was instituted for the Bickerstaffs' missing Datsun and their daughter, although there was no proof of any connection between Teresa and the murders. There was no proof, but there was grave suspicion.

On October 3, 1980, over a month after the murders, U.S. Custom officials at Detroit stopped a Datsun entering the U.S. from Windsor, Ont. Inside the vehicle, inspectors found guns and knives. After extensive questioning, the occupants admitted that they were

Teresa Bickerstaff and her boyfriend Eric Davis.

Teresa confessed that she had killed her mother and brothers. She told detectives that Eric had come to her house in the wee hours of the morning to take her away. Upstairs, her family was asleep. Eric picked up Fred's .357 Ruger and found a box of cartridges. He loaded the weapon and gave it to Teresa, who proceeded upstairs to pack a suitcase. Her mother woke up and called out. Teresa went into the bedroom. An argument erupted immediately, whereupon Teresa shot her mother dead.

Ken was awakened by the shot and ran into the room. He met the same fate as his mother. Fred Jr. ran toward Teresa, cursing at her as he took in the sight of his dead mother sprawled on the bed. Teresa fired twice and her brother fell to the floor. Then the cold-blooded teenager calmly shot both her brothers one more time. Her terrible recital neglected to mention any details concerning the stab wounds found on her brother's bodies.

Eric admitted that he had been in the house. He claimed the killings had not been planned. He was there to steal the Datsun and run away with Teresa. When everything went crazy and Teresa started shooting her family, he had attempted to get her out of the house. After getting Teresa outside, he admitted that he had thrown a five-gallon gas can into the house and had lit it with a match. His statement also didn't account for the stab wounds found on the two bodies and conflicted with the fire marshall's report that the gasoline had been spread throughout the house.

Eric and Teresa made their way to Canada, gaining entry into the country at Niagara Falls on the day after the murders. In Canada, Eric found work as a welder, but when he lost his job the couple decided to flee to Mexico. That's when they were apprehended in Detroit.

On April 22, 1981, Eric stood trial for the three murders. Defence counsel painted Eric as a young man with the best of intentions, who had been caught up in a web of circumstances he couldn't control. Eric's lawyer claimed that his client had broken Teresa of her drug habit and had attempted to have her return to her home to live with her parents. He had also tried to become friends with her parents, but they were abusive and rejected his overtures. Unable to gain parental consent, the couple planned to run away together. Eric claimed he was an innocent bystander when Teresa went berserk and started her shooting spree. He admitted to the theft of the Datsun and setting the house on fire.

The prosecution attorney revealed that Eric had earlier instructed Teresa to gather up the guns in the house. He contended that at least one of the victims had been killed by smoke inhalation, a direct result of Eric having set fire to the house and that he was equally guilty of the other two deaths as they had occurred during the commission of a robbery. The jury agreed. After deliberating for two days, they found Eric guilty of the three murders and a number of lesser charges. He was eventually sentenced to three life terms on the murder charges and three terms of 25 years each on three robbery charges. In addition, he received a sentence of five to 25 years for arson. All sentences were to run concurrently, except for the last, which would start after the other sentences had been served.

At her trial, Teresa changed her story completely, stating that she had initially confessed to the shooting to protect Eric. Now she claimed it was Eric who had killed her mother and brothers. No one believed her. She was found guilty of the three murders and received three concurrent life sentences.

Teresa Bickerstaff has been incarcerated in the Marysville Reformatory for Women since her conviction.

Jerry Brudos

Jerry Brudos didn't smoke or drink. His I.Q. was well above average. He was a skilled electronics technician, as well as a qualified electrician. Jerry was a big man, standing an even six-feet and weighing a solid 180 pounds. When he was 23, an acquaintance introduced him to his first real girlfriend, 17-year-old Ralphine Leone.

In 1962, Jerry and Ralphine wed. That same year Ralphine gave birth to a daughter, Therese. In 1967 their second child, Brian, was born. The Brudos family lived in a pleasant little house on Center St. in Salem, Oregon.

To the outside world, Jerry appeared to be a quiet, happy family man. To Ralphine he was a considerate, sensitive husband. Unknown to Ralphine, there were two incidents in her husband's past which may have served as warning signals had she been aware of their existence.

When Jerry was 17, he became frustrated when a date repulsed his sexual advances. Enraged, he beat the girl badly with his fists. As a result, Jerry was committed to the Oregon State Mental Hospital in Salem. The terms of his commitment allowed him to attend high school during the day. Nine months later he was released to his parents.

The other incident occurred after Jerry graduated from high school and joined the U.S. Army. Stationed at Fort Gordon, Georgia, Jerry fantasized that a woman entered his barracks each night and went to bed with him. Each night he beat her unmercifully. The dreams were so real that Jerry sought out army psychiatrists.

When they heard his story, the recommended that he be discharged as not being fit for military service.

What no one knew, not his high school teachers, not the mental health people in Salem, not the army psychiatrists, and certainly not his wife, was that Jerry Brudos had been stealing ladies' underwear and high-heels for years. Initially, underclothing was taken from clotheslines, but Jerry was not above entering houses while the occupants slept, in order to steal items to satisfy his fetish.

Behind his home in Salem, Jerry had a garage. He outfitted the garage with an intercom connected to the house. When Ralphine wanted him for meals, she called on the intercom. There was a hard and fast rule. Ralphine was never to enter the garage. Jerry told her he developed pictures there, and didn't want sunlight pouring in unexpectedly. Men do have hobbies. Even when her husband moved the family freezer into the garage, Ralphine put up with the inconvenience.

Jerry Brudos was a time bomb ready to explode. He paraded around in women's underclothing and high-heels in the privacy of his own garage. Sometimes he took pictures of himself in the stolen clothing, but the games had become less stimulating. True, he had talked Ralphine into posing in the nude, but she did so reluctantly. No, there was no other way. He had to have his very own woman in order to act out his fantasies.

An encyclopedia saleslady knocked on Jerry Brudos' door on January 26, 1968. Faking interest in purchasing books, Jerry had no trouble enticing her into the basement of his home. Once there, he hit her over the head with a plant. Then he choked her to death.

Jerry was happier than he had ever been in his life. He had his very own model. For hours he dressed and undressed the body in his collection of women's underwear. Slowly the realization came to him. His new friend would have to leave. But surely there was something he could keep.

Jerry took a saw and cut off the left foot of his victim. It would serve him well in the weeks to follow as a form for his high-heeled shoe collection. He placed the foot in the freezer for safekeeping. Jerry tied an engine block to the body. At 2 a.m., displaying unusual strength, he tossed his macabre cargo into the Willamette River. Days later, he weighed down the foot and threw it into the river as well.

Jerry loved the game and could hardly wait for his next victim. Jan Susan Whitney was a 23-year-old University of Oregon student. On November 26, 1968, Jan disappeared while driving her old Rambler from Eugene to McMinnville. It had been Jan's misfortune to have car trouble. It had been her fatal misfortune to encounter a monster posing as a good Samaritan. Jerry told her he could repair her car, but first he had to go into Salem to get his tools.

Jan jumped in Jerry's car and ended up in his garage in Salem. He throttled her with a leather strap. Jerry had outfitted his garage for just such an occasion. He now had the proper photographic equipment. A pulley system had been installed and a hook inserted in the ceiling. The body could be raised to a standing position. Jerry dressed and undressed his victim. To add to his many perversions, he had now become a necrophiliac.

Jerry left the body hanging there in the garage when he and his wife took a trip to Portland. While they were away, a stranger drove into the side of the garage. When Jerry came home he found a card from the police department in his mailbox. It had been a close call. Police inspected the damage. Jerry repaired the garage. The body inside had not been detected. Later, Jerry weighed it down with scrap iron and threw it in the river.

Pre-med honor student Karen Sprinker, 19, was plucked off the streets of Salem four months after Jan Whitney met her terrible fate. Her car was recovered, but gave no clue as to the owner's whereabouts.

Jerry had forced the hapless girl to his garage with a toy gun. Once there, he took pictures before strangling his victim. He then indulged in his fantasies, weighed down the body with a cylinder head and tossed it into the Long Tom River.

A month later, on April 23, 1969, Linda Dawn Salee, 22, became Jerry's fourth victim. After work, Linda had driven her Volkswagen to a shopping centre, where she purchased a birthday gift for her boyfriend. Jerry pointed his gun at Linda's head just as she was about to enter her parked car. She ended up in Jerry's garage. She too was subjected to the madness that was Jerry Brudos. That night he threw her body into the Long Tom River.

Eighteen days later, a fisherman discovered Linda Salee's body. Her killer had been careless and had thrown her into a shallow section of the river. A car's transmission had been tied to the body with nylon cord and a copper wire.

While diving for other clues, police discovered another body, that of Karen Sprinker. The macabre details made the front pages of the nation's newspapers. No one was more interested than Jerry Brudos.

Despite his madness, Jerry was an intelligent, cunning adversary. He read about the bodies, but was sure he had covered his tracks and would not be apprehended.

33

He had no intention of curtailing his bizarre activities.

In fact, Jerry had hit upon a new scheme. He discovered that by phoning the university and asking for a common female name, he could get a girl to the phone. In this way he sometimes enticed girls to meet him for coffee. So far none had appealed to him. By interviewing Oregon State co-eds, detectives learned of the man who attempted to get blind dates.

Finally, they found one girl who had met him for coffee in her dormitory's cafeteria. When interviewed, this young girl stated that the man had kept talking about the two murder victims taken from the river. Police instructed the girl to stall her caller if he ever phoned again. Sure enough, she heard from him again. She told him it would take her some time to dry her hair. In the meantime, she called police. Detectives greeted Jerry Brudos.

A search of Jerry's garage turned up his vast array of women's underclothing and high-heels. Police also discovered photos of the dead girls, as well as one shot which revealed Jerry's image in a mirror. In the same photo was a picture of one of his victims.

Once in custody, Jerry made a full confession. Seven psychiatrists conducted extensive tests. Their conclusions were unanimous. Jerry Brudos had killed in a planned and premeditated manner. He was judged to be sane.

Jerry Brudos pleaded guilty to three counts of first degree murder and was sentenced to three consecutive life sentences in Oregon State Penitentiary.

Ralphine Brudos obtained a court order forbidding her children to visit their father in prison. In 1970, she obtained a divorce.

Officials of the Oregon State Prison in Salem advise

me that Brudos has made a "good institutional adjustment." Initially, as a high-profile inmate whose crimes were committed against women, he was the subject of abuse by other prisoners. One inmate made an unsuccessful attempt to stab him. The Oregon State Parole has decreed that he will never be paroled.

Judi Buenoano

When Ana Lou Weltey was 17 years old, she gave birth to a son, Michael. Ana couldn't pinpoint the father of her baby with any degree of certainty.

Never mind. A year later, in 1962, she met Jimmy Goodyear. A whirlwind romance ensued, culminating with the young couple's marriage. Jimmy adopted Michael. Four years later, Ana gave birth to their second child, a daughter. Jimmy was elated. The family settled nicely in Orlando, Florida.

The Vietnam War interrupted the Goodyears' life, as it did so many American families. Jimmy served in Vietnam, returning home in 1971. He was one of the more fortunate servicemen who returned unscathed by enemy bullets or the ravages of disease. Yet he was no sooner back in the Sunshine State and comfortably employed with a large company that he suddenly took ill.

On September 16, after being rushed to hospital, Jimmy died. The official cause of death was listed as kidney failure. Ana was beside herself with grief. We can only assume the $70,000 insurance money she collected served to alleviate her sorrow to some extent.

A few years passed before Ana met Bobby Joe Morris. Bobby Joe was smitten. When he moved from Florida to Trinidad, Colorado, he took Ana and her children along. All went well until the winter of 1978, when Bobby Joe took ill. He retched, bent over with abdominal pains and in general felt lousy. Doctors said he had an inflamed pancreas and kept him in hospital for three weeks. Much improved, he returned home to Ana's loving care. Two days later he was rushed back to hospital, suffering from severe nausea. He lingered for 48 hours before he lapsed into a coma and died. Death was attributed to liver failure. Distraught Ana cashed in insurance policies totalling $77,000.

Ana was becoming well known in insurance company circles. Every time the name Goodyear popped up, the companies knew it would cost them. As a result, Ana was having difficulty purchasing insurance. To dispense with embarrassing questions, she had her name legally changed to Judi Buenoano.

In 1979, when Michael was 18 years old, he joined the U.S. Army. He spent his first leave with his mother. On his very first night back home under his mother's protective wing, he became ill. Judi took him to the hospital, where his severe nausea cleared up within a day. Upon his release from hospital, his condition progressed from bad to worse. In two months time, he was so ill that he was outfitted with a prosthetic device on his right arm and cumbersome metal braces on both legs. The U.S. Army transferred Michael from hospital to hospital in an effort to find the source of his serious ailment. Finally, when Michael's condition stabilized somewhat, he went back home to his mother.

One day after Michael's return home, Judi had a great idea. She would take Michael and her daughter on a canoe trip on the East River north of Pensacola. The outing didn't go well. A fisherman spotted Judi and Michael struggling in the water. He manoeuvred his boat beside the thrashing pair and managed to pull them out of the water. It was too late for Michael. He had drowned. Judi, as usual, had the foresight to insure her son for a whopping $180,000, which was paid immediately. The tragedy was officially labelled an accident.

Never one to let grass grow under her feet, Judi latched onto a new boyfriend. When he took seriously ill, he told authorities that he had been given some vitamin capsules by his girlfriend, Judi Buenoano. He had some left. These were turned over to authorities at the state crime laboratory for testing. The capsules had been emptied of their original contents and had been filled with poisonous paraformaldehyde.

Judi was taken into custody and charged with the attempted murder of her boyfriend. She was also charged with the murder of her son Michael. Now that Judi's past life was being reviewed, the previous deaths returned to haunt her. Bobby Joe Morris' body was exhumed and found to be laced with arsenic. Remember hubby Jimmy Goodyear? He had been dead for 13 years. Now his body was exhumed and arsenic was found in his hair and fingernails.

Judi was tried for Michael's murder. The prosecution based its case on the premise that she had planned the drowning. The prosthetic apparatus Michael wore on his legs weighed 50 pounds. The entire idea of taking him on a canoe trip was foolhardy. The fisherman who pulled mother and son from the water stated that initially he thought the pair was playing in the water. It didn't appear to him that Judi was attempting to pull her son out of the river. Her motive was clear enough. Judi collected insurance money, as she did from all the other deaths.

After deliberating only six hours, the jury found Judi guilty of first-degree murder. She was sentenced to life imprisonment with no possibility of parole for 25 years. Just as the verdict was announced, she was charged with the attempted murder of her current boyfriend. The old adage that it never rains but it pours was never more true than in Judi's case. She was also charged with the murder of Jimmy Goodyear.

At the trial concerning Judi's current boyfriend, the capsules containing paraformaldehyde were introduced by the prosecution. It took the jury only 40 minutes to find Judi guilty of attempted murder. She was sentenced to 10 years imprisonment to run concurrently with her life sentence.

Before her trial Judi had booked an around-the-world cruise for herself and her daughter. Instead, she entered prison, where it was expected she'd be a guest of the state for 25 years.

Reginald Christie

The draw of Buckingham Palace was too much even for me, a man with a mission and an obsession all rolled into one. I checked into the Rubens Hotel on Buckingham Palace Road, and was relieved to see that the armchairs in the lobby were slightly frayed where thousands of elbows had rested in years gone by, and that the once-beautiful carpet had faded paths leading to doors, worn down by untold pairs of feet, scurrying to dine, scurrying to enter and scurrying to leave.

The year of my visit to England was 1972. I arose bright and early and briskly walked to the lift. Browning's line "Oh, to be in England now that April's there," came to mind. The lift descended ever so slowly to the lobby, and I dashed over to the hall porter.

I inquired of the young man, "Can you tell me how to get to 10 Rillington Place?"

"I never heard of that address myself, sir. Let me get a map," he replied.

I couldn't believe my ears - never heard of 10 Rillington Place! The lad must be pulling my leg. He returned with a street map of London.

"No sir," he said, "there doesn't seem to be a Rillington Place at all."

"But," I stammered, "everyone knows of 10 Rillington Place. It's Reg Christie's place — you know, the murderer."

"The name Christie does seem familiar. Let me get the manager, sir," the young man offered.

A tall balding man with a moustache looked down at me and said, "Yes?" in a manner, which seemed to demand an explanation.

"Have you ever heard of 10 Rillington Place?" I asked.

"Certainly, sir," he said.

This was more like it.

He took me aside, and in the confidential manner made famous by movie spies giving the secret password to enemy agents on street corners, he said, to me, "They changed the name, you know. It was so notorious after the murders, it was changed to Ruston Close. Nothing much there now, but I'll tell you how to get there."

One hour later, I was looking at the demolished houses that had once been Rillington Place. At last I was standing on the same ground as that most classical of all murderers, Reginald Christie.

Reggie was born in Halifax, England, in 1898, to normal parents.

There is nothing in his early life that can even vaguely be construed as a hint of what was to follow. He was a Boy Scout and eventually became an assistant group leader. In his teens he was a choirboy, and to many I am sure this activity will seem an admirable one, but the disproportionate number of choirboys who later in life go around killing people has always made me wonder.

Christie left school at the age of 15, and got his first job as a projectionist in a Halifax movie theatre. It was around this time that he induced a young lady to accompany him to a local lovers' lane for what was to be his first try at sex. Later the young lady, who was apparently a blabbermouth, told one of Christie's chums that Reggie couldn't get it up. From across the streets of Halifax came shouts of "Reggie no dick" and "Can't-make-it Christie." It seems that after this incident

Reggie always felt inadequate around women, and while this experience may not have actually caused his inhibitions, it serves to illuminate the fact that he was never quite normal when it came to members of the opposite sex.

Christie enlisted in the army in September 1916, at the age of 18. He now stood five-feet, eight-inches tall, with blue eyes and reddish-blond hair atop a round, full ruddy face. The young soldier was a model rookie to everyone with whom he came in contact. We suspect that he gave an external impression of efficiency to his superiors and cheerfulness to his acquaintances, but inside smouldered a deep resentment for women. When he looked at the painted young girls flaunting themselves at the uniformed soldiers, we wonder if deep down he still heard the taunts of his chums a few years back.

In April 1918, Christie was sent to the front, and towards the end of June a German mustard gas shell knocked him unconscious. When he regained consciousness he discovered that he had lost his voice. Though he later claimed that he never said a word for over three years, in reality his muteness lasted only a few months and finally gave way to a low whisper. The army doctor diagnosed his affliction as functional aphonia, which means that the explosion scared the wits out of him and left him speechless.

Christie was discharged by the end of 1919, and returned to civilian life to pick up the pieces in Halifax. On May 10, 1920, he married a neighbor, Ethel Simpson Waddington. The young couple, both 22 years old, had known each other for some time. Ethel was a matronly individual, who did not stand out in any particularly memorable way.

Reggie, who now had a nondescript job as a clerk, moved into a new house with his bride. He did not have full use of his voice at this time, and it's fascinating to imagine the whispering Reggie explaining to frigid Ethel that he really wasn't that good at this sex business. We wonder who was more relieved, Reggie or Ethel.

To better his lot Christie changed jobs and became a postman. Almost immediately he started stealing postal orders, and almost immediately he got caught and received three months in jail. When he got out things went routinely enough, but in Reggie's eyes Halifax held no chance for advancement so he headed for London, leaving the wife with relatives in Sheffield.

Once in London, Reggie held a series of dull clerical positions. He took to breaking the law regularly, and just as regularly he received jail sentences for these indiscretions. In 1924, he received a three-month sentence, followed by six months, for two charges of larceny. In 1927, he was caught stealing and received nine months in jail. Two years later Reggie shacked up with a prostitute.

Like many men before him who couldn't hack it with normal women, he seemed to be in his element with prostitutes. No inhibitions here; his sex partners quite simply didn't give a damn one way or the other. One day he had a temper tantrum and hit a prostie over the head with a cricket bat, an indiscretion which earned him six months at hard labor for malicious wounding. In 1933, he got three months for stealing a car; it didn't help him that the owner of the vehicle happened to be a Roman Catholic priest.

After ten years of trying to get ahead of the game and finding nothing for this efforts except jail, Reggie decided to import the wife, who was still staying with those relatives in Sheffield. He wrote to Ethel from prison, and the pair reached a reconciliation during a visit at the jail. Coinciding with the reunion with his wife, Christie was released from prison and became a patient of Dr. Matthew Odess — not that he had any major illness, but he lived in fear of recurring muteness and suffered from such ailments as nervousness and stomach trouble.

In 1938, the sickly Reg and Ethel moved their belongings into 10 Rillington Place. Situated in Notting Hill, Rillington Place was a dead-end street, coming to an abrupt stop at a factory wall. Number 10 was the last building on the left-hand side. Because of the light traffic, Rillington was an active, alive street. Children could play games and dogs could scamper in relative safety from the vehicles. Number 10 consisted of three flats, of which the Christies occupied the ground level. The whole structure was in a state of visible decay. Over the years everything had been painted many times, and was now sadly chipped and cracked; soot from the factory had rained down over the street, coating everything with a greasy deposit.

The flat above the Christies' was occupied by a partially blind old man named Kitchener, and the top flat was vacant. The three flats were connected by narrow stairs that started in the narrow passageway that let to the ground floor past the open door of Christie's flat. Reggie's front room had a bay window covered by curtains. In the evenings, he would part these curtains to watch the goings-on out in the street.

The passageway and stairs were common territory to the tenants of all three flats, but you were almost in the Christies' flat when you were coming and going. Their front room and back room were both only accessible through the passageway or hall. Behind these two main rooms, the Christies had a kitchen with an empty alcove that was used to store coal, and sometimes other things. Behind the kitchen was a wash-house that was mainly used as a storeroom, measuring four feet by four feet. Attached to this section of the house was a lavatory for the use of all the tenants.

The rest of the lot, measuring about twenty feet square, was to become famous as the garden. To gain a proper perspective of the Christie flat, one must try to realize that everything was undersized. Two people couldn't pass comfortably in the hall or on the stairs; the rooms were cramped and small. There was little in the way of comfort at 10 Rillington Place.

Shortly after moving into his new premises, Reggie joined the War Reserve Police. He was assigned to the Harrow Road Police Station, wore a crisp official uniform, and all in all cut a dashing figure. This was more like it. Reggie was a good, efficient cop, and quickly gained a reputation for being very strict with those who didn't obey the air raid regulations.

It was during this rather happy and contented time in Reggie's life that he met, quite by chance, a young lady named Ruth Fuerst. She was an Austrian student nurse who had found herself in England when the war broke out and decided to stay in England rather than return to Austria. When she met Reggie she was working in a munitions factory and living in a furnished room at 41 Oxford Gardens, in the same neighborhood as the Christies. This lonely 21-year-old, who spoke English with a slight accent, was a tall, pretty girl with brown hair and brown eyes. It wasn't long before she and Christie were seeing a great deal of each other.

In the middle of August 1943, Ruth visited Reggie at 10 Rillington Place. Though we only have Reggie's word for what took place that fateful afternoon, in this instance his account is probably accurate. Ethel was away visiting her relatives in Sheffield. While he was having intercourse with Ruth in the bedroom, Reggie strangled her with a piece of rope.

Pause and reflect on Reggie's state of mind then, as he lay spent, just having had intercourse (we must assume he enjoyed it) and having just strangled a naked woman (we can only assume that some perverted thrill was attached to his act) there was a knock on the door. The blood pounding in his temples, Reggie made himself presentable and answered. It was a telegraph-boy with a telegram. The message was from Mrs. Christie. She was returning home from Sheffield that evening with her brother.

Christie was frank about how he solved the problem: "I took her from the bedroom into the front room and put her under the floorboards. I had to do that because of my wife coming back."

A few hours later, Ethel and her brother, Henry Waddington, arrived. Ethel and Reggie slept in the bedroom and Henry slept in the front room, just a few feet from the remains of Ruth Fuerst. Next morning Henry went back to Sheffield, and in the afternoon Ethel went out visiting. At last Reggie retrieved the body from under the floorboards and removed it, and Ruth's clothing, to the wash-house. Then Reggie decided to do a little gardening - he dug a grave. That night, on the pretense of going to the lavatory, he moved Fuerst's body from the wash-house and put it in the hole he had dug. Next morning he tidied up, raking over the grave site and burning Ruth's clothes in a dustbin with some other rubbish.

In September, Ruth was reported missing to the police. No one pressed the matter. She had no relatives, no close friends. The bombs had claimed many victims who were not found for months, even years. Then again, she could be a young girl on the loose. She had probably taken a lover and gone away without telling anyone. No one gave her another thought, except Christie.

Let's let him tell it.

"Months later I was digging in the garden and I probably misjudged where it was or something like that. I found a skull and put it in the dustbin and covered it up. I dug a hole in the corner of the garden, and put the dustbin in the hole about eighteen inches down. The top of the dustbin was open, and I still used it to burn rubbish."

In December 1943, Christie got word that his application for employment at the Ultra Radio Works, Park Royal, Acton, had been accepted. He left the War Reserve Police, and early in the new year took up his new job. Ethel had gainful employment with a light-bulb factory, and again the Christies settled into that humdrum way of life so typical of many who have stubbed their toes on the ladder of success.

Reggie ate his lunch in the company canteen, and it was here that he met Muriel Amelia Eady, a respectable, 31-year-old spinster. Muriel had brown hair and eyes and was rather stout and short. Christie overhead that she had a steady boyfriend, so he asked Muriel to bring him over to 10 Rillington Place to have tea with himself and Ethel. A sort of friendship developed, and Muriel brought her boyfriend over to the Christie's on more than one occasion. In the course of idle conversation, Muriel complained of catarrh, and Reggie hold her he had an inhaling device that would ease her difficult breathing if she cared to try it.

One fine day in October 1944, Ethel was away visiting her brother in Sheffield when Muriel knocked on the door of 10 Rillington Place, wondering if the kind Mr. Christie would let her inhale some of his cure.

"Come right in," said Reggie. He had planned the whole thing for just such an occasion. His inhaling device consisted of a glass jar with a metal screw top that had two holes in it. The jar contained Friar's Balsam, and a rubber tube was inserted into one hole so that Muriel could breathe through the other end of the tube and inhale Friar's Balsam. Another tube was attached to the gas stove, with the other end of the tube inserted into the second hole on top of the glass jar.

Reggie sat Muriel in a chair so she wouldn't see what he was doing, and as she relaxed, she breathed deeply. Gas rushed into the jar and through the tube to Muriel's lungs, soon rendering her unconscious. Reggie carried her into the bedroom, placed her on the bed, took off her panties, had intercourse with her and strangled her. When it came to disposing of the body, this time he could afford to work more leisurely since Ethel wasn't rushing home. Muriel's body was taken out to the wash-house, and that night it was buried in the garden.

Miss Eady was reported missing by relatives, but no trace of her could be found. No suspicion was ever cast in Christie's direction.

The war ended and Christie changed jobs again. He obtained a position as a clerk in the savings bank at the post office. The years passed, and Reggie kept running to Dr. Odess with his minor ailments. Nothing of a serious nature was ever uncovered by the doctor. Perhaps Reggie used these visits to gain a brief respite from his boring existence at home.

A break in the monotony came when another tenant took up residence at 10 Rillington Place. At Easter 1948, Timothy Evans and his wife Beryl moved into the upper flat. Beryl was 19, three months pregnant, and quite pretty, while Tim was 24 and not too bright. He was employed as a van driver and could only read with great difficulty — though he was by no means a simpleton, and had definite ideas on world events as he saw them unfold around him. If his interpretations were erroneous, who are we to criticize? He spent many a night at the pub, and prided himself on his capacity for beer. He was also a compulsive liar, as everyone who ever came in contact with him was quick to point out.

Six months later Beryl gave birth to a little girl whom the Evans christened Geraldine. The cramped quarters, the lack of toilet facilities, the dirty diapers and the inadequate wages Tim brought home were all conducive to bickering. The bickering led to arguments, and the arguments led to screaming fights. What had started out for the young Evanses as a happy, carefree life together had deteriorated to the point where Tim was spending more and more time at the pub and Beryl was slaving away to keep some semblance of a home at 10 Rillington Place.

In the summer of 1949, Beryl found herself pregnant again, and resolved to try to bring on a miscarriage. She tried various pills and home remedies without success, before deciding to have an abortion. She told several people about this, including the Christies. By now the Evanses and the Christies were seeing each other quite often. Tim and Beryl liked the Christies, and the

Christies seemed to take to the young couple living above them.

But seeing an attractive girl like Beryl on a daily basis must have played havoc with Reggie's perverted urges. Every time she entered the house, went up the stairs, or went to the lavatory, she had to pass a doorway leading to Reggie's rooms. Only he knew of the two ladies who had been resting comfortably for years in the garden. Later, Reggie was to say he never thought much about the two bodies. Once, while digging in the garden, a human femur popped to the surface. He nonchalantly used it to prop up the sagging fence bordering his property. The weatherbeaten bone was to remain exposed in this way for years.

In October and November, a series of seemingly common, everyday events started to unfold that were later to come under meticulous study. Mr. Kitchener's sight became so bad that he went to the hospital for an operation. He remained in the hospital for five weeks and was therefore absent from the scene during the crucial weeks that were to follow.

Toward the end of October, the landlord at 10 Rillington Place hired a firm of builders to carry out some repairs to the building. These men were in and around the house on and off for the next 15 days. During this time Beryl Evans told a friend that considerate Mr. Christie was going to perform an abortion on her, despite her husband's objections. The atmosphere between husband and wife was strained over the operation and over a sum of money that Tim had given her to make a payment on their furniture, but which Beryl had spent on something else.

On November 7, it started to rain early in the morning, so the builders, who were not actively engaged in working on the roof, knocked off for the day. When Evans came home from work, his wife told him that Christie would be performing the operation on the following morning. The Evanses argued about the abortion all that evening. Next morning, Tim went to work. The weather had cleared and the workmen were back doing their repairs at eight o'clock. Mrs. Christie went out. Beryl waited upstairs, preparing herself for her operation. Finally, Reggie appeared carrying a rubber tube, which he attached to an outlet on the side of the fireplace. He told Beryl that a few gulps of gas would make the operation less painful.

We do not know exactly what happened next, but it is very possible that Christie made an unmedical improper move, because at this moment she realized what was happening and started to struggle. Christie struck her several blows to the head and strangled her with his rope. He then turned off the gas and had intercourse with her remains.

There was a knock on the door. God, how scared Christie must have been! Remember the telegraph boy arriving at the exact moment he killed Ruth Fuerst? This time Reg didn't know what to do. A friend of Beryl's, Joan Vincent, was surprised to find the door to the flat closed. Beryl had never kept it closed before. She felt her friend was inside and didn't want to see her. Somewhat annoyed, she expressed her feelings through the closed door and left. Reg Christie breathed a sigh of relief.

All the while workmen were scurrying about on the ground floor, in the wash-house and the lavatory. Reggie moved Beryl's body to the bedroom and covered her with a quilt. When Tim came home from work Christie met him at the door and explained that the operation had been a failure, and that Beryl was dead. He showed Tim his wife's body laid out on the bed, explaining that she had poisoned herself by trying to induce a miscarriage and would have died in a few days had he not tried to abort her. Evans, a bit slow-witted, accepted this explanation and went about changing his baby's diapers and giving her something to eat.

Christie explained that he was in a jam for trying to do Beryl a favor, and needed Tim's help. He said that they would dispose of the body and this way no one would get in trouble. Evans, stunned, scared, and slow to comprehend, put himself in Christie's hands. The two men carried the body down to Mr. Kitchener's vacant flat. Evans inquired of Christie just what he planned to do with the body.

Christie replied, "I'll dispose of it down one of the drains." Both men went to bed in their own flats.

The next day the sun's rays couldn't break through the overcast, dreary sky as Tim Evans awoke in his flat and Reg Christie got dressed on the ground floor. It was Wednesday, November 8, and there was the important matter of an infant child to contend with. Evans and Christie met in the hall, and Christie told him not to worry, he would look after the baby for the day, maybe even make some inquiries about adoption. Tim went to work a troubled, confused man.

At eight o'clock the workmen arrived again and went about their tasks. By four in the afternoon they had finished, and stored their gear in the washroom for the night.

When Evans returned, Christie informed him that he had found a couple who would make a good home for Geraldine. Reggie told him to dress and feed the baby before leaving for work the next day, and when

52

the couple came around for the child in the morning, he would let them in and give Geraldine to them. Christie told Evans that if he ever received any inquiries about Beryl and Geraldine, he was to say they were away on vacation.

On Thursday, November 10, Reggie strangled the child with a necktie and placed it beside its mother in Mr. Kitchener's flat. Evans got fired from his job that same day and arrived home by 5:30. Christie told him everything had gone well, the couple had come and picked up the baby. Christie, good friend that he was, had thought of everything — he had even arranged to sell Evans' furniture, so there would be nothing keeping Evans from leaving London.

On Friday, November 11, the workmen finished their repairs and cleaned out all their gear from the wash-house, leaving it bare. That evening Christie, knowing the workmen would not be returning, placed the bodies of Beryl and Geraldine in the wash-house.

By Sunday, Evans had sold the furniture (which he didn't own) and said goodbye to the Christies. He told them he was going to Bristol, but actually he caught a train at Paddington for Cardiff and Merthyr Vale to visit his uncle and aunt, Mr. and Mrs. Lynch. Tim said that he and his boss were touring the area for some vague business reason and had had car trouble in Cardiff. He was wondering if he couldn't stay with them until the car was repaired. In passing, he mentioned that his wife and baby were vacationing in Brighton. Evans stayed with the Lynches for the next six days. He acted perfectly normally, went shopping with Mrs. Lynch and to the pub with Mr. Lynch. Once he talked to his aunt about getting his daughter a Christmas present.

On November 23, Evans showed up on Christie's doorstep inquiring about his daughter. Christie replied that she was well and happy with her new parents, but that it was too early to see her. Disappointed, Evans returned to Merthyr Vale. He had to make up more lies to pacify the Lynches, and told them a not-too-convincing tale to the effect that Beryl had left him and that he had left his daughter with friends.

On November 27, Mrs. Lynch wrote to Tim's mother saying that he was staying with them and that they felt something was wrong because they couldn't get a straight answer from him. Tim's mother wrote back that she hadn't seen Beryl or the baby for a month. Mrs. Lynch read this letter to Tim and accused him of lying to them. Evans, beside himself at being caught in his web of lies and childlike in his indecision and lack of planning, decided to go to the police.

He walked into the police station at Merthyr Vale and told the officer on duty, "I want to give myself up. I have disposed of my wife, put her down the drain."

The officer on duty took this statement from Evans: "About the beginning of October my wife, Beryl Susan Evans, told me that she was expecting a baby. She told me that she was about three months gone. I said, 'If you are having a baby, well, you've had one, another won't make any difference.' She then told me she was going to make herself ill. Then she bought herself a syringe, and started syringing herself. Then she said that didn't work, and I said, 'I am glad it won't work.' Then she said she was going to buy some tablets. I don't know what tablets she bought, because she was always hiding them from me. She started to look very ill, and I told her to go and see a doctor, and she said she'd go when I was in work, but when I'd come home and asked her if she'd been, she'd always say she hadn't.

"On the Sunday morning, that would be the sixth of November, she told me that if she couldn't get rid of the baby, she'd kill herself and our other baby Geraldine. I told her she was talking silly. She never said no more about it then, but when I got up Monday morning to got to work she said she was going to see some woman to see if she could help her, and that if she wasn't in when I came home, she'd be up at her grandmother's. Who the woman was she didn't tell me.

"Then I went to work. I loaded up my van and went on my journey. About nine o'clock that morning I pulled up at a transport cafe between Ipswich and Colchester. I can't say exactly where it is, that's the nearest I can give. I went up to the counter and ordered a cup of tea and breakfast, and I sat down by the table with my cup of tea waiting for my breakfast to come up, and there was a man sitting by the table opposite me. He asked me if I had a cigarette I could give him. I gave him one and he started talking about married life.

"He said to me, 'You are looking pretty worried, is there anything on your mind?' Then I told him all about it. So he said, 'Don't let that worry you. I can give you something that can fix it.' So he said, 'Wait there a minute, I'll be back,' and he went outside. When he came back he handed me a little bottle that was wrapped in a brown paper. He said, 'Tell your wife to take it first thing in the morning before she has any tea, then to lay down on the bed for a couple of hours and that should do the job.' He never asked no money for it. I went up to the counter and paid my bill and carried on with my journey.

"After I finished my work I went home, that would be

between seven and eight. When I got in the house I took off my overcoat and hung it on the peg behind the kitchen door. My wife asked me for a cigarette and I told her that there was one in my pocket, then she found this bottle in my pocket, and I told her all about it...

"I got up in the morning as usual at six o'clock to go to work. I made myself a cup of tea and made a feed for the baby. I told her then not to take that stuff when I went in and said 'Good morning' to her, and I went to work, that would be about half past six. I finished work and got home about half past six in the evening. I then noticed that there was no lights in the place. I let the gas and it started to go out, and I went into the bedroom to get a penny and I noticed my baby in the cot. I put the penny in the gas and went back in the bedroom and lit the gas in the bedroom. Then I saw my wife laying in bed. I spoke to her but she never answered me, so I went over and shook her, then I could see she wasn't breathing. Then I went and made some food for my baby. I fed my baby and I sat up all night.

"Between about one and two in the morning, I got my wife downstairs through the front door. I opened the drain outside my front door, that is No. 10 Rillington Place, and pushed her body head first into the drain. I closed the drain, then I went back in the house. I sat down by the fire smoking a cigarette.

"I never went to work the following day. I went and got my baby looked after. Then I went and told my governor where I worked that I was leaving. He asked me the reason, and I told him I had a better job elsewhere. I had my cards and money that afternoon, then I went to see a man about selling my furniture. The man came down and had a look at my furniture and he offered me £40 for it. So I accept the £40. He told me he wouldn't be able to collect the furniture until Monday morning.

"In the meantime, I went and told my mother that my wife and baby had gone for a holiday. I stopped in the flat till Monday. The van came Monday afternoon and cleared the stuff out. He paid me the money. Then I caught the five to one train from Paddington and I come down to Merthyl Vale and I've been down here ever since. That's the lot.

(Signed) T.J. Evans"

The Merthyr Vale police put in a call to the Notting Hill police, who in turn sent a car over to 10 Rillington Place. Sure enough, there was a manhole in front of Number 10. It took three men to open the lid, but the drain was empty; there was no body. When the Merthyr Vale police told Evans, poor Tim was flabbergasted — the body must be there. Christie said he was going to put it down the drain.

Caught in a lie again, he tried to brazen it out. The detective asked him who helped him lift the manhole cover. Tim said he lifted the lid himself, which was an impossibility. Six hours later he gave another statement. This time he told substantially what he believed to be true, that his wife died during an illegal operation. The police were again dispatched to 10 Rillington Place to make a thorough search, and this time they found the body of Beryl Evans behind some boards under the sink in the wash-house. Geraldine's body was found behind the door with the necktie still around her neck.

Evans was brought from Wales to London, and told of the gruesome find at 10 Rillington Place. He made a further statement telling how he had killed his wife and daughter. He gave plausible, exact details of how he tied the necktie around Geraldine's neck. He said he was happy to get the guilty knowledge off his chest. He kept up these pronouncements of guilt until he met with his lawyers, at which point he abruptly changed his story to put the blame on the shoulders of Reg Christie.

Did the lawyers tell him to cut out his lying and tell the truth? Evans' lies were designed to protect his friend Christie and make it appear as if he, Evans, was confessing to clear up a distasteful, unfortunate death that was unavoidable. Evans didn't start out confessing to murder. Read the words carefully. He only wanted to impart the knowledge that his wife's body was down the drain, not that he killed her. It isn't easy to have murdered your wife and still to have put her down a drain, but poor Evans managed to confess to both without doing either.

On January 11, 1950, Timothy Evans stood trial for the murder of his daughter in London's Old Bailey. Reg Christie, the respected former policeman and neighbor to the accused murderer, was the chief prosecution witness. Evans, begging to be believed, testified that he had found out about his daughter's death only after he had been told by the police. When he was informed of her death he didn't care what happened to him, and confessed, incriminating himself as a double murderer. He started off trying to protect Christie, but now he had to tell the truth to save his own life. He said time and again, "Christie did it," but no one believed him. He further said that the details of the murders had been given to him little by little by the police. They had mentioned that Beryl had been strangled by a rope

58

and Geraldine by a necktie, so that when time came for his to give his statement, he repeated the details. The police denied these accusations.

Evans made a hesitant, unbelievable witness in the dock. Reg Christie's straightforward aloofness was impressive. Wounded serving his country in the First World War, Reg was treated with deference by the presiding judge, even being given a chair to make him more comfortable in the witness box. No one took Evans' irresponsible accusations against him seriously. The jury took only forty minutes to find Evans guilty. All appeals failed, and on March 9, 1950, Timothy Evans was hanged.

And so the Christies returned to 10 Rillington Place. Month after dreary month, Christie complained of minor ailments that necessitated continual visits to Dr. Odess. Black Jamaicans had rented the flat above him, and this increased his bad disposition. Mrs. Christie, too, couldn't stand the blacks coming and going all day long in her hall.

Reggie worked for two years as a clerk for British Road Services, and being back at work and away from home seems to have relieved his nervousness and minor ailments. Then in the spring of 1952, he became ill with fibrositis and was confined to hospital for three weeks. When his doctors decided his trouble was psychological rather than physical, he was released.

At this time, another real problem came to a head. He had abandoned sexual relations with his wife since Evans' execution. Not only that, but Ethel started to get on his nerves about being impotent. Did Reggie again hear those boys from the streets of Halifax shouting "Reggie no dick?" Did he lie beside Ethel night after night with his hands reaching to his ears as the boys' voices taunted him — "Can't-make-it Reggie?" He left his job, and was thrown together with his wife day and night.

On the morning of December 14, 1952, Reg took a stocking that was lying on a chair near his bed, leaned over and strangled Ethel. Her body was to lie in the bed for two or three days while Reggie decided what to do with it. Then he remembered — of course, the loose floor boards in the front room. He rolled back the linoleum, and under the floor she went. Christie covered the body with earth, put back the linoleum, and it was as if Ethel had gone away to Sheffield for another of her visits.

To neighbors and friends who inquired after her, and there were a few, it being Christmas time, Christie explained that she had gone to Sheffield and he was following her there later, as he had accepted a good job opportunity that had suddenly come up. Her friends thought it strange that Ethel didn't say goodbye, but passed it off as a rush trip and let it go at that.

Christmas and New Year's came and passed. Reggie, who by this time was sprinkling deodorant around the front room, made arrangements to sell all his furniture. He received only £12 for the lot. The used furniture buyer wouldn't even take some of the pieces, they were in such bad shape. Reggie stayed on in the flat a little while after the furniture had been removed.

It was now January, and Christie was alone. His wife lay under the floorboards in the front room, Fuerst and Eady were only skeletal remains resting in the garden, the Evanses, mother and child, were gone, and Timothy had met his end at the hangman's noose. Even the furniture was gone. In Reggie's solitude, his mind turned to the necrophiliac thrills that had almost faded from his memory.

On a night in the middle of January, at about eight o'clock, Christie went into the Westminster Arms, where he met a prostitute, Kathleen Maloney. He had met the 26-year-old Kathleen before, and within a short time the pair was seen leaving the Westminster Arms together. Kathleen was quite drunk, and Reggie was taking her home. She didn't require the finesse of deception; Reggie merely sat her down on his chair, attached the rubber tube to the gas, and placed the exposed end of the tube close to her mouth so she was bound to breathe in some of the fumes. Soon Kathleen became drowsy and Reggie strangled her with his piece of rope. He removed her undergarments and had intercourse with her right in the chair. Then he brewed himself a pot of tea and went to bed. When he got up in the morning Kathleen was still in the chair.

Christie pondered a moment — what to do with this corpse? He pulled away a small cupboard, revealing an alcove he knew was off the kitchen. He bundled the body in a blanket, pulled a pillowslip over the head, then hauled the corpse into the alcove, where he arranged it with the legs in the air against the wall. He then covered it with some ashes and earth, and put the cupboard back in place.

The perverse thrill of long ago was now fresh in Reggie's mind, and he wanted more. A few days later he picked up an Irish girl named Rita Nelson, a 25-year-old prostitute who had convictions for soliciting and drunkenness in Ireland. She ended up in Reggie's death chair inhaling gas, and she, too, was ravished after death and her body placed with Kathleen's in the alcove, resting on its neck and head, with the legs extended in the air, propped up against the wall.

61

About a month went by. Then, quite by chance, Christie met Hectorina Maclennan and her boyfriend, a truck driver named Baker, in a cafe. When Christie found out they were looking for a flat he offered to show them his, which he told them he was about to vacate. It was sheer aggravation for Christie when Hectorina brought Baker with her to inspect the flat. Since they had nowhere else to stay, Christie gave them sleeping privileges and they stayed for three days and nights.

On the fourth day Christie had had enough of Baker, and asked the couple to leave. Later the same day Reggie sought out the couple and invited Hectorina to visit him alone. He said he had something to tell her. Hectorina showed up at 10 Rillington Place, and Reggie poured a drink. In a terrible state of nervousness he was fumbling with his rubber tube, connecting it to the gas, when she became suspicious and got up to leave. Christie caught up with her and strangled her in the hall. He lugged her back to the kitchen, and thinking she was still alive, gave her an application of his infernal inhaling mechanism. He then had intercourse with her and put her body with the other two in the alcove.

Baker grew uneasy when Hectorina had still not returned from 10 Rillington Place at 5:30, and he dropped over to inquire. Christie said that he hadn't seen her, and offered a social cup of tea. Later that evening, when Baker went looking for his girlfriend, Christie accompanied him.

Reggie papered over the entrance to the alcove, and set about subletting his empty flat. On the premises, but not included in the inventory, were two skeletons still resting peacefully in the garden, Mrs. Christie under the floorboards in the front room, and the three bodies upside down in the alcove. Not on the premises, but certainly the responsibility of Mr. Christie, was the entire Evans family. Nine bodies in all.

While sauntering down Ladbroke Grove on March 13, Christie met a Mrs. Reilly who was looking at advertisements showing flats for rent. Christie, who never had any difficulty striking up a conversation, told Mrs. Reilly that he had a vacant flat. She was delighted, and with her husband went to inspect the flat.

On March 16, her husband gave Christie £7.13s for three months' rent in advance. Four days later the Reillys moved in, and after borrowing a suitcase from Mr. Reilly, Christie left 10 Rillington Place forever. That very evening the landlord showed up, and was amazed to find the Reillys living there. He informed them that Christie was several months behind with his rent, and that while they could stay the night, they would have to leave in the morning. The Reillys left the next day, unaware that they had spent the night at close quarters with six assorted corpses.

The landlord gave permission to use the vacant Christie kitchen to Beresford Brown, who was occupying one of the Evans' rooms upstairs. He used the kitchen for the next few days and started to tidy up the place. On March 24, he decided to put up a shelf to hold a radio. He was tapping to find a solid wall, but he kept getting a hollow sound from the alcove that Christie had thoughtfully wallpapered over. He tore off a piece of paper, pointed his flashlight into the alcove, and found himself a place in every book ever written about infamous murders. There, in the alcove, with their legs in the air, were the bodies of Kathleen Maloney, Rita Nelson and Hectorina Maclennan.

Scotland Yard descended on 10 Rillington Place, and the three bodies were meticulously removed from the alcove, being photographed at every stage of their removal. Someone noticed that the boards in the front room were very loose, and in due course a fourth body was removed from under the floor.

Old London Town has provided us with some weird murders, and the men who investigate them tend to become blase with the passage of time. But even for them, four bodies in one house on one night was not a routine evening. The word went out — the police would like to question John Reginald Halliday Christie. The days passed and Christie's description was everywhere. The news reached new heights of sensationalism when Fuerst's and Eady's skeletons were discovered in the garden.

Where was the elusive Christie? Not really elusive at all — he was wandering the streets of London. On March 31, Police Constable Thomas Ledger saw a man near Putney Bridge. Constable Ledger asked him a few questions and ascertained that the man was Christie. Reggie was taken into custody.

From the beginning, Reggie confessed to all the murders, except that of little Geraldine Evans.

Christie was charged with murdering his wife, and appeared, ironically enough, in Number One Court of the very court where he had been the chief prosecution witness against Evans nearly four years earlier. Christie's lawyers never for a moment denied his guilt; they pleaded that he was quite mad.

On July 15, 1953, Christie was hanged for his crimes. In January 1966, Timothy Evans was granted a posthumous free pardon by the Queen.

Columbos & De Luca

The bodies were discovered by accident. Police found Frank Columbos' stolen Thunderbird stripped to its frame in Chicago's South Side. Now they were bringing the bad news to Frank in his comfortable suburban Elk Grove Village home. But no news would be delivered on this day in May 1976. Everyone in the Columbos home was dead.

Frank had been bludgeoned about the head with a heavy blunt instrument, stabbed repeatedly and shot four times. His body was found clad only in trousers and socks. His killer or killers had butted out cigarettes on his chest.

Mary Columbos' body was lying in a hallway a few feet from that of her husband. She had been similarly attacked and shot. Upstairs, police came across the body of 13-year-old Michael Columbos. Like his parents, he had been hit over the head, stabbed and shot. A bloodstained bowling trophy had probably been the weapon used by the attacker to strike each of the victims on the head.

Mercifully, pretty 19-year-old Patty Columbos had not been at home when the attack occurred. Two years previously, Patty had had a dispute with her parents. She was madly in love with a married man, 37-year-old Frank De Luca, the proud father of five little De Lucas. When Patty's parents forbade her to see him, she moved out of the family home and into an apartment with Frank. At the time of the murders, it was thought that this move had saved her life.

The perpetrators of the slaughter had apparently ransacked the house, but had taken precious little.

They had left money, jewelry and portable appliances untouched.

Initially, rumors that the murders resembled Mafia execution style killings circulated among the police, as well as the curious in the neighborhood. However, investigators could turn up no organized crime connection to Frank Columbos. He was what he appeared to be — a family man who had worked for years in middle management for Western Auto, an automobile accessory chain.

Detectives attempted to seek out any enemies Frank might have had, but apparently he and Mary led a quiet life, except when it came to Patty. Their slim, beautiful daughter was a handful. At the age of 16, she began dating Frank De Luca, whom she met while working as a clerk in the cosmetic department at a Walgreen Drug Store where he was the pharmacist manager. Patty outraged her parents by quitting school to work in the drugstore full-time. The family had fought bitterly when she moved in with Frank. He, in turn, had left his wife and five children for the shapely teenager.

On one occasion, Patty's father attacked De Luca with an unloaded rifle, knocking out several of his teeth. Yes, there was no love lost between Patty, her boyfriend, and her parents. To add to the tension, Columbos had altered his will, leaving his son Michael the bulk of his estate, amounting to several hundred thousand dollars, and cutting Patty off with a measly $5,000. Significantly, if Michael died, Patty would become the sole beneficiary of the estate.

Patty felt that her parents were the cause of all her troubles, both emotional and financial. She decided to murder her entire family. In true Chicago style, she went about looking for a hit man. She found two. Lanny

Mitchell, a 24-year-old clerk, and Roman Sobezynski, a 34-year-old employee of Cook County. They agreed to kill her parents and brother for $50,000 and sexual favors on demand. There was one thing wrong with the entire scheme. The two men, who were posing as tough professional killers, had no intention of killing anyone. When Patty offered them sex as part payment, they decided to string her along. They delayed her for months, all the while keeping trysts with her at various motels. Five months passed before the men tired of the game and stopped returning her phone calls.

Now that the Columbos family had been murdered, friends approached police, informing them of Patty's relationship with her parents. Patty herself had confided to a girlfriend that she was attempting to have her parents murdered by professional assassins. After the killings, this girlfriend told her father, who marched his daughter down to a police station.

That's how police were to learn that Patty Columbos had actually attempted to hire hit men to kill her parents and her brother. They were even provided with the names of the hit men. Mitchell and Sobezynski were picked up and questioned. They admitted that they had strung along an attractive, promiscuous girl for sex, but claimed they had had nothing to do with the murders.

Upon being questioned, Patty admitted that she had tried to hire Mitchell and Sobezynski, but had changed her mind. When she had attempted to call off the hit, she had been unable to contact them. She further stated that De Luca had been unaware of her plans. Patty wasn't believed. She was arrested and charged with triple murder. De Luca was similarly charged.

While both accused were in jail awaiting their murder

trials, Clifford Childs, a 29-year-old cellmate of De Luca's, informed authorities that De Luca was arranging for him to make bail. He had offered to pay Childs several thousand dollars to kill two witnesses who were prepared to testify against him. Childs also told investigators that De Luca had given him intimate details of the triple murders, admitting that he was actually involved in the shootings.

In one of Chicago's most sensational murder trials in years, the prosecution stated that Patty had tried to hire contract killers to murder her family. When that failed, she and Frank De Luca had done the job themselves. The defence claimed that Patty had tried to call off the killers, but had failed. It was the hit men who had committed the murders, not Patty and De Luca.

Unfortunately for the defendants, they were extremely loose-mouthed immediately after the murders and had confided in several people, including Patty's girlfriend, fellow employees at Walgreens, and a former lover of De Luca's, who swore that Frank had bragged of his involvement. None of these witnesses had anything to gain by giving their damaging evidence. Some of them were provided with police protection, so fearful were they that De Luca would arrange to have them killed rather than allow them to testify.

The Illinois jury took only two hours to find both defendants guilty of three counts of murder, conspiracy and solicitation to commit murder. Each was sentenced to a total of from 200 to 300 years on the murder charges. In addition, Patty Columbos was sentenced to 20 to 50 years imprisonment for solicitation to commit murder. Frank De Luca was sentenced to 10 to 50 years for the same crime. One can only assume the lovers will not walk the streets of Chicago for some time to come.

Fay & Ray Copeland

There are 130 hard-working farmers who call Mooresville, Missouri home. Among them were Faye and Ray Copeland, maybe the hardest-working couple in that northwestern section of the 'Show Me' state.

The Copeland children left the farm while still in their teens. No doubt they were happy to leave the back-breaking labor and stern discipline meted out by their father. In the mid-1980s, Ray had seen 75 summers come and go, while Faye was a work-worn 69 years old.

Despite their advanced years, the Copelands worked harder than many couples half their age. Faye was up before dawn feeding cattle and preparing breakfast for Ray. Then off she went down the road to her part-time job as housekeeper at the Holiday Motel. Ray toiled on the farm all day when he wasn't busy attending cattle auctions. Over and above working the farm, the Copelands were very active purchasing cattle at auction and apparently selling them at substantial profits.

The Copelands had a secret. They would hire strangers as cattle buyers. Usually these men were ecstatic to gain a position with the Copelands. Ray treated them decently enough for awhile. He even took them to area banks and saw to it that they opened accounts, ostensibly to have a place to deposit their paycheques and facilitate the purchase of cattle.

For the first few months, each buyer would successfully bid on small quantities of cattle and pay the auctioneer with his own cheque. Under Ray's direction, when the time was ripe, the buyer would make a large purchase. Ray would have the cattle presold in various counties of Missouri. Nothing suspicious there. The hay hit the fan when Ray's hired cattle buyer's last cheque bounced and the bank attempted to contact him. Surprise! He was nowhere to be found. On those occasions when Ray was questioned, he claimed he had no idea as to the whereabouts of his buyers. These strangers would work for awhile before moving on. The bank was left holding the bag and that, for all intents and purposes, was that.

And now, folks, I'll let you in on a little secret. The two elderly Copelands killed their cattle buyers by shooting them in the head and burying them in lonesome graves on nearby farmland. This substantially decreased their labor costs and effectively brought the cost of their latest cattle purchase to zero.

In a few short years, Dennis Murphy, John Freeman, Wayne Warner, Jimmy Harvey and Paul Cowart disappeared off the face of the earth. In hindsight, we wonder why no one became suspicious. There were some reasons. Ray took his buyers to different banks, so that no one institution got taken more than once. He often recruited inexperienced, rootless men from the Victory Mission in nearby Chillacothe.

Of course, some eyebrows were raised. A neighbor, Bonnie Thompson, thought it strange that young men would appear at the farm in Ray's pickup truck and would drop out of sight in a few short months. She reported the odd goings-on to the sheriff's office. In addition, the number of complaints received from banks concerning rubber cheques had one thing in common. In every case, the passer of the cheque had some connection with the Copelands.

Meanwhile, Ray and Faye were in the market for a new cattle buyer. On July 25, 1989, Ray recruited Jack

McCormick at the Victory Mission. Jack was a bit different from the other cattle buyers. For one thing, he was a 60-year-old who had drifted halfway across the United States. He had worked farms, knew his cattle and loved vodka. Jack could also smell a rat when he saw one, but couldn't resist the $20,000 per annum he was offered. The job seemed a cinch. He was to accompany Ray to auctions and do the bidding, because Ray claimed his sight and hearing didn't allow him to follow the auctioneer.

It all sounded great, but Jack was suspicious from the very first day. Personalized cheques arrived in the mail. Ray asked him to sign a few just in case he couldn't make it to auction. Worldly-wise Jack pieced together the whole scheme. After attending a few auctions, he was in fear for his life. When Ray instructed him to purchase 40 head of cattle, he bought only three because he knew he only had enough money in his account to cover the much smaller purchase. Ray was furious. Jack got out of town in a hurry. He drank his way to Nebraska, where he sobered up long enough to call local authorities and tell them of his suspicions. They, in turn, relayed the information to Missouri.

The sheriff decided to obtain a warrant to search the Copeland farm. Earth-moving equipment rumbled down the county roads. Bonnie Thompson now told her story in detail. Others came forward, advising police Ray had often been seen in isolated areas of little-used or abandoned farms. When police were directed to a barn in Ludlow owned by Neil Bryan, they hit paydirt. There, in the barn, under a light covering of earth, police found the decomposed bodies of Paul Cowart, John Freeman and Jim Harvey. A few days later, Wayne Warner's body was found under bales of hay on another farm.

Farmer Joe Adams remembered the day Ray asked his permission to dump trash down an old abandoned well on his property. Sure enough, the well yielded the body of Dennis Murphy. In removing the body, witnesses were aghast when Dennis' head broke away from his body. Ray and Faye Copeland, who looked as if they had stepped out of a photo depicting rural America, were arrested and charged with multiple murder.

Faye was the first of the unholy duo to stand trial. Her lawyer attempted to paint her as the submissive partner in a dominant/submissive marriage. Her adult son and daughter testified their mother had always followed their father's wishes and demands without question.

The state contended Faye had knowledge of the murders and was a willing accomplice. They produced a list of the victims' names in Faye's handwriting, as well as much of the murdered men's belongings, found on the Copeland farm.

The jury deliberated for only three hours before finding Faye guilty of all five murders. She was sentenced to death.

Ray followed his wife to trial. When a bullet taken from the skull of one of the victims was proven to have been fired from Ray's .22 Marlin rifle, he too was found guilty and was sentenced to death.

The husband and wife team was the first such pair to receive the death sentence since the resumption of the death penalty in the U.S. While incarcerated in Potosi Prison, Ray suffered a stroke and died. Faye Copeland still resides in the Missouri Correctional Facility for Women in Chillacothe. She has the unenviable distinction of the being the oldest woman on Death Row in the United States.

Juan Corona

Strange and unusual murders are remembered for many reasons, but nothing makes violent crime more newsworthy than a large number of victims. Few have surpassed the killing spree of Juan Corona, a transplanted Mexican who made his living as a labor contractor near Yuma City in northern California.

One of Corona's clients was Goro Kagehiro, who owned and operated a successful peach orchard. Kagehiro took pride in his orchard, which he had nurtured for 21 years. As he walked along the straight lines of peach trees, he mused to himself that Corona's seven-man crew was doing a good pruning job. When he came across a large hole between the trees, he couldn't help but wonder why such a hole had been dug. It was big — three-feet deep, over two feet wide and about six feet in length. He would inquire about it later. In the meantime there was work to be done.

That evening, Goro made a point to check on the hole in his orchard. He was surprised to find that it was filled in. That night, he couldn't get the incident out of his mind. Next morning, he decided to inform the sheriff's office. A deputy was dispatched to the peach orchard. Goro and the deputy figured someone had buried garbage on his property. The two men turned over the soil covering the hole. Within five minutes they uncovered a human foot. On that Thursday morning of May 20, 1971, they had no way of knowing they had discovered the first of 25 bodies that were to establish the record for the largest number of murder victims attributed to one person in the U.S. up to that time.

Police knew the murder victim. He was Kenneth Whitacre, one of the thousands of transient laborers who follow California's vegetable and fruit harvests. Many work a few days or weeks, stock up on cheap wine and move on to the next town. Whitacre had been stabbed in the chest and had been struck with five vicious blows to the head, which the coroner thought might have been inflicted by a machete.

For four days, police investigated Whitacre's murder. In the course of their inquiries, they came in contact with labor contractor Juan Corona, who was rather well-known in the area. Corona provided the labor for many of the ranches in the lush fruit belt, including Goro Kagehiro's orchard.

On the fourth day after Whitacre's body was found, a worker on the huge Sullivan ranch nearby noticed an indentation in the ground. Because of the recent murder, he immediately became suspicious and reported his find to police. Sure enough, the body of another transient laborer was found buried on the Sullivan ranch. The unfortunate man had been stabbed in the chest and slashed about the head with a machete. Due to the similarities of the victims and the identical wounds on the two bodies, detectives felt that they were looking for one killer.

Once again, the name Juan Corona entered the investigation. He had also contracted labor for the Sullivan ranch. Police learned that months earlier, Juan had been involved in an altercation in a restaurant where he reportedly wielded a machete. Witnesses said he had a hair-trigger temper.

And so Juan Corona became an early suspect in the case, but other matters occupied investigators. The Sullivan ranch stretched for miles along the Feather

River. Could there be more bodies? Police searched for graves in the orchard. Several suspicious indentations in the earth were uncovered. All contained bodies of transient workers. During the ensuing days, a further 23 bodies were found, making a total of 25 victims. Each had been killed in the same manner.

News of the multiple murders flashed around the world. The most prolific mass murderer in U.S. history had killed in wholesale lots in the lush agricultural section of California. Apparently no one had inquired after the missing men. They were lost souls, who had led a life without friends or family. Later, most were identified as men with troubled pasts made tolerable by alcohol. Many had long jail records for vagrancy and drunkenness. Several have never been identified.

Juan Corona's past was investigated. It was learned that he had spent some time in a mental institution 15 years earlier. Juan had immigrated from Mexico and, by the sweat of his brow, had succeeded in building a lucrative business as a labor contractor. In California's agricultural belt, ranchers don't look for and hire their own part-time labor. They employ the services of a labor contractor. Juan was known to the laborers and ranchers alike as an honest, reliable broker. He prospered, but now the married father of four children was in serious trouble.

Juan's truck and home were searched. Police confiscated a bloodstained machete. They also found a ledger containing nine of the victims' names on a list of 34 transient workers. A plaster impression of a tire track found near one of the graves matched one taken from Corona's pickup truck. Witnesses volunteered that they had seen Corona in the little-travelled area where most of the bodies were found.

Juan Corona was arrested and charged with 25 murders. The entire case against him was circumstantial. The prosecution was criticized for the manner in which they presented their case. Despite these flaws, Juan was found guilty of all the murders and received 25 sentences of life imprisonment. It was specified that the sentences were to run consecutively. So sure was Corona's lawyer that his client could not be convicted on the available evidence that he called no defence witnesses. He was wrong.

A successful appeal was launched, enabling Corona to stand trial for a second time after he had served 11 years in prison. This second trial lasted seven months and cost the state of California in excess of $5 million. Juan was not the same man. The years had taken their toll. He had suffered three heart attacks while serving his time. In addition, he had lost an eye when he had been attacked by a fellow prisoner.

The prosecution produced one new witness, a Mexican official, Jesus Rodriquez Novarro, who had visited Juan in 1978 between the two trials. In a private interview, Corona told Novarro, `Yes, I did it, but I am a sick man and a sick man cannot be judged by the same standards as other men.' Once more, the accused man was found guilty and again received 25 sentences of life imprisonment.

Tony Costa

Tony Costa was an exceptional gardener. He planted only two crops: marijuana and female bodies.

Aside from his horticultural pursuits, Tony made a precarious living as a part-time carpenter in and around Provincetown, Massachusetts. In 1969, Provincetown, located on the northern tip of Cape Cod, was a home away from home for hundreds of youths who felt that the drug scene took precedence over that dull but necessary activity known as work.

Tony married young. He was a high school student when he met 14-year-old Avis, who quickly became Mrs. Costa. In the succeeding years Avis gave birth to three children, while Tony chafed under the responsibility of providing for a family.

Tony entered the drug scene with a vengeance. He was rarely without his supply of pills. In fact, he kept such a large supply on hand that he secreted it in some woods near Truro, a few miles down the road from Provincetown.

Tony spent less and less time at home, until finally he and Avis were divorced. Free to play the field, Tony was often in the company of girls who were either visiting Provincetown or were among the hordes of youths who made the hippie resort town their home.

In January 1969, Pat Walsh and Mary Anne Wysocki were reported missing. The two girls had left Providence, Rhode Island, to spend the weekend in Provincetown, but had not returned. Police traced the girls' last known movements. On Friday, January 24, Pat and Mary Anne had checked into a guest house owned by Mrs. Patricia Morton. They had paid $24 in advance for two nights' lodging.

The girls left on Saturday morning. When questioned by police, Mrs. Morton said that she had seen a note from a permanent resident, Tony Costa, pinned to the girls' door. He had asked them for a lift to Truro. He, too, had not been seen by Mrs. Morton after Friday night. It appeared to the police that the girls had given Tony a lift in Pat's light blue 1968 Volkswagen on Saturday morning and had not been heard of since.

When Provincetown police checked with Truro's two-man police force, they learned that a light blue Volkswagen had been reported parked by the woods near Truro. The Truro police informed them that when they had checked out the parked car, they found a note on the windshield. It said, "Engine trouble, will return." They now returned to the South Truro woods and found that the Volkswagen was gone.

Upon examining the wooded area beyond the road, police found torn insurance documents and sales slips in the name of Patricia Walsh. There was the very real possibility that the two friends had wandered away from their car and become lost in the woods. Exposed to the frigid January weather, they could easily have frozen to death.

Next morning, one hundred men searched the wooded area. Three hours after the search began, a slight depression in the ground was detected by the searchers. The men dug and soon uncovered a human foot. Further digging revealed a leg and two arms. Police believed they had recovered the dismembered remains of Pat Walsh but they were mistaken.

Returning to Mrs. Morton's guest house, detectives found that Tony Costa had left his personal belongings in his room. Obviously, he had departed in a hurry. His mother thought that he had gone to Boston. His ex-wife Avis had no idea as to his whereabouts.

Provincetown police were surprised to receive a phone call from Tony. He called from Burlington, Vermont. His mother had informed him of the body found in the Truro woods and of the two missing girls. He was calling to clear up matters. According to Tony, he had met the girls at a Provincetown bar. Pat wanted an abortion and was going to meet a man named Russell, who would accompany her and Mary Anne to Los Angeles, where she would undergo the operation. The last Tony saw of the girls, they were heading down the road towards Hyannis.

Tony returned to Provincetown driving Pat Walsh's Volkswagen. He now told police a different story. He said that he knew the two missing girls from the previous summer. They had purchased dope from him and skipped without paying. When he spotted them in Provincetown, he bought the Volkswagen from Pat for $900, paying $300 cash and deducting $600 Pat owed him. This was the first of many stories Tony was to tell officials to account for his possession of Pat Walsh's Volkswagen.

It was while interrogating Tony's acquaintances that police stumbled upon Tony's horticultural bent. Somewhere in the Truro woods he maintained a marijuana garden and had often taken girls into the woods when he watered his plants. Tony also kept his cache of drugs close by, but none of his girlfriends had actually seen the drugs.

One girl, Marsha Mowery, was willing to lead police to Tony's garden. In freezing rain they passed by the open grave where the remnants of the still unidentified body had been uncovered. Walking along a partially obscured trail through the woods they came to a clearing. This was the site of Tony Costa's marijuana garden.

Six weeks had passed since Pat Walsh and Mary Anne Wysocki had left Mrs. Morton's guest house. On March 5, the two girls' bodies were discovered in shallow graves near Tony's garden. Both had been viciously attacked with a knife, horribly mutilated and sexually ravished. Several organs had been removed from the bodies. Clothing found in the graves identified the victims. Dental charts verified the identification. An autopsy indicated that the two girls had been shot with a .22-calibre weapon.

While removing the remains of the two girls, police uncovered another body. The dissected sections of this female body were in an advanced state of decomposition and had obviously been buried for a much longer period of time. A fingerprint check of missing girls identified the body as that of Sydney Monzon, who had been reported missing the previous May 28.

By tracing a ring found on the very first corpse, detectives were able to identify 17-year-old Susan Perry. She had at one time lived with Tony Costa and was last seen in his company.

Tony was taken into custody, but steadfastly denied any guilt in any of the four deaths. He claimed that he was being harassed and persecuted because of his involvement in the Provincetown drug scene.

Tony twisted and elaborated on his original story to cover all the circumstances concerning the murders already known by the investigating officers. He vehemently swore that his brother had loaned him the $300 he required to complete the purchase of Pat Walsh's car. At first Tony's brother verified this story, but as the case developed he admitted that he had lied to protect his brother.

Tony had a handwritten bill of sale for the Volkswagen signed by Pat Walsh. FBI handwriting experts stated that Pat's signature was in Tony's disguised handwriting.

Gradually, Tony opened up. Initially, he would only admit to being on the scene while a friend killed the girls and dissected the bodies. Slowly, he gravitated to helping his friend mutilate the bodies. Finally, he admitted to the killings.

Tony Costa was examined by psychiatrists and adjudged to be legally sane. He was also considered to be a psychopath, caring only for the fulfillment of his immediate needs with no thoughts or feelings for others. In short, a monster.

Tony was tried, found guilty on two charges of murder and sentenced to two life terms in prison with no possibility of parole. On May 12, 1974, Tony Costa fastened his leather belt over the upper bars of his cell at the Massachusetts Correctional Institute at Walpole and hanged himself. He was 29 years old.

Richard Cottingham

Richard Cottingham was employed for over a decade with Blue Cross and Blue Shield of Greater New York. He was a valued and highly regarded member of the company's large computer staff.

Richard and his wife Janet lived in a pleasant three-bedroom home in Lodi, New Jersey. They had three children: two boys, Blair and Scott, and a daughter, Jenny. Richard commuted to New York each day. Because of the nature of his employment, he had the option of reporting to work at any hour convenient to him. He normally worked from 4 p.m. to 11 p.m.

Among his colleagues, Richard Cottingham was a regular guy. Janet was the first to become aware that her husband was not what he appeared to be to the outside world.

In 1976, after Jenny's birth, 28-year-old Richard refused to have sexual intercourse with his wife. As a result, she gravitated to spending more and more time with her own friends. Richard, in turn, spent most of his time at home in his own private room. After work, he rarely drove directly home. Indeed, it was common for Richard to arrive home at dawn with the smell of alcohol on his breath. Sometimes he stayed away for several days.

One day, Richard inadvertently left his private room unlocked. Janet walked in. She was amazed to find an assortment of ladies' used underclothing and cheap jewelry scattered about the room.

No, Richard Cottingham was not normal. He was clever and cunning, but far from normal. For years he had led a double life, committing abnormal criminal acts which had not been attributed to one man.

On December 16, 1977, the body of 26-year-old nurse Maryann Carr was found in the parking lot of the Quality Inn in Hackensack, New Jersey. Maryann, who had been married only 15 months, had been handcuffed hand and foot before being strangled to death. Despite an intensive investigation, her murder went unsolved.

Two years later, New York firemen were called to the Travel Inn Motor Lodge on West 42nd St. The blaze was localized in Room 417. Firemen had no trouble extinguishing the flames which originated from a double bed. When the smoke cleared, even the hard-nosed New York firemen recoiled in horror. There, on the bed, were the bodies of two nude, partially burned females. They were headless and their hands had been removed.

The investigation into the gruesome murders revealed that both girls had been prostitutes. Lighter fluid had been sprinkled over their bodies and ignited. New York detectives surmised that the strange mutilations had a purpose. With no heads, there were no teeth to check against dental records. With no hands, there were no fingerprints to compare. It would be six weeks before one of the girls would be identified. The identify of the other girl has never been established.

The man who had checked into Room 417 at the Travel Inn had given his name as Carl Wilson of Merlin, N.J. Both his name and the name of the town were fictitious. The room was clean. No fingerprints, no cigarette butts, nothing that would lead to the identity of the killer. He had checked in on Wednesday evening, November 29, and for four days was rarely seen by hotel staff. The "Do not disturb" sign hung from the doorknob of 417 for almost all of those four days.

After weeks of tedious legwork, detectives identified

one of the victims as Deedeh Goodarzi. Jackie, as she was known, plied her trade in Atlantic City and New York City. The beautiful five-foot six-inch Kuwait native had left Atlantic City to attend a meeting with her pimp in New York during the last week of November. She never kept the appointment. Instead, she ended up in Room 417. It has never been ascertained whether a headless corpse greeted her when she entered the room or whether she was the first of the two to die. For the time being, the Times Square Torso Murders, as they came to be known, remained unsolved.

Valorie Street found Miami too hot for comfort. She had been arrested for prostitution several times. Once more on the street, she decided to try the Big Apple. Valorie arrived in New York City on May 1, 1980. Four days later, using the name Shelly Dudley, she signed herself into the Quality Inn Motel in New Jersey. Valorie was assigned Room 132. Her nude body was found under the bed. She had been handcuffed, bitten, beaten and raped.

Twenty-five-year-old prostitute Jean Mary Ann Reyner's body was found in the Hotel Seville on May 15, 1980. She had been stabbed to death and her breasts had been removed. The police had only a composite drawing of the fictional Carl Wilson to work on, provided by employees of the Travel Inn Hotel off Times Square.

Three days later, on May 18, 1980, Leslie Ann O'Dell, 18, arrived in New York by bus from Washington, D.C. Alone in the big city, without money or friends, Leslie was approached by a friendly man who bought her breakfast. The man explained that he could put her in touch with another man who would see to it that she made plenty of money. Within

24 hours Leslie was walking the New York streets under the protection of a pimp.

Leslie, on her fourth night as a New York streetwalker, was motioned over to a blue and silver Chevy Caprice. The man, who called himself Tommy, suggested a drink at a bar in New Jersey. Leslie was happy to comply. Tommy proved to be a pleasant companion. He even seemed interested in her problems.

They left the bar and dropped into a restaurant for a bite to eat. Over coffee they negotiated, finally agreeing to the fee of $100 for a half hour of Leslie's time. Dawn was breaking when they pulled up to the Quality Inn Motel in Hasbrouck Heights, the very same motel where Valorie Street had been murdered. Tommy paid $27.77 in advance for the keys to Room 117.

Soon they were in bed. Without warning, the now wild-eyed Tommy pulled a knife from his attache case. He quickly fastened handcuffs about the helpless girl's wrists. Gruffly Tommy ordered, "You have to take it. The other girls did. You're a whore and you have to be punished."

For the next three hours, Leslie endured sexual perversions and torture rarely equalled in the annals of crime. Her attacker threatened her with a pistol if she screamed. Leslie bit her lips until blood ran down her chin as she muffled her cries of pain.

At one point, while being whipped, she fell to the floor beside Tommy's gun, which he had put down so that he could wield his whip to better advantage. Leslie picked up the gun. Tommy advanced towards her with his knife. Leslie, who had never before held a firearm, pulled the trigger again and again. Nothing happened. The gun jammed. Figuring she was about to die, she screamed at the top of her lungs.

It was 9 a.m. A maid doing her rounds heard Leslie scream and called the front desk. Todd Radner, the assistant manger, called police. Together with head housekeeper Paula De Matthews, Radner headed for Room 117. Inside, the man known as Tommy had clamped a hand over Leslie's mouth. Radner knocked on the door.

Under instructions Leslie, leaving the chain intact, opened the door. Her eyes were black and blue, her cheeks swollen. "Everything is okay. I have no clothes on. I can't open the door." As she talked, Leslie attempted to signal that she was in trouble. Radner and De Matthews walked away.

Just then a police car arrived. Tommy saw the car pull up. He frantically dressed and gathered up his implements of torture. As he ran down the hall, Leslie hollered, "Stop him, stop him! He tried to kill me!"

Tommy, carrying a small calibre weapon, unknowingly ran directly toward Patrolman Stan Melowic. The police officer raised his shotgun and commanded, "Hold it right there and don't move!"

The hunt for the madman who had raped, mutilated and murdered prostitutes for years had come to an end. Tommy was identified as computer expert Richard Cottingham. Costume jewelry and bits of clothing found in his home enabled detectives to link him with the previous killings, as well as several vicious rapes that they had thought were perpetrated by several different men.

After a series of trials in New Jersey and New York, Cottingham was convicted of assault, kidnapping, rape and murder. His accumulated sentences total 250 years in Trenton State Prison, where he is currently incarcerated.

Annie Crawford

Some families have no luck.

Take the Crawford family of New Orleans, for example. In June 1910, Mary Agnes, the elder of a seemingly inexhaustible supply of daughters, suddenly became ill and just as suddenly died. A few weeks later Walter, the head of the family, passed away with hardly a whimper. Would you believe that 13 days after his untimely demise, his ever-loving wife also departed this cruel world?

Surviving daughters Elise, Gertrude and Annie moved in with an aunt and uncle, Mary and Robert Crawford, on St. Peter St. Elise was a pleasant-looking secretary employed with the railroad. Gertrude, 19, was the youngest member of the family. She too was an attractive young woman. Annie, the eldest surviving sister was 28, and presumably had never been kissed. Annie's forehead was too wide and her eyes seemed to be placed much too far apart. They resembled two little green peas. Her hair, which should have been blonde, was a dirty yellow, which she accentuated by having it done up in a huge ball at the back of her head. You could say that Annie was not attractive.

Annie had been working for six years at the New Orleans Sanitarium, but was unemployed when the series of tragic events befell her family. Soon she emerged as the dominant sister, demanding obedience from Elise and Gertie. In all fairness, she seemed to have their best interests at heart.

The three sisters had barely adjusted to living with their aunt and uncle when Elise suddenly took ill. She seemed to be constantly vomiting. It got so bad that one day she couldn't go to work and was confined to bed. Fortunately, Annie took charge. She consulted with the family physician, Dr. Marion H. McGuire, who prescribed capsules of calomel and soda for his patient.

Annie rushed down to the corner drugstore to purchase the medicine. Later that same night she summoned Mrs. Crawford to inform her that Elise appeared to be much worse. Mrs. Crawford took one look at Elise, who was in a coma, and agreed. Annie phoned Dr. McGuire, who arrive a short time later. After conducting some preliminary tests he decided the best thing for his patient would be to get her on her feet. The treatment apparently worked. Slowly Elise came around.

The next day, a Tuesday, Elise seemed to be much better, and the following day she was up and around. On Friday she suffered a relapse and again was confined to bed. That evening Annie brought her sick sister some tea. Elise complained to Gertie that the tea tasted bitter and refused to take it. Finally, Gertie brewed another cup, which Elise drank.

Then a strange conversation took place between the two younger sisters. Elise took off her rings and locket and presented them to Gertie. Despite Gertie's objections, Elise forced the jewelry upon her stating: "I won't need them any more."

Later that night Elise began breathing with great difficulty. Her aunt was most concerned. Remembering the doctor had once before brought Elise around by keeping the poor girl moving, Mrs. Crawford tried to get Elise on her feet. She was shocked when Annie exclaimed: "Why don't you let her alone and let her sleep?" Mrs. Crawford looked at Annie. For the first time the thought entered her head — was it possible that Annie was responsible for Elise's illness?

While these thoughts were dancing through Mrs. Crawford's head Annie made an appearance with a steaming cup of tea for dear Aunt Mary. Mrs. Crawford threw the teacup to the floor. At this precise moment Dr. McGuire made his entrance, ordered an ambulance, and thus the tense moment between aunt and niece passed. Next morning Elise died.

That Sunday Elise was buried, but not before a curious coroner had extracted two containers of liquid from her stomach and bladder. Upon examination the liquid was found to contain three grains of morphine.

The entire family was taken to police headquarters where the chronological events leading up to Elise's death were related to the police. It was revealed that Annie had placed a small insurance policy on Elise's life amounting to $132. Elise's funeral had cost more then the insurance payoff. After the questioning only Annie was detained by the authorities. Despite vehemently denying giving her sister the morphine, Annie was charged with murder. While confined in jailed she admitted to being a morphine addict who was accustomed to stashing it around the house. She also admitted she may have giver her sister morphine tablets instead of calomel and soda by mistake.

Authorities delved into Annie's history, with special emphasis on her family's unfortunate inability to live to a ripe old age. It was discovered that when Annie's sister Mary Agnes and her parents had died, a different doctor had been summoned on each occasion. Annie was always the one doing the summoning. Each doctor had mildly suspected poisoning, but had dismissed the suspicions from their minds.

Elise Crawford's body was exhumed. An autopsy was performed and revealed she had died of opiate poisoning. Annie was charged with her sister's murder.

It was felt at that in there was nothing to be gained by exhuming the bodies of Annie's parents of her sister Mary Agnes. After more than a year, if any morphine had been administered to them it would have decomposed.

There matters stood. Annie was tried for Elise's murder and admitted she may have given her sister morphine tablets by mistake. Circumstantial evidence weighed heavily against her but without a confession murder was difficult to prove. Annie stated time and again during her trial that she had no motive for killing Elise and to even suggest she was responsible for the deaths of other members of her family was preposterous.

The prosecuting attorney's could only state that it was possible Annie had pure hatred for her entire family. That was motive enough for them. Defence attorneys put forward the strong argument that Elise might very well have committed suicide.

The jury deliberated all night before reporting they were hopelessly deadlocked. The presiding judge declared a mistrial. Annie was released from custody and left for Texas the same day. Many believe that one of the cleverest and most diabolical killers in U.S. history walked out of the New Orleans courtroom that day in 1912, having successfully killed her mother, father and two sisters.

Fred Deeming

Fred Deeming was a boisterous, free-spending, fun-seeking fellow. He loved to dress in tweed from his head to his toes. Fred could usually be found in the local hotel regaling fellow patrons with his tales of humorous and sometimes dangerous exploits around the world. Sucking on his ornately carved meerschaum, with a mug of stout before him on the bar, Fred kept the good citizens of Rainhill, England, amused all through the summer of 1892.

Rainhill was a fitting stage for Fred and his stories. Located in Lancashire, not far from Liverpool, his audience had no way of knowing that their drinking companion, whom they knew as Albert Williams, was really an ex-con who had been convicted of robbery, extortion, arson, bigamy, fraud, and embezzlement.

Williams, as he called himself, was of average height, sported a moustache, and was of medium build. One day he just showed up, ostensibly to purchase a home for a Colonel Brooks, whom he claimed was planning to retire in Rainhill. Williams explained that both he and the colonel had recently returned to England from Australia. He neglected to point out that in reality he had a wife and four children stashed away in Birkenhead, living with one of his brothers.

Albert, fast worker that he was, noted a rather plain but well-turned-out lass clerking at a stationery store close by his hotel. Emily Mather, who lived with her widowed mother, was attracted to the tweed-bedecked Albert. Within two weeks Al had proposed to Emily. Nothing like this had ever happened to her before. Would she marry Al? You bet your life she would.

Quick like a bunny, the pair became engaged.

In the meantime Al went about securing a home for the fictional Colonel Brooks. He rented a semi-detached, seven-room house known as Dinham Villa, with the stipulation that after the colonel occupied the house for six months the lease could be renewed. Al made one small request of the owner. It seems that Colonel Brooks had a chronic phobia about uneven floors. Al noticed that the kitchen floor was definitely uneven. Did the landlord have any objections to Al's cementing over the floor? With an eye to having a floor replaced at no expense, the owner of Dinham Villa consented to the renovations. Al immediately ordered copious quantities of cement. Later it became obvious that cement was positively Al's favorite manufactured product.

Down at the hotel Al passed the summer evenings pleasantly enough. He informed his drinking companions that his sister and her four children were planning a short visit. Fortunately, he explained, they would be able to stay at Dinham Villa as the colonel did not plan to take occupancy of the place for some time yet.

A short time later the townsfolk noted a middle-aged lady and her four offspring dashing about Dinham Villa. No doubt Al's sister and her children had arrived. Strangely enough, all five occupants of the house didn't venture far from the backyard. As Al explained it, it was all quite logical. His sister and her children would be joining her husband in California in a few days. They simply wanted to spend as much time with Al as possible before moving on. Six days after arriving, they apparently left the quiet and comfort of Dinham Villa, for they were never seen again. Once the relatives departed, Al went about laying a new cement floor. He supervised the workmen himself. In a few days the job was completed.

Al, who was chock full of schemes and ideas, informed his dear Emily and her mother that he had accepted an attractive job in Melbourne, Australia. He and Emily would sail in November, but first they would marry. On September 22, the vows were duly exchanged. Six weeks later the newlyweds bid farewell to the good folk of Rainhill and departed for Melbourne. Mrs. Mather was never to see her daughter again.

The Williamses landed in Windsor, a suburb of Melbourne. Emily was somewhat puzzled as to why her husband insisted that they use the name Mr. and Mrs. Droven. However, times were different before the turn of the century. It was not Emily's place to question her husband. If he said their name was to be Droven, then Droven it would be.

At this time Emily's letters to her mother indicated that she was having the adventure of her life. In all of them she praised her husband. Then according to neighbors, the love affair between the Drovens seemed to cool. Actually, it turned to ice water. Sometimes, late into the night, it was obvious that they were not throwing kisses at one another. Neighbors figured that it sounded more like chairs and dishes.

On December 24, a particularly loud piercing scream emanated from the Droven residence. Later, the only unusual occurrence noted by neighbors was a rather large delivery of cement to the Droven domicile. On January 5, Mr. Droven left for Sydney and informed the owners of the dwelling that he was vacating the premises. They proceeded to list the property with a rental agency, which immediately commenced to show it to prospective tenants.

As time wore on these potential tenants complained about the decidedly repugnant odor evident as soon as they entered the house. The rental agency people were inclined to agree. They called in the police to locate the cause of the offensive smell.

In the bedroom fireplace, under freshly poured cement, the police found Emily's body. Her head had been smashed in with a blunt instrument and her throat had been slashed. On a table in the bedroom was a Bible. Inside the cover was the name of the previous owner, Mrs. E. Mather, Rainhill, England.

While the police searched for the elusive Mr. Droven they also began tracing his trail back to Rainhill. Mrs. Mather sadly confirmed that the murdered woman was no doubt her daughter. She also informed police that while Droven, whom she knew as Williams, had lived in Rainhill, he had redone the floor of Dinham Villa with cement. Not only that, but a woman and four children had stayed in the house.

Dinham Villa, which was still vacant, was searched by police, who tore up the kitchen floor. The bodies of a woman and four children were recovered. All except a baby had had their throats cut. The infant had been strangled. The victims were identified as Deeming's wife and children.

Now Deeming's murderous activities occupied the front pages of newspapers on two continents. Indeed, most of the English-speaking world awaited his capture. All of this activity seems not to have bothered Deeming at all. Posing as Baron Swanston, he met a cute little number named Kate Rounsfell on the boat from Melbourne to Sydney. By the time the sweet-talking Baron disembarked, he and Kate, believe it or not, were unofficially engaged.

The pair made their way to Bathurst, where Kate introduced her fiancé to her parents. They were duly impressed. Making some excuse or other the Baron left Kate and her family and made his way to Southern Cross.

He wired Kate enough money so that she could join him. En route to her lover she was informed that the police had picked up her Baron as a suspected multiple murderer. Kate turned right around and went back to her parents. For the rest of her life she knew that she had come within a whisker of ending up under some cement floor.

Deeming was transported from Perth to Sydney, to Adelaide, to Melbourne. Everywhere the prisoner was taken, huge crowds formed to catch a glimpse of the infamous murderer.

At his trial Deeming's attorneys attempted to prove that he was insane, but their efforts were futile. A jury brought in a verdict of guilty with a rider that, in their opinion, the prisoner was sane and knew the difference between right and wrong.

When asked if he had anything to say before sentence was passed, Deeming surprised the court by speaking for over an hour, claiming that he certainly was insane because he didn't even remember killing his wife and children back in Rainhill, England.

Deeming was hanged in Australia for the murder of Emily Mather. Had he managed to evade punishment for this crime, he would have been extradited to England to stand trail for the murder of his family.

The memorabilia of Deeming's crimes have gradually been obliterated. For years his wax image was displayed in Madame Tussaud's Chamber of Horrors in London,

England. In more recent years, new monsters have taken his place in infamy. Dinham Villa, where five innocent people were murdered, was a sore reminder of the Deeming case. The owner of the property had it demolished, giving strict instruction that not one brick remain.

Harry De La Roche Jr.

Harry and Mary Jane De La Roche were justifiably proud of their home and the lifestyle they had carved out for themselves. This was middle-class America, the way it should be.

Harry and Mary Jane lived in the New York City suburban town of Montvale, New Jersey. Most of Montvale's 8,000 citizens were interested in the high school football team and Little League baseball. With three sons, Harry Jr., 18, Ronnie, 15, and the always smiling Eric, 12, the De La Roches were no exception. Encouraged by their father, the boys took part in sports. Ronnie was an exceptional athlete. All three were introduced to guns at an early age by their father. They practised at a rifle range located a short distance from their comfortable home.

In 1976, when six-foot, three-inch Harry Jr. graduated from high school, the family was thrilled to learn that he had been accepted by The Citadel, a liberal arts military college in Charleston, South Carolina.

Harry Jr. was the first to leave the De La Roche nest. His parents wished him well. Harry Sr., a Ford Motor Co. employee, had always emphasized the need of a good education. His son would be an officer some day. The strict discipline, which Harry had stressed in his relationship with all three sons, would stand young Harry in good stead now that he had chosen a career in the military. Even his familiarity with guns would be an asset.

Photographs of Harry Jr. in his snappy cadet uniform were sent home during those first few months. The family couldn't wait until November, when Harry would be coming home for Thanksgiving. Many of the De La Roches' friends in town shared the family's pride in Harry.

Finally, November rolled around. Harry didn't talk much about his life at The Citadel, but his parents let him know how very pleased they were with him. Unknown to the De La Roches, Harry had made up his mind not to return to The Citadel. He knew the news would be devastating to his parents, particularly his father. Harry decided that he wouldn't break the news to them until after Thanksgiving dinner.

The meal was a culinary and social success. The boys' grandparents joined in the celebration. The three De La Roche boys wolfed down turkey and all the trimmings. Harry was in turmoil. He couldn't get up the courage to break the news to his family of his decision to leave The Citadel. The gnawing thought that sooner or later his mother and father had to be told preyed on his mind. He thought of little less.

While Harry Jr. struggled with his dilemma, his brother Ronnie also faced potential problems. Ronnie was actively using drugs. He kept a stash under his bed and was delighted to show it to his older brother. Harry admonished Ronnie, warning him that if their father ever found out about his involvement with drugs, there would be hell to pay.

And so the middle-class American family had flaws, invisible to the outsider, but flaws nevertheless. The oldest son, a disgruntled student, was fearful of being a failure in his ambitious father's eyes. The middle son was involved with drugs. Above all, gun enthusiast Harry Sr. had the ever-present instruments of death in his home.

Three days after Thanksgiving, Harry Jr. drove his

1970 Falcon downtown and blurted to Officer Carol Olsen, "Quick come to my house! I have just found my parents and younger brother dead and my middle brother is missing!" It was 4 a.m. Olsen rushed to the De La Roche home and took in a scene of wanton carnage. One bed held the bloody body of Mary Jane De La Roche. Harry Sr. lay dead in another bed. Eric's body was on the floor. All had been shot.

Other officers were quickly at the scene. Harry Jr. was questioned. He related that he had come home and discovered the three murdered members of his family and that his younger brother Ronnie was missing.

Meanwhile, police swarmed over the De La Roche home. Around noon the next day, two officers made their way upstairs leading to the attic, where they opened a metal locker. Stuffed inside, under Christmas decorations, was the body of Ronnie De La Roche. Like his parents and brother, he had been shot to death.

Shortly after the body was discovered, detectives found the murder weapon, a .22-calibre pistol. It was wrapped in a blood-soaked rag and had been placed in a basement drawer. In Harry Jr.'s room, police found a Citadel t-shirt and a pair of long underwear. Both were bloodstained. Harry Jr. was subjected to a lie detector test, which indicated that he was not telling the truth concerning the murders.

That same day, Harry confessed. It was a cold-blooded confession, describing in detail how in a few minutes he had annihilated his entire family. He revealed that he had removed his clothes except for the t-shirt and long underwear. He desperately thought of his dilemma. He simply would not return to a life he hated in Charleston. Yet, he couldn't tell his parents of this decision. He approached his parents' room several times, but each time returned to his own room without saying a word.

Finally, he made his way to their room and said, "I can't go back." At the same time, he closed his eyes and pulled the trigger of the .22-calibre pistol he clutched in his hand. He then turned the weapon from his father to his mother. Operating in a frenzy, he entered Ronnie's room and turned on the lights. According to Harry, Ronnie opened his eyes and was shot dead.

In his twin bed, Eric stirred. He too was shot. But Eric wasn't dead. when Harry returned to his own room, he heard noises coming from his brothers' bedroom. He went back to find Eric attempting to speak and get out of bed. Harry put his hand over his brother's eyes and said, "Eric, go to sleep, go to sleep. It's just a dream." Eric, if he heard at all, paid no heed. He managed to get up. Harry pistol-whipped him until he was dead.

In an attempt to divert blame from himself to Ronnie, he lugged Ronnie's body up to the attic and hid it in the locker. Noticing blood on Ronnie's bed, he had the presence of mind to realize that he would have to account for it. He transferred his father's body to Ronnie's bed. Harry then hid the gun, placed his two pieces of bloody clothing in his drawer, took a shower and raced downtown to tell officer Olsen that someone had killed Eric and his parents and that Ronnie was missing.

Harry De La Roche was charged with four counts of first-degree murder. He later recanted his confession, claiming that his brother Ronnie had been caught with drugs by their father. Ronnie had killed the family.

Harry, in turn, had killed Ronnie. Harry's story was not believed.

On January 26, 1978, after deliberating six and a half hours, the New Jersey jury reached a verdict. They found Harry De La Roche guilty on the four murder charges. He was sentenced to four terms of life imprisonment to run concurrently.

Because the sentences were not to run consecutively, Harry was first eligible for parole in 1987. However, at that time he was denied parole. He currently resides at New Jersey's Garden State Prison.

Arthur Devereux

To look at Arthur Devereux, you'd never think he was one of the most cold-hearted fathers who ever drew breath. At the same time, weird Art loved one of his sons more than life itself.

Art wasn't tough to take in the looks department. He was a tall, slim charmer who could talk the birds out of the trees. One fine day in 1898, when he was displaying his charm, as well as his physical attributes, Art met Beatrice Gregory. Beatrice and her mom were vacationing in Hastings, England. Beatrice, who felt life was passing her by, took one look at Art and fell madly in love. Even her mom had to admit that on the surface Art appeared to be the genuine article. The attractive young couple were married after knowing each other for only a few months.

The marriage didn't go well. Charming Art turned out to be decidedly disinterested in his new wife. Well, that's not exactly true. He was attentive enough to put Beatrice in the family way only a few months after the minister had assisted in tying the knot.

Little Stanley's arrival was a joyous occasion, but it did tax the family's already stretched income, which was derived solely from Art's efforts as a chemist's assistant. Art did what he could. He changed jobs, moved to London. Nothing seemed to alleviate the financial pressure.

Art blamed Beatrice for all the family's problems. He yelled at her, insulted her and was an absolute boor. Strangely enough, while he grew to hate Beatrice, he was extremely fond of little Stanley. Nothing was too good for his son. Eventually, Art's world revolved around the boy.

Timing is everything. Of necessity, Beatrice had to inform her husband, that due to a lunar miscalculation, she was pregnant again. Art threw a tantrum, but that didn't prevent Beatrice, after the prescribed nine months, from presenting Art with a newborn babe. Make that babes. Beatrice had twins.

Human behavior is a strange phenomenon. Just as Art doted on Stanley, Beatrice had eyes only for the twins. The split in parental affection did nothing to cement the Devereux marriage. As the months turned into years, Art grew not only to hate his wife, but also the twins. In his warped mind, he felt if he had only to fend for himself and Stanley, everything would be fine. His income would do nicely. It just wasn't adequate to support five individuals.

Art was a man with a problem. He thought and thought and finally formed a diabolical plot. He purchased a large trunk, which he placed in the middle of the living room. Beatrice, in that annoying low voice of hers, inquired why, with money so scarce, they needed a big trunk. Art informed her he planned to store some useless articles that were hanging around the house. The explanation seemed to satisfy Beatrice.

Next day, Art brought home a bottle of tonic for Beatrice and the twins. She had complained all three were feeling poorly. Art volunteered to bring home a sure cure for what ailed them. The sure cure was laced with fatal quantities of morphine. Beatrice and the twins took liberal doses of the deadly concoction. Art placed all three bodies in the large trunk.

Next morning, Art made a substantial breakfast for himself and Stanley before venturing forth to make arrangements for the trunk to be picked up and placed in long-term storage. Art moved out of his flat and took new lodgings in London. He left his job and got another. He enrolled Stanley in a private school. Life was going to be perfect. He and Stanley were on the threshold of a new beginning.

If it weren't for Art's mother-in-law, it is quite possible Art might have pulled off the perfect triple murder. Mrs. Gregory had remained close to her daughter throughout her marriage, although in recent years, because of Art's vile temper and gross behavior, she hadn't visited as often as she once did. Now, all of a sudden, she couldn't locate her daughter's entire family. It took Mrs. Gregory several weeks to trace Art. She was dumbfounded to discover that Beatrice and the twins were not with him. Art appeared ill at ease when interrogated by the not-so-calm Mrs. Gregory. He told her some cock-and-bull story about Beatrice and the twins being away in the country on vacation. When pressed, Art refused to give Mrs. Gregory their address.

Mrs. Gregory, who may have had police blood coursing through her veins, made not-so-discreet inquiries around her daughter's former neighborhood. No one could remember anything unusual, except for an extremely large trunk being removed from the Devereux flat just before Art moved out. Mrs. Gregory tracked down the moving company, dashed down to their facilities and demanded in no uncertain terms that the trunk be opened. We all know what was found inside.

Meanwhile, Art knew his mother-in-law only too well. He realized she would trace the trunk, and he was right. By the time Inspector. Pollard of Scotland Yard knocked on Art's front door, he was gone. Art made his way to Coventry, where he obtained a job at his profession of chemist's assistant. The inspector knew his quarry would have to seek employment to support himself and Stanley. He advised all chemists to report any recent applicants for a position. In this way, Art was located working in Coventry.

When Pollard showed up at Art's place of employment and introduced himself, the wanted man volunteered this rather unfortunate statement: "I don't know anything about a trunk." The inspector knew he was in the right place.

Art was tried for the murder of his wife and two children in London's Old Bailey. He claimed Beatrice had killed the kids and then committed suicide. He realized no one would believe he wasn't the killer. He admitted he had purchased the trunk and placed the bodies inside. It was a fanciful story, believed by no one. The Crown produced telegrams proving Art had applied for a new job before Beatrice's death. One telegram stated he was a widower with one child.

When Arthur Devereux was sentenced to death in the Old Bailey, Mrs. Gregory sat in court clutching the hand of her seven-year-old grandson, Stanley. He was all she had. The man in the prisoner's box had killed the rest of her family.

Arthur Devereux, who left something to be desired as a father, was hanged on August 15, 1905 at Pentonville Prison.

The Black Donnellys

They came from County Tipperary in the mid-19th century to settle in a new land. Most made their way to Lucan, Ontario, about 14 miles north of London, to be with their own countrymen and to carve small farms out of the wilderness. It was a tempting proposition. Land could be purchased for a mere 13 shillings an acre. The new immigrants worked hard and they played hard.

One of their number was Jim Donnelly, a small, handsome man, who preceded his wife Johannah and son James to the new land. Two years after Jim's arrival, Johannah and her little son joined him in Lucan. A year later, Johannah gave birth to a second son, William, who was born with a club foot. In the years to follow, five more boys, John, Patrick, Michael, Robert, Thomas and a lone girl, Jenny, would bless the union.

Whatever reputation Jim Donnelly was to later attain, no one has ever claimed that he was a lazy man or that he lacked ambition. He settled on a piece of vacant land along the Roman Line, so called for the large number of Roman Catholics whose farms faced the road. The lot that Jim settled on belonged to John Grace. In 1855, Grace sold half the site to Michael Maher, who, in turn, leased it to Patrick Farrell.

Patrick Farrell wanted his land and therein lies the crunch. One must take sides when studying the saga of Jim Donnelly and his family. At every turn he could be painted either as a moody bully or a man justified in fighting for his rights and maintaining his principles. It is for the reader to decide.

The Irish had brought with them to the new world

all the superstitions and feuds which had been passed down through generations back in Tipperary. Alliances were soon formed along the Roman Line. Neighbor fought neighbor. Disputes about land boundaries, livestock and rights of way were sometimes settled in court. More often, they were settled with fists outside Keefes Tavern, one of 12 watering holes which prospered in the small town.

Now Patrick Farrell wanted the land which he legally owned. There was Jim Donnelly. He and his wife, with the help of their small boys, had worked year after year, from dawn to dusk, clearing the land until it was a functioning farm. By all that was holy, it was his property. After all, others had squatted on land with little regard for legal formalities.

Farrell rode up to the Donnelly homestead. Jim came out of the barn, which still stands, 111 years later, grim witness to the events which were to follow. Farrell gave Jim an hour to get off his property. Words were exchanged. Blows were struck. Farrell towered over Jim and outweighed him by at least 40 pounds. Despite these inequalities, Jim is reported to have given Farrell a severe beating, as Johannah and the boys cheered him on.

Farrell took his case to court. The results of the court action didn't sit well with Jim Donnelly. Farrell was awarded the south 50 acres, while Jim was given legal title to the north 50.

The two men became blood enemies. Donnelly is said to have taken a pot shot at Farrell, who lived close by his farm. The shot missed, but Farrell was convinced that his enemy had attempted to kill him. He formally charged Jim with "felonious shooting." Just before New Year's 1856, Jim stood in the Goderich Courthouse and swore to keep the peace for one year and not to molest Patrick Farrell.

For the next two years, Farrell would claim that Jim was responsible for the string of misfortunes which befell his farm. Cows took ill and suddenly died. Farrell's barn mysteriously caught fire. Legend has it that it was Farrell who first coined the phrase 'Black Donnellys.' As things turned out, he had good reason to be the originator of the derogatory description.

The second confrontation between Jim Donnelly and Patrick Farrell took place on June 27, 1857.

In pioneer days it was the custom to hold bees to clear land or raise a barn. The menfolk of the community donated their labor and animals to complete the work in record time. On that fateful hot day in June, several men were engaged at a logging bee on the small property of William Maloney. Some of the men brought jugs of whisky. Others relied on Maloney to provide the sauce for the day's labor. Pat Farrell was there. So was Jim Donnelly.

Oxen grunted and chains were pulled taut. Sweat stained men stripped to the waist. It was hard work, conducive to taking long deep slugs of whisky from Maloney's liberal supply.

According to reports of the events which transpired, it is certain that both Farrell and Jim were drinking that day. Most likely, Farrell was intoxicated. Each time the two men came close to each other, a nasty remark would pass between them. Jim and Pat teed off against each other, but were separated before any harm was done. Jim is reported to have taunted Farrell into continuing the fight. Big Pat grabbed the nearest weapon, a big handspike. The handspike, a three-foot-long piece of hardwood, was used as a lever to move large logs. It made a formidable weapon.

Within minutes, Farrell faced Jim, who had also picked up a handspike. Once again, cooler heads prevailed. The two adversaries were separated. It is reported that Pat fell to his knees, either from a push or from the effects of Maloney's whisky. At that precise moment, Jim raised his handspike and brought it down full force on Farrell's head. A few moments later, Patrick Farrell died. The logging bee came to an abrupt halt. Ashen-faced men looked at Jim Donnelly. Jim slowly left the scene and walked home.

Two days later, an inquest was held into Farrell's death. Jim Donnelly didn't show up, but the inquest jury managed just fine without his presence. They came to the conclusion that Jim had murdered Pat Farrell and a warrant was issued for his arrest.

Jim was nowhere to be found. He had fled, but not far. Tough Jim was hiding out in woods, which skirted the rear of all the farms along the Roman Line. Jim's older boys, James, 15, Will, 12, and John, 10, brought their father provisions. Sometimes Jim donned women's clothing and managed to work his distant fields while being sought by the law.

With the coming of winter and the severe windswept snows which swirled along the Roman Line, Jim had much more difficulty staying at large. Often he would spend the cold nights in a farmer's barn. There is some evidence that friends of the Donnellys allowed him to stay in their homes for short periods of time.

Still, life in hiding was no life at all. Johannah needed her man. Jim's children needed a father. On May 7, 1858, after being at large for a year, Jim Donnelly turned himself in to the local sheriff. Jim was tried, found guilty of murder and sentenced to hang.

Johannah Donnelly's nature wouldn't allow her to sit back while her husband's life was in jeopardy. She went about getting signatures on a petition for clemency. Some of the citizenry's hatred of Jim Donnelly was overcome by their sense of fairness. The death had taken place during a drunken brawl. Had Pat Farrell's wild swings connected with Jim's head, it would be Farrell who would be in the shadow of the hangman's noose.

Johannah wandered far afield to London and Goderich in search of men who knew her husband and regarded him quite differently than his enemies in Lucan. No less a personage than Attorney General John A. Macdonald, who would later become prime minister of Canada, commuted Jim's sentence from death to seven years imprisonment.

The cold iron gates of Kingston Penitentiary closed behind Jim Donnelly. Two months later, Johannah gave birth to Jenny, her only daughter.

One can only imagine the plight of Johannah Donnelly, with seven boys and a baby daughter to care for and a farm to run, living amongst many who hated the Donnelly clan with a passion. It is a tribute to this remarkable woman's resolve that she was successful in running and improving the farm during her husband's absence.

Seven years passed. Despite petitions, Jim served every day of his prison term. Now 48 years old, he returned to his family. His oldest son, Jim, was a young man of 23.

Jim Donnelly was back in town and life in Lucan would never be the same.

After Jim's return, every mishap which befell those who had testified at his trial seven years earlier was laid at the feet of the Donnelly family. The boys could scrap like hellions and there is no record of them ever losing a fight.

The Donnellys prospered. In the 1860s, they went into the stagecoach business. Will and young Jim discovered they had a knack for business. From all reports, their small line was the cleanest, most efficient of any in service in the area. Their competition, old Bob Hawkshaw, planned to retire. Will and Jim offered to purchase his line, but Hawkshaw sold out to John Flannigan. John was well liked and was confident that customers would patronize his stagecoach line rather than the Donnellys'. He was right.

Then, as if willed by the Devil himself, strange and unusual misfortunes befell Flannigan's stagecoach line. One day an axle broke, shaking up the passengers, severely damaging the coach and injuring a horse. Accident, maybe. Sabotage, possibly. One of Flannigan's barns burned to the ground. Five days later, another Flannigan barn inexplicably caught fire. A stagecoach was burned beyond repair, but eight horses were rescued from the blazing building. It is even reported that on one occasion Flannigan found his horses with their tongues cut out.

Flannigan was understandably incensed at the Donnellys. Together with 17 men, who believed that the Donnellys had gone too far, he advanced toward the Donnelly farm. Will and James were preparing the stagecoach for the run to London. The unruly mob stopped in front of the Donnelly barn. Jim, Sr. and all seven sons looked at the mob and rolled up their sleeves. Jim, Sr. spoke first: "You gentlemen seem to be looking for trouble. If so, the boys and I will be pleased to oblige you."

Flannigan hesitated at the cockiness of Jim Donnelly. That hesitation was to cost him dearly. The eight Donnellys tore into the 18-member mob. Several witnesses observed the Donnelly boys as they clubbed and punched until their enemies lay prostrate on the ground or took flight. It was all over in 10 minutes, but the scene of the fearless family fighting against better than two to one odds remained indelibly etched in the minds of the witnesses, who never tired of telling the story of the epic battle.

To gain some perspective into the terror that was the Donnelly family, one has only to scan the criminal charges placed against them in the first three months of 1876. It is an impressive list of 33 charges, including assault, arson, wounding, robbing and shooting with intent.

Like all pioneer families, the Donnellys had their share of personal tragedies. Jim, Jr., is reported to have died of pneumonia. Like everything about the Donnellys, his death is shrouded in mystery. Some say he was shot to death and the shooting was kept secret by the family. Whatever the truth, he lies today in the country graveyard beside St. Patrick's Church. Later, brother Michael was stabbed to death in a barroom brawl. He is buried beside his older brother.

The feuds continued, fiercer and crueler than before. Word of the acts of terrorism and the law's inability to cope with the Black Donnellys slowly trickled to the outside world. Inside the tight pocket of pioneer Canada, desperate men had had enough. If the law couldn't tame the Donnellys, they would mete out their own brand of justice.

Jim Carroll was the catalyst which was required to ignite the local citizenry into action. Jim was born in the area, but had moved to the U.S., returning in 1878, at age 26. He was quickly made aware of the scourge known as the Black Donnellys. Big Jim let it be known that he had no fear of the Donnellys.

Robert Donnelly was hustled off to Kingston Penitentiary for taking a potshot at Constable Sam Everett. Everett was given a severe thrashing soon after Robert's conviction. He couldn't or wouldn't identify his attackers and, soon after, resigned his position.

Jim Carroll became a Lucan constable with the promise, "I will drive the Donnellys out of Lucan." In a way, he did just that.

On the night of February 3, 1880, grim-faced men met at the Cedar Swamp Schoolhouse. They called themselves the Biddulph Vigilance Committee. The stone schoolhouse had been the gathering place for socials and political meetings, but this was different. By lantern light, jugs of whisky were passed from man to man. Although the weather was not overly cold, the whisky was necessary for the task at hand.

Some say there were 31 men in attendance, some say over 40. It matters little. They walked down the road toward the home of Jim Donnelly. Other men joined them en route. Into the Donnelly home they marched. Patrick Grouchy Ryder was among their number. Grouchy's barn had been burned. After many postponements, Johannah and Jim, Sr., were to appear in Granton to answer to the charge of arson the next day.

Farming is a demanding occupation. Chores must be carried out and farm animals must be fed. To that end, the Donnellys had a neighboring youngster, 11-year-old Johnny O'Connor, sleeping over that night. Johnny was to take care of the animals the next day, while the Donnellys drove to Granton to appear in court. A niece, Bridget, was visiting from Ireland. Tom was at home with his parents.

Constable Jim Carroll led the group. He sighted Tom Donnelly asleep in a tiny bedroom off the kitchen. Jim snapped handcuffs on his wrist. Tom awoke with a start and cried out, "What the hell!" Carroll responded, "You're under arrest."

The noise woke up Johannah, who in turn woke up her niece Bridget. Jim, Sr., was sleeping with Johnny O'Connor. He pulled on his trousers and joined the rest in the kitchen. He saw his son in handcuffs, "What? Tom, are you handcuffed?" he asked.

"Yes," Tom replied. "He thinks he is smart." By candlelight, Jim, Sr., went back to the bedroom for his coat. Johnny O'Connor had been using the elder Donnelly's coat for a pillow. Now he held it out for Jim, who returned to the kitchen.

There, in the eerie glow of the candle, Johnny O'Connor's eyes met Jim Carroll's. Later, Johnny would state there was no way Carroll was unaware of his presence. In light of future events, it is a minor mystery that Johnny O'Connor's life was spared.

Did the men intend only to beat up the Donnelly clan? Bill Ryder, a great-great-great nephew of Grouchy Ryder, says, "I believe the intent was to rough up the Donnellys, but something went wrong and, once started, the mob got out of hand."

All but one of the inhabitants of the house that night were beaten and clubbed to death. Tom Donnelly fell. So did his parents and so did his cousin Bridget. Johnny O'Connor, trembling with fear, hid under a bed, where he could see a shovel being brought down time after time on a Donnelly skull.

The house was set ablaze and in moments the mob

was gone. Johnny O'Connor escaped from the burning house and ran barefoot to a neighboring farm. The mob's work wasn't completed. Down the road they marched to the home of Will Donnelly. It was his brother John who answered the door. Silhouetted in the light of the doorway, he was an easy target. John died moments after being shot. The mob thought it had killed the hated Will. Now the carnage came to an end. The men dispersed, leaving five members of the one family dead in their wake.

Next day, word of the tragedy spread. Initially, 13 men were held on suspicion. Of these, six were charged with murder — James Carroll, John Kennedy, Martin McLaughlin, Thomas Ryder, James Ryder and John Purtell. The six men were lodged in the jail behind the London courthouse.

On January 24, 1881, Jim Carroll stood trial for the murder of Johannah Donnelly for the second time. This time, he was found not guilty. Because the case against Carroll had been so strong, it was felt that it would be futile to try any of the remaining men. They were all released from custody. No one has ever been convicted of the five murders which took place in the wee hours of the morning of February 4, 1880.

In the years which followed the massacre of the Donnelly family, members of the Vigilance Committee were buried in the little graveyard beside St. Patrick's Church. Ironically, they rest forever beside the Donnelly family, victims of Canada's most infamous crime.

Albert Fish

Cannibalism! The word itself screams out from the page as no other word in the English language. Incidents of human flesh being consumed by fellow humans to sustain life are well recorded. Marooned sailors, bush pilots, and surviving victims of plane crashes have all forced themselves to eat human flesh in order to survive. North American Indians and some African tribes ate portions of their fallen enemies as an act of respect, in the belief that they would acquire some of the admirable qualities of their former foes.

Those cases where cannibalism is practised for the sheer perverted pleasure of the act are much rarer. In the 20th century, the case most often referred to as an example of pure cannibalism is the bizarre saga of Albert Fish.

"Young man, 18 years old, wishes position in the country for the summer." The ad appeared in the Situations Wanted column of a New York City newspaper on Monday, May 21, 1928. Edward Budd was to regret placing the ad for the rest of his life.

The Budd family lived in West 15th St. apartment house in what was then the edge of New York City. Edward Budd, Sr., and his wife, Delia, had four children, the oldest being Edward Jr., and the youngest Grace, 12. Ed Budd had made up his mind. This summer he would escape from the city heat and noise. He placed the ad for summer employment in the newspaper.

Two days after the advertisement appeared an elderly, respectable looking man arrived at the Budd's door. He explained to Mrs. Budd that he had a large vegetable garden operation near Farmingdale, Long Island,

and could use help over the summer months. Edward was enthusiastic. A deal was struck then and there. The elderly gentleman, who had introduced himself as Frank Howard, would pick Edward up the following Thursday or Sunday. The Budds invited Howard to come early on Sunday and have dinner with them. The old man promised to try. Later in the week, the Budd family received a telegram advising them that Howard would arrive early on Sunday.

Sure enough, Mr. Howard arrived the following Sunday and broke bread with the Budds. He said grace and proved to be a charming conversationalist. At the conclusion of the meal he informed his hosts that he had a surprise. His sister, who lived in New York, was having a birthday party for her daughter, who just happened to be Grace Budd's age. He was planning on attending and would take Grace along if it was all right with her mother. When they returned he and Ed could then leave for the country. Mrs. Budd was at first apprehensive, but with exuberant coaxing by her daughter, she finally consented. Hand-in-hand, little Grace and one of the worst monsters who ever lived strolled out of the apartment and, in Grace's case, into oblivion.

By subway, Frank Howard led Grace to Westchester County near Irvington. There, in a ram-shackle house called Wisteria Cottage, the old man choked the life from the little girl. He then dissected his victim and wrapped a portion of the body in his bandanna. Frank Howard left the house of death and proceeded to his rented room. Next day he ate the portion of meat that had once been Grace Budd. Every few days the old man would return to Wisteria Cottage. Each time he left with a parcel, which he later consumed. Nine days after the murder he made his final trip. What remained of Grace Budd was thrown out of a window into a weed-infested back yard.

Grace was reported missing. The case, considered to be a kidnapping perpetrated by an old man, presented only one clue. The missing person's bureau of the New York City Police Force was able to trace the telegram sent to the Budd family. This provided them with a sample of the kidnapper's handwriting, but nothing further turned up.

Years went by, and the little girl's disappearance was all but forgotten. From time to time the Budd family received crank notes and letters, which they routinely turned over to the police.

Six years after the kidnapping, one of these letters, thought to be from a crank, proved to have been written by the same hand which had written the old telegram to the Budds. The contents of the unsigned letter described Grace Budd's fate in detail.

Police were able to trace the writing paper to a type used by an organization known as The Private Chauffeurs Benevolent Association. A janitor for this organization admitted taking some of the stationery to his rooming house for his personal use. He told police that he had left some in his room at 200 East 52nd St. when he had moved out.

The police proceeded to Room 11 at the janitor's former address. The landlady gave the police a description of the occupant of Room 11. There was no question about it — the occupant was Frank Howard, who had abducted Grace Budd almost six years previously.

The landlady informed police that Number 11 was often vacant for most of the month, but her tenant, known to her as Albert Fish, always returned to pick up a cheque sent to him by a son in North Carolina. This time when Fish returned to his room, police were waiting for him.

The mild-mannered old man readily confessed to the abduction. His story was one of perversion, which had begun at the age of five, when he discovered that he enjoyed pain after being spanked by a teacher. Brought up in an orphanage, he later married and had several children. His wife always considered him strange, but lived with him for 20 years before leaving him. His grown children later testified that their father often thought he was Christ, and from time to time would disappear without an explanation.

Police uncovered the skull and some bones of Grace Budd, which had lain where they had been thrown so many years before. In the same weeds, they found a rusty knife and cleaver.

Fish was examined extensively by both psychiatrists and police. It was discovered that he had visited various communities in the northeastern U.S. at the exact time when young children had been murdered. Fish denied any knowledge of these crimes, but admitted to leading a life of molesting children, while he wandered from one job to another, usually as a house painter.

In a case as weird as any ever recorded, there was still more to come. While X-raying Fish, doctors found 29 metal needles in various parts of his body. Some were as large as those used to repair canvas. All had been inserted by Fish to cause pain. Doctors stated that some of the needles had been in his body for as long as seven years.

When Fish related his life story to doctors, he revealed that over the years he had been in several mental institutions for short periods of time. On each occasion he had been released as harmless.

Albert Fish stood trial for the murder of Grace Budd on March 11, 1935 in White Plains, N.Y. Despite the efforts put forward by his defence counsel, pleading that his client was insane, the jury deliberated only a few hours before finding Fish guilty of murder.

Just before being transferred to Sing Sing, Fish confessed to four additional murders of small children.

As the end drew near, Fish told the guards that he was delighted at the chance of experiencing the ultimate thrill of being put to death. Albert Fish was electrocuted on January 16, 1936.

Harvey Glatman

Harvey Glatman was a specialist. He robbed only women.

In 1945, Harvey spent a year in the Canon City, Colorado prison for a series of armed robberies perpetrated against women. Shortly after his release, he was apprehended for stealing purses from women as they walked along dimly-lit streets. This time he spent five years in Sing Sing, before being paroled to his mother's loving care in Denver.

In 1957, Harvey migrated to Los Angeles, where the strange desire he had bottled up in his psyche came to the surface. Nondescript, owlish Harvey, with the oversized ears, shell-rimmed glasses and large nose, did not take L.A. by storm. You see, Harvey, at age 30, was a virgin. He had tried to become acquainted with members of the opposite sex in the past, but had always been rejected. Swinging Los Angeles would be different. Besides, Harvey had a plan.

Using the alias Johnny Glynn and posing as a professional photographer, Harvey had no trouble making contact with model Judy Dull. Judy, a beautiful blonde, was only 19, but had already been married and divorced. She lived in a rather plush apartment at 1302 Sweetzer Ave. with two equally beautiful models.

Harvey met all three girls, explaining that he had an assignment for one of them. It was to pose for the cover of a detective magazine and would involve some nude shots. He thought Judy Dull was exactly the type. A fee was established. The shooting would take place in the girls' apartment. Harvey explained that his studio was undergoing renovations.

On August 1, 1957, Harvey pulled up in his black Dodge bearing Colorado plates. He told the girls that there was a slight change of plans. He had been able to borrow the well-equipped studio of a friend. He wouldn't have to use their apartment after all. One of the girls mentioned that Judy had appointments for later that same afternoon. Could she have a telephone number where Judy could be reached? Without hesitation, Harvey jotted down a number on a piece of paper and passed it over.

Judy and Harvey sped away. They drove to a dreary building on Melrose Ave. Judy, carrying her model's suitcase, briskly walked to a second floor apartment. She was no doubt reassured by the tripods, lights and other photographic equipment already set up. Harvey took several shots of Judy fully clothed before asking her to take off her blouse. He took more photographs. Then he suggested she slip out of her skirt.

Harvey approached Judy with a five-foot piece of white sash cord. Initially, Judy objected, but Harvey calmly explained that he had to tie her up for a few shots in order to fulfil his obligations to the detective magazine. Reluctantly, Judy allowed her hands and feet to be tied and a gag to be placed over her mouth. Harvey took more pictures. He then produced a gun and informed Judy that was going to release the gag and untie her hands and feet. If she didn't comply with his every wish, he would shoot her in the head.

Once free of the gag, Judy pleaded for her life. She tearfully explained that she and her husband were in the midst of a divorce. She was about to receive custody of their little girl. She promised to keep Harvey's secret. She just wanted to be spared. Weird Harvey raped the terror-stricken girl and forced her to watch

122

TV with him. Every so often, Judy pleaded to be released, but Harvey was deep in thought.

Finally he agreed. He would drive out to the desert, take a few more photographs and then set her free. The pair drove for hours into the San Jacinto mountains. Harvey stated, "Just a few quick shots. Then we'll go back to the highway and you're on your own. Sorry we had to come so far, but there wasn't any other way, Judy."

Harvey was lying. He realized that Judy knew his address, knew he had Colorado plates on his Dodge and could describe him in far more detail than her roommates. Harvey once more tied Judy's hands and feet and gagged the hapless girl. He took another piece of rope and wrapped it around Judy's neck. In minutes the girl was dead. There, on the lonely desert, Harvey dug a shallow grave with his hands for Judy Dull.

Judy's roommates went to the police with the phone number given to them by photographer Johnny Glynn. It proved to be a bogus number.

Seven months later, posing as plumber George Williams, Harvey joined a lonely hearts club and managed a blind date with 24-year-old Shirley Ann Bridgeford. Shirley, who had recently been divorced, had two small sons and lived with her mother. To "mix with new friends," she answered a lonely hearts club ad. It was Shirley's misfortune to answer an ad extolling the virtues of Harvey Glatman. As soon as Shirley entered his car, Harvey pulled out his gun. He drove into the desert and took a series of photographs before raping and killing his victim.

Shirley's mother reported her daughter missing to police. A quick check with the lonely hearts club revealed that plumber George Williams had given a fictitious name and address.

Two months later Harvey, posing as Mr. Johnson, called a nude modelling service. He required a model for an hour or two, and was put in touch with Ruth Rita Mercado, who had her own studio. A date was set and Harvey showed up in his beat-up Dodge.

On this occasion, he didn't waste time. Ruth opened the door and stared into the barrel of Harvey's trusty black automatic. In minutes, she was tied, gagged and helpless. Harvey took his pictures. At gunpoint, he untied his quarry and led her to the Dodge. They sped into the desert. The usual outdoor pictures were taken. Ruth was raped and then murdered in the usual hideous manner with the rope draped around her neck. Acquaintances reported Ruth Mercado's disappearance to police.

Harvey was confident. After all, hadn't he had his way with three lovely women and no one had the slightest idea why they had disappeared? In fact, no one even knew they were dead.

Harvey was referred to model Lorraine Vigil by another model. Lorraine was newly arrived in Hollywood from San Francisco and was eager for work. Harvey called at Lorraine's apartment. During the drive to his non-existent studio, Lorraine sized up her companion. He didn't seem right. She couldn't quite categorize her anxiety, but this strange man just didn't act like a professional photographer. When she realized her silent companion was leaving the city far behind, she knew her instincts were correct.

Lorraine didn't have long to wait. Harvey braked the car, pulled out his gun and told her he would kill her unless she complied with his every desire. Lorraine replied, "All right, just please don't hurt me." When

Harvey took out his rope, Lorraine pleaded not to be tied up. She promised over and over that she would obey his every wish. Lorraine knew intuitively that she was in a life and death situation. The previous three victims possibly felt they would be spared. Lorraine knew better. This man was going to kill her.

Without warning, she pushed Harvey's gun aside. The two desperately struggled for possession of the weapon. The gun went off, but only slightly seared Lorraine's thigh. She moaned and slumped against him, feigning death. Harvey stared at the gun in a stupor. Slowly, Lorraine inched her hand toward the door handle on Harvey's side of the car. She moved the handle mechanism until she knew the door was ajar. Then, with all her strength, she shoved Harvey out the door.

The force of her thrust landed her on top of the gunman. Desperately, she fought to get control of the gun. Her teeth clamped down on Harvey's gun hand. With a yelp, he let go. Lorraine pounced on the gun, picked it up, pointed it and fired it at Harvey. The gun jammed. As Harvey crouched like an animal, about to attack Lorraine, the courageous girl had one stroke of incredible good luck that day.

Tom Mulligan of the California Highway Patrol drove up on his motorcycle at that moment. Instantly realizing what was taking place, he barked at Harvey, "You stay right were you are!"

Harvey confessed in detail to his crimes and led police to the three lonely graves in the desert. On August 18, 1959, Harvey Glatman was quietly strapped into the gas chamber in San Diego and put to death.

John Gilbert Graham

A few years ago John Wayne Gacy paid the ultimate price for murdering 33 young men and boys, thereby becoming the most prolific mass murderer in U.S. criminal history. Twenty-five years earlier another citizen of the U.S., John Gilbert Graham, actually murdered a larger number than Gacy. Only a technicality deprived this earlier day monster from being the all-time champ.

John first saw the light of day in 1932 in Denver, Colorado. His father passed away when he was only five years old. Left destitute, Jack's mother Daisy had little choice but to place her son in an orphanage, where he remained for six years. In 1943, Mrs. Graham remarried a wealthy rancher, John Earl King and brought her 11-year-old-son to his new home. For a while he was joined by his sister, who later moved to Alaska.

Jack was not a contented child. While he got high marks, he never really showed any interest in school work. He is mainly remembered for an explosive temper, which could flare up at the slightest provocation. When Jack didn't get his way he ran away from home. At the age of 16 he lied about his age to join the Coast Guard. Nine months later his deception was uncovered and he was dismissed from the service.

Jack returned to Denver and found a job, but quickly succeeded in getting into trouble. He stole several of his company's blank cheques, forged the name of one of the company's directors, and cashed $4,200 of the bogus paper. With the proceeds he travelled to Texas, where he became a bootlegger. He was apprehended, and after serving a few months in jail was returned to Colorado to face forgery charges. Daisy King stepped in and made restitution in the amount of $2,500, with the firm promise that her son would pay off the balance of $1,700 in instalments.

Jack secured work in a garage, married pretty Gloria Elson, and for a while seemed to settle down. The attractive young couple promptly had two children. Daisy doted over her grandchildren.

In 1954, tragedy once again entered Daisy King's life. Her husband Earl died. This time Daisy was left with a comfortable fortune. She decided that her wayward son would reform if given a proper opportunity. Daisy presented Jack with a new home. She would live with her son and daughter-in-law, but the house was in his name. Daisy had also found a drive-in restaurant, which she purchased for $5,000, and asked Jack to run it. No son could ask more of a mother.

But things just didn't work out. Jack always seemed to be short of cash at the end of the day. Daisy couldn't understand how an intelligent 23-year-old man could not manage to balance his cash with his cash register tapes. Mother and son began to argue over the operation of the restaurant. To relieve the tension, Daisy decided to visit her daughter in Alaska. During October 1955 she bought Christmas presents to take north.

On November 1, Jack and Gloria, accompanied by their two children, drove Daisy to the airport. Daisy was catching Flight 629 for the first leg of her trip to Alaska. There was a slight delay at the weigh-in counter when it was discovered that her luggage was in excess of the allowable weight of 66 pounds. She was over by 37 pounds. When an attendant was told that one suitcase contained Christmas presents, he suggested that those items could be mailed a lot cheaper than the $27 he had to charge. Jack would hear none of it. He talked his mother into paying the $27.

It is to be remembered that there were no security measures at airports 40 years ago, but insurance was available from vending machines. Jack sauntered over to the machines and popped in quarters. You could buy $6,250 protection for a quarter. Jack bought several policies totalling $87,500. His mother joked with him as she signed the policies.

Daisy hugged her grandchildren, kissed her daughter-in-law, and clasped her son to her bosom. Flight 629 took off. Before the Graham family was out of the airport word was received that the DC6 had exploded in mid-air. There were no survivors. A total of 44 men, women, and children had perished. Among them was Mrs. Daisy King.

The FBI lab in Washington quickly ascertained that the plane had been blown up by dynamite. Traces of sodium nitrate and sodium carbonate were found in the gaping torn metal believed to be the location in the baggage compartment.

Authorities could not locate the baggage of one Daisy King, leading them to believe that her luggage may have contained the dynamite. They did find Daisy's handbag, which had been carried aboard the ill-fated plane. It was then they found newspaper clippings concerning her son, Jack Graham, who four years earlier had been sought by Denver police as a forgery suspect. FBI agents dug into Jack Graham's life and discovered that he had a penchant for getting into trouble with the law.

Nine days after the disaster, FBI agents knocked on

Jack's door. He denied any knowledge of the crime. A search of his home uncovered a roll of wire used in connecting up dynamite. Agents also discovered gaily wrapped Christmas presents. Had Jack, unknown to his mother, substituted a dynamite bomb in place of the presents?

After three hours of questioning, Jack Graham calmly changed his story and confessed to perpetrating the horrendous crime. He told the FBI of actually working as an apprentice electrician for ten days so that he could manufacture the bomb without blowing himself up. He had bought 25 sticks of dynamite and all the accessories to construct the bomb. Later clerks in hardware stores identified him as the purchaser of these supplies.

Jack Graham stood trial for the murder of his mother only, thereby escaping the historical notoriety of becoming the greatest convicted mass murder in U.S. history. After deliberating only an hour and a half, a jury found him guilty of murder in the first degree.

Graham was one of the coolest men ever to be executed. A few days before his death he reminded a guard, "if any mail comes for me after next month you can readdress it to hell."

On January 11, 1957, he calmly entered Colorado's gas chamber, inhaled deeply, lost consciousness, and was pronounced dead twelve minutes later.

Albert Guay

Three times a week, a Quebec Airways flight left Montreal for Seven Islands, with stops at Quebec City and Baie Comeau. It was so punctual and reliable that people along the route used to set their watches by the roar of the engines.

On September 9, 1949, Patrick Simard was fishing for eels near his home at Sault-aux-Cochon, Quebec. He glanced up, idly following the flight of the Douglas DC-3 as it approached Cap Tourmente. Then he heard a loud explosion, and as he watched in horror the plane veered crazily to the left and went into a power dive, heading straight for the peak of Cap Tourmente. Simard ran through thick bush towards the crash; it took him an hour to get to the scene. Scattered among the wreckage of the aircraft were the remains of the passengers and their luggage. Surprisingly, there was no fire, but the ominous smell of leaking gasoline hung over the entire area. The propellers had been turned when the plane smashed vertically into the ground. There was no swath of torn trees, only the aircraft with its wings ripped off and its horribly mangled nose sticking into the earth.

The plane had held four crew members and 19 passengers. Simard checked to see if there were any survivors. Finding none, he started down the mountain for help. He met some men who were working on railway tracks nearby, and they took the news to St. Joachim, where it was relayed to Quebec City. Within hours Canadian Pacific Airlines, the parent company of Quebec Airways, had their investigating officials at the scene of the crash.

The left front luggage compartment showed signs of an explosion, and it was this explosion that had destroyed the control system of the aircraft, causing the disaster. They examined everything aboard the aircraft that could have caused an explosion. Items such as fire extinguishers and storage batteries were checked, but none of these was found to be the cause of the crash. The four crew members and 19 passengers had been killed instantly upon impact, but the lack of fire made identifying the bodies relatively easy, and the next of kin were quickly notified. Because of the explosion in the baggage compartment, the authorities concluded that they were dealing with a criminal case and not an accident.

On September 12, the entire matter was turned over to the RCMP. The Mounties were to be assisted by the Quebec Provincial Police and the Quebec City Police Force.

The left front compartment had been loaded in Montreal with cargo destined for Quebec City. It was completely emptied in Quebec City and reloaded with cargo destined for Baie Comeau. This was routine practice, and was employed to reduce unnecessary delay during the flight's many stops. The authorities realized that the explosive material must have been put into the left front baggage compartment at Ancienne Lorette Airport in Quebec City.

The passenger list of the ill-fated craft was closely scrutinized, as was the list of insurance policies taken out on the passengers' lives. A cursory check turned up nothing unusual, and the police decided to place all relatives of victims who boarded the plane in Quebec City under observation and to conduct an investigation into their private lives.

Undertaking the investigation from another direction, the police started with the plane on the ground in Quebec City and the left front baggage compartment empty. They questioned Willie Lamonde, the freight clerk who had been on duty on September 9, but he could recall nothing of significance except that several pieces of freight had been placed on the aircraft, in addition to the passengers' regular luggage. From company records the police were able to obtain the names of the senders and prospective receivers of all the air freight shipments, and they set about checking every name on the list. This approach bore fruit with the discovery of a 28-lb. parcel sent by Delphis Bouchard of St. Simeon, Quebec, to Alfred Plouffe, 180 Laval St., Baie Comeau. Neither sender nor addressee existed, so it seemed reasonable to assume that someone had walked up to Willie Lamonde with a bomb and shipped it air freight to Baie Comeau.

The police begged Willie to try to remember who had given him the parcel. Willie's memory was now jarred by names and addresses he could relate to, and he came up with a mental picture of the person who had given him the bomb. He said it was a fat woman who had come to the airport by cab. He remembered this because the cabbie had carried the parcel to the scale for the fat lady. The cost of shipping the 28-lb. parcel to Baie Comeau was $2.72, which she paid to Willie, who gave her a receipt. The police started the tedious task of questioning every cabbie in Quebec City, and almost immediately they found the right man.

Paul Pelletier, who worked for the Yellow Cab Co., had picked up the fat lady on September 9 at the Palais Railroad Station. He described her as middle-aged and overweight, with dark hair and eyes. She didn't say one word to him on the trip to the airport, but because she was returning to the city with him, he had carried the parcel to the freight clerk. When they returned to the city she got out of his cab at the rear of the Chateau Frontenac Hotel, and Pelletier recalled seeing her walk toward Lower Town, the older section of the city.

Then, upon checking the relatives of victims, the police for ty the authorities. The girl still worked at the restaurant and the police decided to question her about her relationship with Guay. The detectives confronted an attractive, shapely young girl who would have caused heads to turn anywhere.

Marie-Ange openly admitted knowing Albert Guay, and when asked if Guay had anything to do with a fat middle-aged woman, she immediately gave the police the name of Marguerite Pitre who lived at 49 Monseigneur Gauvreau St. The police stationed the cab driver outside Marguerite Pitre's house, so that when she came out he would be able to identify her. On September 20, a taxi drove up and Pelletier had a good look at Marguerite as she got in. He positively identified her as the lady he had driven to the airport on September 9. Marguerite had taken an overdose of sleeping pills, and the taxi had been summoned to rush her to Infant Jesus Hospital. The police decided to arrest her as soon as she was released.

Who was this strange woman? What circumstances tied her to the young waitress, Marie-Ange Robitaille? How was Albert Guay connected to the two women?

The tangled plot started to unfold. Albert Guay was born in 1917 to a working-class family. As a child, he liked games in which he played the part of a ship's captain or commander of great armies, and always had illusions of power and wealth. By the time he was 22, he was working in a war plant and selling watches as a sideline.

During the war he married the former Rita Morel, and when peace came he gravitated to the jewelry business as a full-time occupation, opening up a store in Seven Islands, Quebec. In 1948, he closed his store and opened a shop on St. Sauveur St., which he soon owned.

Guay was having a prolonged affair with Marie-Ange. It is almost certain that Rita Guay had knowledge of the affair, but being wise to the ways of men with wandering eyes, she figured Albert would have his fling, tire of the waitress, and return to her. Marie-Ange had lived in a room in Marguerite Pitre's house, and it was here that Albert Guay would come to make love to his mistress, with Marguerite's complicity. The heavy-set Marguerite, who always wore black, and as a result came to be known as The Raven, had met Guay during the war when they both worked in the same munitions plant. Another member of The Raven's family, her crippled brother Genereux Ruest, worked for Guay as a watch repairman in his jewelry shop.

The Raven had come under Guay's influence when she started borrowing small amounts of money from him during the war. This led to more and more loans until finally she was compelled to comply his every wish. When first questioned, the Raven at first denied taking the bomb out to the airport, but when faced with the cab driver she confessed that she had delivered the explosives. Once started, the Raven continued to sing. She admitted getting in debt to Albert, until finally she owed him $600. He always demanded favors of her, and when Marie-Ange was only sixteen she had set the good-looking young girl up in her own apartment at his insistence.

The Raven claimed that Guay promised he would forget the debt if she would get him some dynamite, knowing that her neighbor had acquaintances in the construction business who had access to explosives. The Raven told her neighbor that if she could get her hands on some dynamite it would be her chance to get out of Albert's clutches once and for all. Guay had told the Raven that he needed the dynamite for a friend who was removing tree stumps. In the end the Raven succeeded in obtaining ten pounds of dynamite and 19 blasting caps.

On September 23, Albert Guay was arrested and taken into custody. He admitted everything except murder. Albert said he knew the Raven very well because she brought him leads for watch sales, and her crippled brother worked for him. He even admitted having the affair with Marie-Ange, but claimed it was over before the plane crash. Through it all he swore he loved his wife dearly, and that the Raven was a barefaced liar.

The police descended on Genereux Ruest's workshop to search it for any evidence that a bomb had been manufactured there. They found an insignificant piece of corrugated cardboard coated with black deposits. It was the only thing in the shop that looked unusual in any way. The cardboard was rushed to a Montreal laboratory for testing. In the lab, blasting caps were exploded using a piece of corrugated cardboard as a shield. The explosions left black deposits on the cardboard matching the ones on the cardboard taken from Ruest's workshop. The same tell-tale black deposits appeared on the inside of the left front luggage compartment of the downed aircraft.

Armed with this incriminating evidence, the authorities faced Ruest. Finally he confessed that he had constructed a time mechanism, and that he and Albert had experimented with setting it off. He claimed Albert had brought him all the materials for the bomb, and that he had no idea that Guay planned to use it for anything other than clearing stumps. He said he was afraid to volunteer the information earlier because he thought the police would believe he knew of Guay's intentions.

Meanwhile, Marie-Ange Robitaille added her chapter to the increasingly well-documented life and loves of Albert Guay. She said she had met Guay at a dance in 1947, when she was 16 years old. She thought he was a glamorous man-about-town in the jewelry business, and even though she knew he was married, it wasn't long before they were having sexual relations. Rita Guay had even complained to the girl's parents, but Marie-Ange moved out of her parents' home and into a spare room that the Raven provided. Several times she tried to break up with Guay, but each time he went after her and brought her back. There is little doubt that Marie-Ange was physically attracted to Guay, but in the end she could see no future with a married man. She had only seen Guay once after the crash. On the occasion he had begged her to come back to him, pleading that since his wife was now dead, no obstacles stood in their way. She told him the affair was over, and she now told police she knew nothing about the bomb.

Despite the incriminating statements of the Raven and her brother, Albert steadfastly maintained his innocence. On February 23, 1950, Albert Guay stood trial for murder. The jury took only 17 minutes to find him guilty, and he was sentenced to death by hanging. Once in Bordeaux Jail awaiting death, he made a full confession, implicating the Raven and her brother as willing accomplices. Both had been motivated by money he had promised them from a small insurance policy he had taken out on his wife's life, and both had been well aware that he planned to blow up the aircraft.

Albert Guay was hanged on January 12, 1951, and Genereux Ruest followed him to the gallows in 1952. The Raven was hanged in 1953.

Fritz Haarmann

This little tale of terror concerns Fritz Haarmann, a man who was unique in that he had three distinct motives for murder. He received sexual gratification from the act, simply enjoyed killing and also murdered for cold, hard cash.

Fritz was born in Hanover, Germany in 1879. His father was a stoker on the German railway but quit working when Fritz's mother received an inheritance sufficient to support the family of six children, the youngest of whom was our Fritz.

The three Haarmann daughters all took up the profitable but precarious occupation of prostitution. One son, Wilhelm, was institutionalized as a teenager when he attacked a 12-year-old girl. Lest you think that I am leading you to believe that all the Haarmann brood were bad seeds, let me hasten to add that one son led an average, reputable life. And then there was Fritz.

He was an odd kid. No sooner was he able to walk than it was observed that he preferred to play with dolls. Sometimes he dressed in his sisters' clothing. You get the idea.

As he grew into his teens, Fritz developed into a rather good-looking, chubby lad. At 16, he attended a military academy. One day he took a sort of fit while on parade. Some records indicate his fainting spell was the result of sunstroke. After this incident, Fritz left the academy.

At 17, Fritz was accused of indecent acts against children and was sent to the Provincial Asylum at Hildesheim. Six months later, he escaped and spent two years wandering around Switzerland, before returning to Hanover and joining the army. Fritz stayed in the army until 1903. Upon being discharged, he practised every vice imaginable. He stole, committed indecent acts and spent more time in prison than outside. When World War I broke out, Fritz was confined to prison and sat out the entire war. He was released in 1918 into a Germany in turmoil.

In Hanover, Fritz found a city fraught with swindlers, thieves and cutthroats, all intent on exploiting a poorly clothed and hungry populace. The centre of the illicit activity was the Head Railroad Station and the Schieber Market across the street. Here, for a price, one could purchase literally anything from the thousands of little stalls where hawkers merchandised their wares. Among the sellers and buyers were the destitute, the prostitutes, the sneak thieves, the perverts and the fugitives from justice. Hanover truly attracted the dregs.

Fritz took one look and felt right at home. Within six months he had established himself in two professions. He prospered as a butcher and also acted as a police informer to the grossly undermanned Hanover police force. Fritz Haarmann had found his niche. He managed to undercut his competitors' meat prices, making him very popular with his customers. His semi-official police work earned him the nickname of Detective Haarmann.

To the outside world, Fritz even appeared to be performing charitable acts. He was known to befriend homeless boys. On many occasions, he would take a homeless waif and, with the promise of a meal and a mattress, lead the hapless youngster to the warmth of his rooms. The boys never left the butcher's quarters alive.

It is impossible to relate exactly what happened to all of Fritz's victims. It will suffice here to follow the fate of one as representative of all.

Seventeen-year-old Friedel Rothe ran away from home and headed directly for Schieber Market. Two days later, his mother received a brief postcard from him. The Rothes were certain that if they could find their son, they could bring him home. All would be forgiven. A friend of Friedel's told the Rothes that their son had visited a male friend at 27 Cellarstrasse. That's how the Rothes ended up knocking at Fritz Haarmann's door.

With police at their side, the Rothes were shocked to find Haarmann performing a sex act with a young boy. A rather casual search of his rooms uncovered no evidence of the missing Friedel Rothe. We know the search was perfunctory because four years later, at his trial for murder, Fritz remarked, "At the time when the policeman arrested me, the head of the boy Friedel was hidden under a newspaper behind the oven. Later on I threw it into the canal."

In the meantime, Fritz was sent to prison for nine months for indecency. Upon his release, he moved and continued his murderous ways in his new location.

In 1919, he met Hans Grans, a well-built young man with the face of an angel. Fritz and Hans became close friends. Now, with a confederate, it was even easier for Fritz to entice young boys to his quarters for a good time. Certainly, Grans knew of his companion's murderous ways. Later Fritz would accuse Grans of being his willing accomplice in all the murders.

From 1919 to 1923, Fritz, with Grans as an accomplice, brought young boys to his rooms. Here, they were killed. Every stitch of the victims' clothing was sold on the black market, with the exception of certain items young Grans fancied. These he kept for his own use.

Around this time, rumors spread about the district that human flesh was being sold on the open market. Suspicion fell on Fritz Haarmann, mainly because of his association with young boys and also because his meat prices were always the lowest. No one did much about the suspicions. That's all they were — suspicions, nothing more.

How did Fritz kill with impunity over a lengthy period of time? Several conditions existed which favored his nefarious deeds. The disruption of post-war Germany lent itself to a laissez-faire attitude toward criminal activity. The police were desperately understaffed. Finally, there was Fritz's occupation. What was more natural than a bloody apron or a bloody knife in a butcher's premises? Fritz acted quite openly. In hindsight, neighbors remembered him carrying buckets of bloody water through the halls. No one thought much about it. After all, he was a butcher.

On May 17, 1924, youngsters playing on the banks of the Leine River found a human skull. Twelve days later, another skull was found further down the river. In July, boys playing along the river bank found a sack of human bones and a skull. News of the gruesome finds spread like wildfire. There was a killer on the loose. Maybe those rumors about someone selling human flesh were authentic after all.

Citizens gathered by the score to stare at the waters of the Leine River. Police searched the murky depths. They were not disappointed. On the first day they recovered 500 human bones. Doctors agreed that the bones had come from 22 different bodies, all young boys.

Fritz was immediately suspected. Police imported detectives who were not known to the suspect. When Fritz and a young boy were observed arguing on the street, the detectives intervened. Fritz claimed the young man had travelled on a train without a ticket. The youngster charged Fritz with an indecent act. Police seized the opportunity to haul both off to jail while they searched Fritz's rooms.

Blood-smeared pieces of clothing were found and were readily traced to many of the missing boys. One wall of Fritz's room was caked with human blood.

Under extensive questioning, Fritz confessed to "30 or 40" murders. He couldn't remember the exact number. His trial for mass murder brought forth sensational evidence of cannibalism and the butchering of humans. Evidence pointing to the sale of human flesh was suppressed. The German government thought that the conviction of a mass murderer was sufficient.

Hans Grans was found guilty of murder and sentenced to life imprisonment. Fritz Haarmann, one of the most prolific and despicable mass murderers of all time, was found guilty of the murder of 24 young boys. He received the death sentence. In 1925, he was decapitated by a swordsman.

William Heirens

The city of Chicago has long been familiar with violent death. The citizens of that community take a gangland killing as casually as we take our morning coffee. It takes a bizarre and baffling case to arouse public interest. Here is such a case.

On June 3, 1945, Mrs. Josephine Alice Ross was found dead in her apartment. Her body had horrible knife wounds about the head and neck. The jugular vein had been cut, allowing her to bleed to death. A nylon stocking and skirt were wrapped around her neck. The bed she lay on was completely soaked in blood. The investigating officers knew immediately that this was no ordinary crime when they discovered that the body had been washed clean of blood and adhesive tape had been applied to the cuts and abrasions. Mrs. Ross had not been sexually attacked, but her murderer had lingered in the apartment and had meticulously wiped the entire apartment clean of fingerprints.

For the next five months, police investigated several attacks on women in the general area of the University of Chicago. Some were shootings and some were beatings, and all could have ended in tragedy but for the fact that the attacker was either interrupted or was successfully fought off by the women.

Then on December 10, the murderer struck again. Frances Brown's nude body was found draped in a kneeling position over the bathtub of her apartment. She had been stabbed repeatedly in the head and neck, and had been shot as well. Again the murderer had taken great care in washing the body. He had also stayed in the apartment long enough to wash every piece of furniture free of fingerprints. This time he missed one lone print - the right index finger. An attempt to trace him through this print failed.

Overshadowing all other evidence in the Brown case was an actual message left by the killer. On a wall in the living room, written in lipstick, were the words:

For heavens
sake catch me
Before I kill more
I cannot control myself

The similarity of the two murders as well as the several other attacks on women convinced the police that they were looking for one sick man. On the morning of January 7 they were to find out just how sick.

A little six-year-old girl, Suzanne Degnan, had been abducted from the first-floor bedroom of her two-storey home. Her father found a ransom note on her bed.

Get $20,000
Reddy &
Waite
For word
do not notify
FBI or
police
Bills in 5's and 10's

One fingerprint was found on the note. It was the print of the left little finger. A check of police files again proved fruitless, as no match could be found.

A search was started for Suzanne in the immediate

vicinity of her home. An officer noticed that a sewer lid looked as if it had been recently pried loose. He lifted the lid and peered into the sewer. There floating on the surface was a human head. A search of other sewers revealed the rest of pathetic little Suzanne's body. She had been abducted and dismembered on the same night.

In scouring the neighborhood for any clues to the killer's identity the police found an apartment building close by where Suzanne had been dismembered. The basement, like many of the buildings in that area, was equipped with a washbasin for the tenants. Here the police found bloody rags, and not a great deal more. It was estimated that the killer had spent over two hours cleaning the washroom. Again despite an all-out effort by the police, there was a vacuum of concrete clues to the wave of wanton killings. Months dragged by, and then in a completely unrelated incident, the police found their killer.

A young man was interrupted as he was ransacking an apartment. He dashed out of the building, and into an adjoining building at 1320 Farrell Ave. He stopped at the back door of an apartment occupied by Mrs. Frances Willett, and asked for a drink of water. He picked the wrong door. Mrs. Willett was the wife of a policeman. She sensed something wrong and told him to sit down on her porch. She then hooked the door from the inside and pretended to get the water. Instead she called the police.

In the meantime, an off-duty policeman, Abner Cunningham, was coming home from the beach wearing swimming trunks and a t-shirt. He saw the youth dash out of one building and into another. Cunningham started a door-to-door search of the second building.

The police, responding to Mrs. Willett's call, arrived at the back of her building. She called out, "He's up here on the back porch!"

Det. Tiffin P. Constant started up after him. As he looked up the stairs he saw a young man pointing a gun at him. He was pulling the trigger but the gun failed to fire. The detective caught up with the youth and they started to fight and roll on the porch. Officer Cunningham heard the noise and started up the stairs. As he did so he picked up three flower pots. When he reached the pair, he hesitated for a minute, not knowing which was the fugitive. Det. Constant sensed the hesitation. He screamed, "That's him!" Cunningham brought the flower pots down on the young man's head with all his might. The fight was over.

The young man was William Heirens, a 17-year-old University of Chicago student. William was a clean-cut, good-looking boy, weighing 155 pounds and standing five-feet, 10-inches. In a routine check of the boy's room at the university, police found two suitcases. They contained several pistols, $1,800 in War Bonds, and a surgical kit. Upon checking Heirens' fingerprints, it was found that the print of his left little finger matched the print found on the Degnan ransom note.

In one fell swoop, the William Heirens case was transformed from that of a prowler to one receiving world-wide publicity as a mass killer.

At first the young student would say nothing, and for a while there was some question as to whether the flower pot had resulted in permanent damage to his brain. A thorough examination proved these suspicions to be unfounded, and gradually young Heirens started to talk. He claimed he was dominated by another person, whom he referred to as George.

George, he said, did the bad things, while he, William tried to stop him.

In the end though, William Heirens took the responsibility for his crimes. He confessed in detail to the three killings, and to an estimated 300 robberies. He led police to various caches of loot throughout Chicago. Thousands of dollars in bonds and cash were recovered. Heirens never spent more than five dollars a week on himself. He went to the three murder locations, and while the officers watched, he reenacted every horrible detail of his crimes.

The authorities were baffled on one point—what was his motive?

Heirens revealed that while ordinary people received sexual satisfaction from a relationship with a member of the opposite sex, he received this same satisfaction only by breaking into and robbing a house or apartment. He would get this sexual urge that had to be satisfied. He never molested or interfered in any way with the three women he killed. In each case, he panicked when they made too much noise.

Heirens stood trial and pleaded guilty to three indictments of murder, and 26 of assault with intent to kill, burglary, and robbery. He received three life sentences to run consecutively, and a one year to life sentence for the 26 non-murder charges to follow the three life sentences.

He was committed to Statesville Penitentiary at Joliet, Ill., where he is to this day.

Hickock & Smith

Perry Smith met Dick Hickock while both were non-paying guests of the State of Kansas. They were cellmates at Kansas State Penitentiary in Lansing.

Dick was a high school graduate with an above average I.Q. His parents, who lived on a small farm, had high hopes for their athletic son. Dick had received offers of baseball and football scholarships, but even with assistance he felt that attending university would place too great a financial burden on his parents. He took a mechanic's course instead and worked off and on in garages. At the age of 19, he married a 16-year-old girl, but the marriage didn't last. Dick played around with another girl. When she became pregnant, he divorced his wife and married for the second time. This marriage fared no better than the first.

Good looking, pleasant Dick Hickock had no trouble passing bad cheques. Even his victims admitted that he could charm the birds out of the trees. When he wasn't passing rubber cheques, he was stealing, and when he wasn't doing either he was in prison serving time. That's how Dick met Perry Smith.

While cellmates at Kansas State Penitentiary, Dick and Perry became good friends. Dick had an obsession. A fellow inmate, Floyd Wells, had told him that years before he had worked for a wealthy farmer named Clutter in Holcomb, Kansas. The Clutter farm was rather isolated and easy pickings for anyone with brains. Wells claimed that Herb Clutter was known to keep large quantities of cash in a safe in his home. When Wells helped with the crops on the Clutter spread the occupants of the house were Herb Clutter, his wife Bonnie, a son Kenyon, and a daughter Nancy.

Dick constantly repeated the story to Perry. The two men arranged to get in touch with each other once they were paroled. On July 6, 1959, Perry Smith walked out of the Kansas State Pen. Five weeks later Dick Hickock was paroled. The two friends met as they had promised and agreed to rob Herb Clutter. Wells had provided the pair with details of how to reach the Clutter farm. Dick had one stipulation. There would be no witnesses. Perry agreed.

Herb Clutter had worked hard all his life. At 48 he was lean, suntanned, and tough as leather. As a young man he had majored in agriculture at Kansas State University. Soon after graduation he had purchased a piece of land. His wife Bonnie was of some concern. She suffered from bouts of depression and from time to time had been admitted to rest homes. Nancy, at 16, was an outgoing, good-looking young girl who planned on attending university. It was Herb's hope that Kenyon, 15, would some day run the ranch.

The Clutter home was a sprawling, ranch style, modern dwelling with every convenience. Herb did have one idiosyncrasy. He didn't believe in keeping money around his house. In fact, he hardly ever carried more than a few dollars with him. Everyone in Holcomb knew that Herb Clutter always paid by cheque.

In the early morning hours of November 15, 1959, the two small-time hoodlums, Dick Hickock and Perry Smith, drove up to the Clutter ranch. Equipped with adhesive tape, rope, a shotgun, and a knife, the two desperate men had little difficulty gaining entrance to the house. The side door was unlocked. Quietly they made their way to Herb Clutter's panelled office. Try as they might, they couldn't find the safe which was supposedly located there. Herb Clutter woke up and was herded into his office. He explained that he didn't keep any appreciable amount of money in his home. He offered the two men the few dollars he had in his pocket.

Frail, nervous Bonnie Clutter was the next member of the family to be awakened that night. She confirmed that there was no money in the house. Herb Clutter and his wife were locked in a bathroom, while Perry and Dick went looking for Nancy and Kenyon Clutter.

Now the whole Clutter family was gathered together. Herb Clutter's hands were tied and, while Dick stood guard over the remaining three members of the family, Herb was marched down to the basement of his home. Here Perry forced Herb to lie down while he tied his feet. One by one each member of the Clutter family was tied hand and foot. Kenyon was taken down to a separate room in the basement. The two women were taken to their bedrooms and placed on their beds.

Without blinking an eye Perry Smith slit Herb Clutter's throat. Then he shot the dying man at point blank range in the head. One by one each member of the Clutter family was annihilated. Later in the car the two men counted their take: Under $40 in cash, a pair of binoculars, and a transistor radio. Four mutilated corpses were all that was left of a hard-working, loving family.

Next morning the bodies of the Clutter family were found. Law enforcement officials were amazed at the viciousness of the senseless attack.

Dick and Perry were disappointed at the meagreness of their score, but it was too late. They read about the murders in the newspaper, but later admitted they felt no sorrow or remorse at what they had done. Their minds contained only two thoughts - to survive and to have some fun. Dick managed to pass enough bad cheques in one day to finance their getaway to Mexico. Once there Dick became disillusioned, and as the money ran out the pair made their way back to the U.S.

The Clutter massacre was considered to be one of the most vicious crimes ever perpetrated in the state of Kansas. News of the murders remained on the front pages of the area's newspapers for several days. Floyd Wells heard of the murders on the radio in the penitentiary and immediately became the one person in the world who knew the identity of the killers. He couldn't believe that Dick Hickock had actually taken him seriously and tried to rob Herb Clutter. Prisons are full of desperate men trying to impress each other. Men brag, rumors of the big score pass the lonely months and years. Such haphazard information is rarely acted upon once the prisoner is on the outside. Dick Hickock was an exception.

Tempted by a newspaper's offer of $1,000 reward, Wells went to the authorities with his story. He was believed. As soon as the police knew who they were looking for, Dick Hickock and Perry Smith became the most wanted men in 10 states. Ironically they made their way back to Kansas City, where Hickock passed several bad cheques. This time the men decided to make their way to Miami for the Christmas season. Unbelievably Hickock used his own name while passing the phony cheques. A storekeeper became suspicious when Dick purchased a TV set. He had the presence of mind to jot down Hickock's license number.

After a short stay at a sleazy hotel in Miami, the

wandering killers decided to move on through New Mexico, Arizona, and on to Las Vegas. On the last day of 1959 two Las Vegas police officers in their patrol car spotted a Kansas licence number which was on their hot list. They edged the stolen car over to the curb. It was the end of the road for Dick Hickock and Perry Smith.

Both men later had conflicting stories of the exact events which had taken place inside the Clutter home on that fateful night. Both were sure of one thing. They admitted being the murderers.

Dick and Perry were tried and found guilty. They survived three execution dates on Death Row, before being hanged on April 14, 1965.

Fritz Honka

It didn't seem to matter how often the tenants in the two bottom flats complained. The night watchman and handyman, Fritz Honka, at 74 Zeiss St. in Hamburg, Germany, didn't take their complaints seriously, even though he admitted that the old house smelled to high heaven.

Klaus Kienzle, who lived in the first floor flat had, at Fritz's suggestion, checked the pipes leading into his bathroom. No clogs or leaks were found. John Fordal, a 46-year-old sailor, who was so drunk most of the time his sense of smell left much to be desired, often complained of the nauseating odor as well. Fritz himself lived in the third-floor flat, which was little more than an attic hovel. Occasionally he sprinkled deodorant throughout the building.

Now I must reveal that 74 Zeiss St. would never be featured in Better Homes and Gardens. The dilapidated structure was located in Hamburg's worst slum. It goes without saying that the occupants of 74 Zeiss were not among the upper rung of German society. The lives of many inhabitants of the area revolved around the popular Golden Glove, a low-life saloon where prostitutes, thieves and pimps, confirmed alcoholics all, hung out until the management closed up in the wee hours each morning.

The alcoholic haze of the area's residents was disrupted somewhat on November 1, 1972, when a woman's head was found in a nearby yard. Police conducted a search of the district. They located two arms and two legs, but no torso. Even though the body parts had been lying in the yard for some months, technicians were able to lift fingerprints, which were instrumental in identifying the unfortunate woman as Susi Braeuer, a 42-year-old licensed prostitute with a police record. Evidently Susi had had a penchant for rolling drunks, which had necessitated her arrest on more than one occasion.

The investigation into Susi's murder involved the questioning of many of her clients, all of whom had nothing but compliments for her in the sex department. They swore they only wanted to love Susi, not kill her. The murder went unsolved.

Meanwhile, as the months turned into years, that annoying odor continued to linger over 74 Zeiss St. Fritz did what he could. He sprayed the attic with more deodorant. The handyman had good reason to keep the odor in check. From time to time virile Fritz, who relished sex of the rougher variety, enticed assorted women to live with him in his attic flat. Eventually, they all moved out, complaining of the vile smell.

No one except her husband paid much attention when Anna Beuschel went missing. Every day like clockwork, Anna showed up at the Golden Glove to get sloshed and to ply her chosen profession. Toothless Anna, well in her 50s, was married to Thomas Beuschel, who was in his 30s and actually held down a legitimate job. No one knew what Thomas saw in the alcoholic prostitute, but he apparently loved Anna and provided her with enough money to stay intoxicated when her business dried up. Each evening on his way home from work, he checked at the Golden Glove to see if Anna was all right. On the evening of August 4, 1974, Anna wasn't there. In fact, she was never seen alive again. Thomas reported her missing to police.

On Christmas Eve 1974, prostitute Rita Roblick, a

regular patron of the Golden Glove, didn't show up at her usual table. Hamburg's finest believed there might be a connection between Rita's disappearance and that of Anna Beuschel. Who knows, maybe the four-year-old Susi Braeuer case was connected in some way. All three women were prostitutes who frequented the Golden Glove.

The next lady of the night to go missing was something of a local celebrity. Ruth Schultz was a member of the 50-something gang whose claim to fame involved a penchant for practising her varied talents in public. This behavior was frowned on by authorities, licensed prostitute or not.

For years it was Ruth's habit to have her hasty midday meal on the same park bench each day. Intoxicated or sober, she never missed her ritual of having something to eat on that park bench. On January 10, 1975, when she failed to show up as usual, one of the local merchants, fearing that she might be ill, informed the police. Because she fit the pattern of the other missing women and hung out at the Golden Glove, her disappearance received immediate attention.

On June 17, 1975, in the early morning, John Fordal tipped over a candle in a drunken stupor. The fire raged upward into the attic and onto the roof. Fordal was fortunate to escape the blaze. It took well over an hour for firemen to bring the flames under control. Once the fire was extinguished, they entered Fritz's apartment, fearing that the night watchman may have been trapped inside. Such was not the case. Fritz had been at an all-night drinking party and had missed the fun.

Conscientious fireman Walter Aust sifted through the debris in Fritz's apartment. He made his way behind a cardboard partition which appeared to have escaped the brunt of the fire. Walter peered down and gazed in horror at the mummified torso of what had once been a woman. Later he learned, as did the rest of Germany, that he had found the missing torso of Susi Braeuer. There was more. In that confined storage space, firemen unearthed the bodies of Anna Beuschel, Rita Roblick and Ruth Schultz in various stages of decomposition.

As authorities pondered their gruesome find, the occupant of the death flat showed up to discover police, firemen and medical personnel scrambling about his humble abode. He knew very well why they were there.

Fritz was taken into custody. Faced with the undeniable fact that four bodies had been found only a few feet from his bed, he confessed to strangling the women. He told the police that he liked his sex on the rough side. When the women protested, he strangled them. Fritz had decided to dissect his first victim Susi Braeuer, but found it a difficult task, working as he did with elementary tools in the confined space of his kitchen. After disposing of her head, arms and legs in the field, he placed her torso in the storage space. The next three women were simply put in the storage space behind the cardboard partition. Fritz always feared he would be exposed because of the repugnant odor. He never dreamed his murderous ways would be revealed due to a drunken sailor knocking over a lit candle.

Fritz Honka stood trial for the murders of the four women. He was found guilty and was sentenced to life imprisonment.

Ray Jackson

Annette Stewart was fed up with her job and, as a result, had an interview lined up for the following Monday morning. She had no way of knowing that she wouldn't live through the weekend.

On the pleasant Friday night of September 16, 1989, Annette dropped into a bar in downtown Kansas City, Missouri. The work week was over and she figured she deserved a few minutes to relax with a tall cool one.

As 33-year-old Annette was leaving the bar, a young man struck up a conversation with her. Together they walked along the city's Gillham Park. Suddenly, the young man clutched Annette by the throat and dragged her into some nearby bushes. When she went limp, he carefully removed her clothing. Annette didn't utter a sound. She was dead.

As quickly as he had struck, the young man disappeared into the darkness. Next morning, a businessman discovered Annette's nude body and called police. The murder of Annette Stewart, although tragic, was considered to be another routine big-city homicide, if homicide can ever be called routine. Her death would take on far more sinister connotations four days later.

On September 20, the nude body of 22-year-old Kimberly Creer was found in Gillham Park, about four blocks from where Annette Stewart had been strangled. As at the previous crime scene, Kimberly's clothing had been spread around the body, but nothing had been torn or ripped. Both women had been strangled. It appeared that Kimberly may have screamed for help as her killer carefully wrapped her brassiere across her mouth and around her head to prevent her from shouting.

While there was no direct proof that the killings were connected, investigators suspected the two similar murders committed in the same area only four days apart had been the work of the same perpetrator.

On October 23, the body of 22-year-old Teresa Williams was found adjacent to Gillham Park. She had been manually strangled and her clothes had been removed. For the first time, the dreaded words serial killer were used to describe the murderer who was stalking women in and around the park. He had taken three lives, yet no one had seen him, nor had he left any traceable clue to his identity. None of his three victims had known each other.

Seven days later, the Gillham Park strangler struck again — 36-year-old Janice Berryman's body was found in the same condition as the previous three victims.

November and the Christmas holiday season came and went. It was as if the madman, who had struck terror into the hearts of the citizens of Kansas City, had taken a vacation or moved out of the area.

On January 18, 1990, with the discovery of 23-year-old Tonya Ward's body, investigators knew the killer was still in their midst. All the tell-tale signs were there. Tonya had been strangled, her body stripped of clothing. Nothing had been torn or ripped.

Winter gave way to spring. Maybe the urge to kill had left the murderer, but such was not the case. On April 6, Michelle Mitchell was strangled in Gillham Park. Only hours before her body was discovered by a passerby, Michelle, her girlfriend and two men were stopped by police. When drugs were found in their vehicle, one of the men was arrested. Michelle and her girlfriend were released.

Michelle's girlfriend was traced through the licence

number of the vehicle. She told investigators that after their run-in with the police, she and Michelle had given a lift to another man. She had let this man and Michelle out of the car after he helped pay for some gasoline. With the help of a police artist, Michelle's friend was able to provide enough details to come up with what she felt was an extremely good likeness of the possible suspect.

The artist's sketch was widely distributed on TV and in the local newspapers. Tips poured in to police headquarters. One woman told how she was attacked and dragged into bushes in Gillham Park. Her attacker was intent on strangling her, but just as she was losing consciousness a man walking his dog came upon the scene and her assailant ran away. She thought the man in the composite sketch was the same man.

Now police had two witnesses who could identify the strangler, but still had no name to go with the picture. One lead appeared promising. A woman called police. Although she didn't know the name of the man in the newspaper sketch, she said she was a neighbor of his and could point out his house.

Following up on this tip, police picked up 22-year-old Ray Jackson. He bore a stunning resemblance to the sketch featured in the newspapers. Within minutes, Jackson was confessing to the string of Gillham Park murders. He described in detail how he had struck up conversations with the women and had pounced upon them just as he had gained their confidence. He was very strong and, struggle as they might, once he had clamped his hands around their throats, they had no chance of escape.

His last victim, Michelle Mitchell, had managed to scratch his arms. Jackson proudly displayed the scratches to his interrogators. She was the only one of the six women who had been able to fight back. Jackson also admitted that he had attacked the woman who had escaped when the man with the dog stumbled upon them.

Michelle's girlfriend and the surviving woman positively identified Ray Jackson from a police lineup.

In December 1991, Jackson's lawyers and the prosecution came to terms regarding a plea bargain agreement. In exchange for Jackson's guilty plea to all six murders, as well as an aggravated assault charge, the prosecution did not request the death penalty. Jackson was sentenced to six terms of life imprisonment for the murders and a further term of life imprisonment for the aggravated assault. The sentences are to run consecutively.

It is interesting to note that Ray Jackson had never been in any trouble in his entire life before he went on his killing spree.

Jack the Ripper

Jack the Ripper holds a fascination for criminologists and the general public that has not diminished for over 100 years.

He appeared in the East End of a turbulent London, England in 1888. The Whitechapel District of London was the last stop on the road down for the derelicts of the nation, and indeed a great portion of Europe. It is estimated that 15,000 men, women, and children did not have a roof over their heads. Workhouses held over 128,000 souls. There were 80,000 prostitutes plying the oldest profession throughout London. Large ethnic groups from the continent who could neither read nor write English tried to eke out a living.

Gin was the cheapest alcoholic beverage, and it was consumed in great quantities in the pubs that dotted the area. Beds were sold several times in one night. Crime in general and murder in particular ran wild in Whitechapel.

Jack the Ripper was the tip of the iceberg. The horror, audacity and method of his killings were so terrible that they brought the plight of the general population of the worst slums in the world to the attention of the authorities.

Mary Ann Nicholls was a 42-year-old prostitute. She had five front teeth missing. Dental care did not rank high on Mary Nicholls' list of priorities. On the night of August 31, 1888, she passed her old friend Nelly Holland. Nelly was later to say that Mary was so drunk she could hardly walk.

In the darkness of Bucks Row just off Whitechapel, a hand clamped over Mary's mouth from behind. A razor sharp knife held in Jack's other hand made a wide arc, starting under the left ear and ending across the throat under the right ear. The rip was so vicious it nearly decapitated the victim. His work not finished, the Ripper plunged his knife into the lower part of the abdomen and cut upward and to the right. Again the knife was plunged into the body, and from the lower abdomen the cut proceeded up the centre of the body to the breastbone. The two slashes just described became the trademark of Jack the Ripper.

Eight days later, Annie Chapman was walking the streets at two o'clock in the morning. She couldn't raise the two pennies for a bed for the rest of the night. Annie was 47, and suffered from consumption. Her body was found next morning behind a house on Hanbury Street. The throat cut, the body laid open were plainly in evidence, but there was much more. The body was disembowelled and the womb had been removed. The intestines had been lifted out of the body and placed on the shoulder of the corpse. The doctors examining the body suggested that some of the incisions indicated knowledge of formal medical training.

On September 30, the Ripper struck again, twice on the same night. Louis Diemschultz drove his horse into a yard at 40 Berners Street. The horse shied and Diemschultz noticed what he thought was a bag of something lying against a wall. What he found was the remains of Elizabeth Stride. Only the throat had been cut. There was no mutilation. The Ripper had been interrupted in his work. It is believed that he may have still been at the scene, and was the cause of the horse shying as it did. Certainly he made a hurried exit out the back yard. A few minutes later Catherine Eddowes fell into his grasp. He mutilated her in the style of Annie Chapman. Poor Catherine Eddowes was, like her fellow victims, a middle-aged alcoholic prostitute. A man she was currently living with identified the body.

A German immigrant came forward and said he had seen Eddowes with a man shortly before she was killed. He described her escort as a man of about 30, well-dressed, fair complexion, moustache, medium build and about five-feet, eight-inches tall. The description fit thousands of men in London. Then the police released this letter they had received just before the double killing:

Dear Boss,

I keep on hearing the police have caught me, but they won't fix me just yet. I have laughed when they looked so clever and talk about being on the right track. The joke about Leather Apron gave me real fits.

I am down on whores and I shan't quit ripping them till I do get buckled. Grand work, the last job was. I gave the lady no time to squeal. How can they catch me now? I love my work and want to start again. You will soon hear of me and my funny little games.

I saved some of the proper red stuff in a ginger beer bottle over the last job, to write with, but it went thick like glue and I can't use it. Red ink is fit enough I hope. Ha! Ha!

The next job I do I shall clip the lady's ears off. Keep this letter back till I do a bit more work, then give it out straight. My knife is nice and sharp. I want to get to work right away if I get a chance. Good luck.

Yours truly
Jack the Ripper

Don't mind me giving the trade name, wasn't good enough to post this before I got all the red ink off my hands curse it. No luck yet they say I am a doctor now. ha ha

A few hours after the double murder the police received this postcard:

I was not kidding dear old Boss when I gave you the tip. You'll hear about Saucy Jack's work tomorrow. Double event this time. Number one squealed a bit. Couldn't finish straight off. Had no time to get ears for police. Thanks for keeping last letter back till I got to work again.

Jack the Ripper

The police considered both the letter and card to be genuine.

A Whitechapel Vigilante Committee was formed and was now actively engaged patrolling the streets late at night. The chairman of the committee, a Mr. George Lusk, received a letter enclosed in a box.

It read:

Mr. Lusk
Sir I send you half the Kidney I took from one woman presarved it for you, other piece I fried and ate it was very nice. I may send you the bloody knife that took it out if you only wate a while longer.

Signed Catch me when you can

This letter too is considered to be genuine. The kidney that had been enclosed with the letter had been removed from a human body not more than two weeks previously. It was in an advanced state of Bright's Disease. Eddowes was suffering from Bright's Disease, and her kidney had been removed by her killer.

Mary Kelly was the last to die at the hands of Jack the Ripper. She was a heavy drinker and a prostitute. Unlike the previous victims she was attractive, and only 25 years old. She even had her own room at 13 Miller's Court. Mary was on the skids but had not made the complete trip. On Thursday night, November 8, she picked up a customer and took him to her room. For the first time Jack the Ripper had no fear of discovery or interruption. He had reached the pinnacle of wanton mutilation and savagery in his treatment of Mary Kelly. Her body was hacked beyond recognition. The police officers who witnessed the scene at 13 Miller's Court were never to forget the sight that greeted them on November 9 when the body was discovered. Mary Kelly had been three months pregnant.

On Wednesday Nov. 21, the police received this letter:

Dear Boss. It is no use for you to look for me in London because I'm not there. Don't trouble yourself about me until I return, which will not be very long. I like the work too well to leave it alone. Oh, it was a jolly job the last one. I had plenty of time to do it properly in Ha, ha, ha! The next lot I mean to do with Vengeance, cut of their head and arms. You think it is a man with a black moustache. Ha, ha, ha! When I have done another one you can try and catch me again. So goodbye dear Boss, till I return.

Yours,
Jack the Ripper

Jack the Ripper was never heard from again. It was generally agreed by the police in 1888 that while there were murders before the outbreak and some after it that were similar in nature, it is only those described here that are attributed to the one person. There were five in all, starting on the night of August 31, and abruptly ending 70 days later in the early morning hours of November 9.

Who committed these horrible crimes? There have been many theories.

Dr. Neill Cream is erroneously believed to be Jack the Ripper by many students of the case. He was born in 1850 in Glasgow, Scotland and immigrated to Canada in 1863. At the age of 26, he received his medical degree from McGill University in Montreal. In 1881, he was found guilty of poisoning a friend in Chicago and was sentenced to life imprisonment in Joliet, Illinois, but was out in 10 years. He appears on the London scene in October of 1891, where he started killing prostitutes by poisoning them. He would write letters to newspapers keeping the unsolved cases alive. In this way he brought suspicion to himself, and was finally tried and found guilty. He was hung on November 15, 1892. On the scaffold Dr. Cream's last words were "I am Jack the —."

It is unfortunate that positive documentation exists proving beyond a doubt that Dr. Cream was confined to Joliet Prison in Illinois during the 10 weeks Jack was committing his murders in London.

The Duke of Clarence was Queen Victoria's grandson, and was in a direct line to the throne of England. In 1970, Dr. Thomas Stowell wrote an article claiming that the Duke was Jack the Ripper. It seems the Duke was quite a ladies' man. The story goes that he contracted syphilis in his early twenties. As a result he was under the care of a doctor, Sir William Gull. The good doctor tried to restrain the Duke, but after the Kelly murder he knew he had to have him confined to a mental home.

Queen Victoria was accustomed to consulting a spiritualist named Lees. It is said that Lees saw the face of the murderer in his dreams. One day while travelling on a bus he saw the man who had appeared in his dreams sitting beside him. He followed this man off the bus to the home of Sir William Gull. Dr. Stowell's theory received wide publicity, and it is disheartening to report that there is documentary proof that Clarence was at Sadringham from November 3-12, 1888, and could not have killed Mary Kelly in London.

And so the theories go, from a Jewish butcher, to a medical student, to a secret agent of the Russian Czar.

There is only one theory and one man who fits all the known facts.

During the course of research for a television program in 1959, Lady Aberconway was interviewed. She was the elderly daughter of Sir Melville Macnaghten, who was Assistant Chief Constable of Scotland Yard in 1889, only a few months after the killings. Surprisingly, after all these years, Lady Aberconway produced her father's notes. Here was a direct link to the man who had actually hunted Jack the Ripper. From these notes we learn what the police believed at the time of the hunt.

Montague J. Druitt was born on August 15, 1857. His father was a doctor and the entire family was highly respected. Young Druitt whizzed through school and ended up with a B.A. degree from Oxford University in 1880. On March 30, 1885 he received his law degree.

It seems that he was unsuccessful in his practise of law, and in 1888 he was teaching at a private school and living in rooms at Kings Bench Walk. On December 31, 1888, M.J. Druitt's body was recovered from the Thames, his pockets full of stones. He had leaped to his death on December 4, twenty five days after the last Ripper murder.

Shortly before the first Ripper murder, Druitt's mother became insane, and Druitt thought he was going mad. He left a suicide note expressing his fear. The Macnaghten notes reveal the fact that all police agencies as well as vigilante committees were given the word to stop looking for the Ripper after Druitt's body was found. The police kept all information from the general public in order to save the respected Druitt family from unnecessary embarrassment.

The eyewitness reports fit Druitt. The idea that he was a gentleman fit Druitt's station in life. The Ripper's letters have been analyzed by experts, and they believe they were written by an educated man disguising his handwriting and using poor grammar to throw the police off the track. Would a real illiterate write the word "knif" or would "nife" be more natural?

It has always been believed that the Ripper had medical knowledge, or at least medical instruments. Druitt's father, uncle and cousin were all doctors, so he had ready access to medical instruments and could easily have picked up some knowledge from attending post mortems with his father. Druitt also lived in the centre of the area where the killings took place. This would give him the knowledge that the killer obviously had of the general area. It also gave him a place to go immediately after each killing.

Dr. Peter Druitt lives in Christchurch, New Zealand.

He is the great grandson of Robert Druitt, Montague's uncle. He says that having Jack the Ripper as a possible ancestor is most enjoyable, and really livens up his otherwise dull family tree.

Bela Kiss

The tiny village of Czinkota, Hungary, is one of the most beautiful spots in the world. Before the First World War it could have appeared on a postcard, representing all the quaint villages of Central Europe. It has a few commercial establishments — a general store, post office, and blacksmith shop were as near as you got to big business in Czinkota — and nothing exciting ever happened in the village.

Then Bela Kiss and his wife arrived and immediately bought the only imposing house in the area, a huge greystone structure on the outskirts of the village. Bela was about 40 years old, and his wife was fifteen years his junior when they took up residence.

Mr. Kiss immediately impressed the locals with his acts of kindness towards the less fortunate in the village. He made it his business to find out who was ill and who needed assistance; nothing seemed too insignificant for the unselfish Bela to lend a hand.

He owned a dashing red roadster, and many a night it would be seen roaring up the main drag, sometimes to deliver a food basket to a needy citizen, sometimes to bring some much-needed medicine to a sick friend. Everyone agreed that Bela was the greatest thing that ever happened to Czinkota. He seemed not to worry about money at all, though he had no visible means of support. But the villagers must have felt that it was not for them to look a gift horse in the a mouth.

Despite his magnanimous gestures, Bela was a shy, introverted man, short of stature but with considerable presence. He sported a black handlebar moustache, which accentuated his oval face, and made him appear somewhat chubby. His wife, Marie, was a real knockout in the looks department, with a voluptuous figure to match. She and Bela hired two girls from the village to act as servants, but they only stayed during the day, returning to their own homes each night. As for Bela, he sometimes left in his red car for a few days, but generally could be found at home, in his great greystone house, living the life of a country gentleman.

It is too bad that such scenes of marital bliss and tranquillity should have to come to an end. In Bela's case, the whole thing came to an abrupt stop when he learned that Marie was seeing an artist, Paul Bihari, on the side. Actually, she was doing more than seeing him; she was sharing his bed. Imagine Bela's disappointment when he found out that the one woman he ever cared about was being unfaithful to him, particularly since it coincided with his purchase of their new home and their good life in Czinkota.

At about the time that this revolting development came to Bela's attention, the village constable paid a social visit to the Kiss residence. Constable Adolph Trauber, who didn't have that much to do in the village anyway, occasionally did a little public relations work to pass the time of day. He wanted to know if there was any way he could be of service to the village's most illustrious resident. Bela said that he would appreciate it if Trauber would keep an eye on the property on those nights when he was away and Marie was left alone in the house, and the constable said that he would be delighted to do so. Trauber, a big, friendly man, immediately liked and admired Bela, and a warm friendship grew between the two men.

In the meantime, every time that red roadster disappeared over the hill, who would show up but Marie's lover, Paul. In a village the size of Czinkota it was impossible to keep tongues from wagging, and the townspeople passed the days wondering about the outcome of the triangle. All agreed that the shabby artist couldn't be half the man kind Mr. Kiss was, but there were a couple of things — the artist was tall, slender, and above all, the same age as Marie.

One day just before Christmas, when the two servants reported for work in the morning, they were surprised to find Bela in his study with his head buried in his arms. They gingerly asked him what was wrong. Bela passed them a letter written to him by his wife to the effect that she had left him for the artist Paul Bihari. Bela, beside himself with grief, informed the two servants that he wouldn't be needing them any more now that he was alone in the big house, and that anyway he wanted to be alone in his sadness.

As the weather grew colder and the grey house remained dark and quiet, the only break in the monotony of village life came when one evening a wagon pulled up at Bela's door and deposited two large metal drums. Then the cold winter descended like a blanket, leaving the villagers with only one piece of gossip to discuss during the long dark evenings — poor Bela's beautiful wife running off with an artist.

Weeks passed into months, and one day it dawned on Constable Trauber that he had not seen his friend Bela since his wife ran away. He decided to pay him a visit. When he knocked at the door, though he pounded long and hard, nobody answered. He broke the lock and entered the dark interior. In the study he found Bela, looking half-starved, his clothes in rags and the house a shambles. It was obvious to Trauber that his friend had not taken care of himself or the house since his wife left him.

"I have nothing to live for, Adolph," said the down-hearted Bela.

"Nonsense," said the constable. "First we will get someone to look after you and the house. You are both a mess."

The very next day an old woman knocked on Bela's front door, announcing that she was the widow Kalman and that Constable Trauber had sent her to take care of him and the house, and that was that. Under the widow's supervision Bela once more began to look like his old self. He started to gain weight, and with the improvement in his health, his old cheerful but reserved disposition returned. By spring he appeared to be back to normal.

One fine day, when the snow had melted and flowers were beginning to show their buds, Bela had a little tete-a-tete with the widow. He thanked her profusely for being such a great help to him, but felt that he was sufficiently recovered so that he no longer needed her at night. She could return to her home each evening and come back each morning. The widow didn't know whether to take this new arrangement as an insult or a compliment, but eventually she found out that when Mrs. Kiss lived in the house the two servants had returned to their homes each night, so all things considered she decided not to take offence. At least nice Mr. Kiss was well enough to take care of himself.

Mr. Kiss had some strange ideas, thought Mrs. Kalman. Take the upstairs closet which he always kept locked — she had once asked about cleaning in there, but was told that it wasn't necessary. It was none of her business, mind you, but a body couldn't help but be curious.

Shortly after Bela's little meeting with the widow, he left the village in his smart red car and returned with a lady. The widow Kalman was given to understand that the visit would be more or less a permanent one. The Madame, as Bela called her, was an overweight blonde in her late fifties. She was just getting settled in when a wagon pulled up to the Kiss residence and deposited another metal drum. Bela had the delivery man carry it to the upstairs closet which already held the other two drums.

Kiss, who never ceased to amaze the widow Kalman, then offered to send her on a week's vacation with full pay. The widow took her boss up on the offer, and was on her way the same day the proposition was put to her. When she came back from her unexpected vacation, she noticed that the Madame was nowhere to be seen. Bela nonchalantly told her that the Madame had left. This puzzled Mrs. Kalman, because when she had set off on her travels a few days earlier it had appeared that the Madame would be a permanent resident.

Maybe Bela realized the widow was having some misgivings about her boss, because he came to her and invited her into his study. The widow, who was becoming accustomed to their little chats, nevertheless shifted uneasily in an overstuffed chair. Bela coughed once or twice, and then confessed to Mrs. Kalman that he liked women and he intended to indulge himself with them. He was sorry if he shocked her, but out of respect for her he thought it best to let her know that he planned to invite several ladies to the house in the future. She could, of course, leave his employ if she wished, but Bela would rather — indeed positively insisted — that she stay. To sweeten the pie, Kiss let it drop that there would be quite a few paid vacations during the coming months. The widow Kalman made up her mind. Women or no, she would be happy to remain in his employ.

Next day Bela took off in the red roadster and returned with a six-foot, 300-pound Amazon. He winked knowingly at the widow Kalman. "Madame will be with us for some time," he said. Mrs. Kalman nodded understandingly and started to unpack Madame's bags. She then went on one of her periodic vacations, so she didn't see the wagon when it delivered the fourth steel drum. Upon her return she inquired after the new Madame, and was told she had left. The widow Kalman nodded her head and went about her dusting.

One day Constable Trauber, who by now was justifiably proud of butting into Bela's life and bringing him out of the doldrums, paid his friend a semi-official visit. Two Budapest widows had mysteriously disappeared of late, and as Bela had recently entertained two ladies, would he mind answering a few questions? Evidently a man named Hofmann had enticed the ladies to his flat, and they were never heard of again. The Budapest police had found the flat, but Hofmann had long since gone. The police felt that the women had been murdered, because both had withdrawn their life savings immediately before their disappearance.

Trauber and his friend had a good laugh. Such gullible women almost deserved whatever fate befell them. The two men had a glass of wine, a good cigar out of Bela's humidor, and spent a pleasant few hours, as good friends will. Bela told Trauber that he had something he had been wanting to show him. He took the constable upstairs and unlocked the closet door. Inside were four metal drums which Bela started to bang on with a stick. They all gave off a dull thud as if they were full of liquid. Bela took the cover off one of the drums and told his friend to look in.

"Petrol," Trauber said.

"Yes," replied Bela. He had a friend who could only pay off his debts in petrol, which was just fine with him. With the sabre-rattling that was going on throughout Europe, Bela explained, it was only a matter of time before the world would be at war and petrol would be better than hard cash. Trauber agreed, as Bela replaced the lid. Bela tapped the other three. "See," he said, "they contain petrol, too. Here, take the keys to this room. If anything ever happens to me, you take the petrol. I wouldn't want my wife and her artist friend to have any claim to it."

The two friends returned to the study to have a few more glasses of wine, Trauber protesting that nothing was about to happen to Bela.

In 1914, the war broke out. Time and again Bela was seen with middle-aged ladies by his side as he roared from Budapest to Czinkota in his red roadster. Mrs. Kalman was taking more and more paid vacations, and the man with the drums kept reappearing at Bela's door. Bela, always an impressive figure around the village, distinguished himself by acting as a voluntary recruiting officer. The young, able-bodied men had to be on their guard if they shirked their duty, because Bela didn't take his job lightly.

Then one day it actually happened to him. He was taken without notice from his house to Budapest to join the army. He never even got a chance to return to his home to tidy up his affairs, and nothing further was heard from him. Often on a cold winter evening the very old, for they and the very young were the only people left in Czinkota in 1914 and '15, wondered how their distinguished little neighbor was making out at the front.

In May 1916, Adolph Trauber received word that Bela Kiss had been killed in action at the front. Constable Trauber had lost a friend, the village its most illustrious citizen, and Hungary a true patriot, in one fell swoop. Having spent many an afternoon in his cups with Bela, Adolph felt that he had suffered a personal loss. He went down to the village square and inscribed Bela's name on the roll of honor. Grief-stricken villagers jointed the constable, and with bowed heads they mourned the passing of Bela Kiss.

Not long after the touching scene in the village square, representatives of the government entered Czinkota looking for the most precious of all commodities — petrol. They looked up Constable Trauber and made their mission known to him. It was only then that the constable remembered the hoard of petrol which Bela had shown him so many months before. He took the soldiers to the austere gray house, and up the stairs to the closet where the petrol was stored. The soldiers tilted the first drum and one peered inside. He said, "My God!" and started to stammer, pointing into the drum. The second soldier took a look, and he too became incoherent. Finally the constable looked into the drum and saw the well-preserved body of a woman, submerged in alcohol.

In all there were seven drums in the closet. All but two contained the bodies of middle-aged ladies; in the sixth was the body of Paul Bihari, and the seventh contained petrol — the same petrol that Adolph had peered into when Bela showed him his secret.

A top detective was dispatched from Budapest to

take over the strange case of Bela Kiss. Detective Nagy pasted together the baffling pieces of the case. He searched Bela's house, and found his desk full of letters from women all over Europe.

The mass killer had used the simplest of schemes, that of placing matrimonial advertisements in newspapers and luring rich widows to his home in Czinkota, where he had strangled each of his victims with a rope and pickled them in alcohol. Detective Nagy traced the supplier of the drums and found out that he had delivered many more than the seven that were found. As a result, a thorough search of the entire area was conducted, and several more drums were uncovered.

Each of them contained the well-preserved body of a strangled lady.

When news of Detective Nagy's gruesome find spread, several farms came forward and told of turning up skeletons when they were ploughing fields adjoining Bela's property. In all it seemed that Bela Kiss had murdered 23 women, including his wife, and one man, the artist Paul Bihari.

Then, in 1919, people who knew his face reported seeing him in Budapest. The reports were so positive that Detective Nagy went to the hospital in Belgrade where Kiss had died of his wounds during the war. He was shocked to find out that Bela was a tall, blond, blue-eyed Nordic type. It was obvious that Bela had managed to switch papers with a critically wounded soldier. When the soldier died, Kiss had assumed the dead man's identity, and had been discharged at the war's end.

Cunning little Bela Kiss had made good his escape. Years passed without word of the mass killer, until in 1952, a deserter from the French Foreign Legion told of a companion named Hofmann, who used to amuse his fellow in the desert with stories of how he had loved and strangled woman in Hungary. When Detective Nagy heard these stories he recognized details that had never been made public, and he knew that the teller was in reality Bela Kiss. But by the time Nagy got in touch with officials of the French Foreign Legion, Bela had deserted.

Though some criminologists who have studied the Bela Kiss case believe he emigrated to the United States, he has never been apprehended.

Fritz Klenner

Susie Newsome had all the credentials of the proverbial southern belle. She was good looking in that delicate way which girls from the southern U.S. seem to inherit at birth. Her family was respectable, upper-middle class.Susie hailed from Charlotte, North Carolina, so it was only natural that she attend Wake Forest University. It was there in her junior year that she met and fell in love with Tom Lynch, a pre-dental student.

In 1970, Susie and Tom were married. While I would like to report that the wedding was a gala affair enjoyed by all, such was not quite the case. Susie and her mother-in-law, Delores Lynch, got into a tiff over one of the wedding party's dresses. It was a matter soon forgotten by everyone but Susie. She was one to hold a grudge. Would you believe years and years?

After spending the next four years at the University of Kentucky, where he obtained his dental degree, Tom joined the navy. He and Susie moved to Beaufort, S.C. Susie proceeded, in the succeeding two years, to give birth to two sons, John and Jim. Now I would be amiss not to inform you that while these happy events were unfolding, Susie was decidedly cold to her mother-in-law. To give you an idea, Delores didn't see her grandson Jim until he was a full year old.

Tom received his discharge from the navy and decided to practise dentistry in Albuquerque, New Mexico. Our Susie didn't like the heat. She didn't like the food. She didn't like Albuquerque, period. She was inclined to blame Tom for the town's perceived deficiencies. Susie stood the place for an argumentative three years before she piled the two boys into her Audi and took

off. She didn't stop until she hit the comforting con-
fines of North Carolina. Only then did she call the
understandably worried Tom, advising him that she
would not be returning. Not ever.

The once devoted couple formally separated. Susie
obtained custody of the two boys. She busied herself
becoming reacquainted with old friends. One fine day,
she visited her doctor, Fred Klenner, who just happened to be her uncle.His son Fritz had been assisting
him around the office. It was in this way that he and
Susie got to know each other.

Fritz had an interesting history. Back in 1970, he had
flunked out of the University of Mississippi's pre-med
school. He returned to his father's office,where he
passed his time wearing a white jacket with a stetho-
scope conspicuously sticking out of his pocket. Dad was
disappointed, but was given some cause for hope when
his rather weird son informed him that he had been
accepted at Duke Medical School in Durham, N.C.

Fritz rented an apartment near the campus. As far as
anyone was concerned, he was only a smidgen away
from becoming a doctor. It was all a sham. For years,
Fritz spent his days frequenting gun shops and biker
hangouts. Even they thought he was a couple of cards
short of a full deck. One of his so-called friends decided
to check up on him. It didn't take more than a telephone call to the university to verify that there was no
one remotely resembling Fritz enrolled at Duke.

When the sham was exposed, Fritz returned to being
an almost doctor, assisting his father. In 1984, Dr.
Klenner died and left Fritz $25,000, which he used to
buy guns and survivalist paraphernalia.

This, then, was Susie's new companion. For some
unknown reason, she didn't find Fritz that strange at

all. In fact, she was very attracted to her first cousin. Friends attempted to have her reconcile with her husband, but Susie wouldn't hear of it. For his part, Tom obtained a divorce and married his dental assistant, Kathy Anderson. Tom's only contact with his former wife were his constant efforts to be allowed to spend more time with his two sons. Slowly, Susie was losing the friendship of her entire family. Her mother and brother Rob didn't approve of Fritz. Her mother-in-law hated her and any spark that Tom may have felt for her had been long extinguished. Let's face it, Susie had weird Fritz and that's about all she had.

On July 24, 1984, Delores Lynch was found murdered in her home in Kentucky. She had been shot in the face. The body of her daughter Janie was located in an upstairs bedroom. She too had been shot in the head. Nothing had been taken from the house and no clues to the killer's identity were uncovered. Back in Albuquerque, Tom was devastated to learn of the murders of his mother and sister.

Susie was not disturbed by her mother-in-law's untimely demise. In March 1985, Fritz moved in with her. Susie's main aim in life was to prevent her ex from having access to their two sons. To add insult to injury, her own parents felt that Tom should be allowed more time with the boys.

On May 18, 1985, police were called to the home of Susie's parents. They found her father's body in the hallway. Bob Newsome had been shot in the head, arm and stomach. Susie's mother Florence had been stabbed to death and her grandmother had been shot through the temple. Expensive jewelry and cash lying around the house had not been touched.

When Tom Lynch heard that his former wife's

mother, father and grandmother had been murdered in North Carolina, it was just too much. After all, only a year earlier, Susie's mother-in-law and sister-in-law had been murdered in similar fashion in Kentucky. He informed police of his suspicions. Sweet Susie was questioned. Yes, it was true. A horrible coincidence had taken place. Perhaps that evil husband of hers was behind it all.

Police conducted an extensive investigation, attempting to connect the two sets of killings. Naturally they learned of Susie's close relationship with her first cousin Fritz. He was questioned and came up with an alibi. On the day of the murder, he had been with Ian Perkins, a student friend. Ian was interrogated. He admitted knowing Fritz and considered him quite a guy. According to Ian, Fritz had told him that he was a CIA agent. On occasion Fritz claimed that he was a hit man for the agency.

Rather than providing Fritz with an alibi for the night of the murders, Ian's story tended to incriminate him. He told police that on the night in question he had driven Fritz to within a mile of the Newsome home and had let him out. Fritz had been equipped with two guns and a bayonet. Ostensibly, he was going to rub out a drug dealer under instructions from the CIA. Fritz returned to the pickup point sometime later and told Ian that the job had been successful. After hearing Ian's incriminating statement, it was decided to keep a close surveillance on Fritz and Susie.

On June 3, Fritz, who sensed the heat was on, pulled up in front of Susie's apartment. Police watched as he loaded his Chevy Blazer with survivalist equipment. Susie, her two sons and the family's two dogs, jumped in. Fritz took off with the police in pursuit. All pretense

183

of secretive surveillance was out the window. Fritz fired one of his weapons and wounded a pursuing police officer. Finally, he sighted a roadblock and pulled up. In seconds, the Chevy Blazer and all its occupants blew up. Fritz had set a bomb under the vehicle. When he felt he was trapped, he set off the device. Every living thing in the Chevy was blown apart.

In all, nine individuals had lost their lives. Many believe that one man, Fritz Klenner, was solely responsible for all eight murders. Others feel that Susie may have had guilty knowledge in the first five killings. The most popular theory is that Fritz acted independently in all the murders in some misguided belief that he was acting on Susie's behalf.

Peter Kurten

Henri Landru burned his lady friends. Reg Christie liked to plant bodies in the walls of his flat. George Haigh disposed of his victims in sulphuric acid. All of them either had a certain type of victim or a definite pattern of perpetrating their murders.

Peter Kurten did it all. He didn't care who the victim was and he used any means he saw fit to dispose of his victims. If one man can be held up to the light of criminal history and be described as the worst monster who ever lived, it is Peter Kurten who must be given this rather macabre honor.

Kurten was one of 13 children whose father was a hopeless drunk. The lived in Dusseldorf, Germany, and each night the father would beat up the whole family just for fun. The father once spent three years in prison for having an incestuous relationship with Kurten's 13-year-old sister.

Kurten became inquisitive and aroused at the open sex taking place in the confined quarters at home. At the age of nine he achieved some perverted thrill from torturing dogs. He became fascinated with the sight of blood, and as a teenager received complete sexual gratification from killing animals.

With this training-ground Peter graduated from experimenting with animals to humans. He took to living with prostitutes who let him inflict beatings upon them. In order to feed his sexual habits, he engaged in petty robbery. He was caught and received two years in prison. Rather than suppressing his sexual urges he found that solitary confinement gave him the peace and quiet he required to take part in sadistic daydreaming.

Once released from prison, he made his first attack on a woman. He raped and stabbed her, but she didn't die and probably never reported the incident to the authorities. We only have Kurten's word that this was his first offence against another human being.

After this original attack, Kurten attacked women, girls, and even men. He received sexual satisfaction from the sight of blood, and had no remorse or feelings of any kind for his victims. Because he devoted himself so completely to his sexual gratification, of necessity he had to steal to live. He was continually being caught and sent to prison. In all, he was to spend 20 years behind bars.

On May 25, 1913, when he was 30 years old, he was robbing an inn at Mulheim where the owners lodged above the drinking area. While rummaging through the rooms he discovered 13-year-old Christine Klein asleep in her bed. He strangled her and cut her throat. He returned to Dusseldorf, but came back the next day to Mulheim and lingered in a cafe opposite the Klein's Inn. In this way, he was able to savor the horror and excitement his crime had caused the people in the immediate vicinity.

For the next 17 years, Kurten kept killing and raping. He would have killed more, but he was continually being put in prison for robbery. He got progressively worse until finally the people of Dusseldorf realized a living monster was in their midst.

On the night of August 23, 1929, a suburb of Dusseldorf named Flene was holding its annual fair. At around 10:30, two foster sisters, Gertrude Hamacher, aged five and 14-year-old Louise Lenzen were on their way home from the fair. A pleasant man stopped them and asked the older girl to run back and get him a package of cigarettes. The Dusseldorf monster strangled Gertrude and cut her throat. When Louise returned with the cigarettes he did the same thing to her.

Only 12 hours later a servant, Gertrude Schulte, aged 36, was wondering what to do on her night off. A mild-mannered, pleasant man stopped her and suggested they take in the fair. While walking through a wooded area the man turned on her. He became furious when she resisted his advances. As he had done so often before, he brought out his knife and with quick, sure arcs plunged it into the poor woman's body. Finally the monster literally threw her away. Gertrude Schulte did not die. Her screams caught the attention of a passerby, and she was rushed to a hospital.

It became apparent that the Dusseldorf monster had lost all control of his desires. He was stalking victims on a full-time basis. In short order two servant girls, Ida Reuter and Elisabeth Dorrier, were raped and stabbed to death.

As summer turned to winter, Kurten attacked and wounded a girl of 18, a woman of 37, and a man of 30, all in a half hour. One child, Gertrude Albermann, was found dead with 36 stab wounds.

On the night of May 14, 1930, Maria Budlick arrived in Dusseldorf looking for work. A young man engaged her in conversation at the railway station. He offered to show her the way to a hotel that catered to young women. As they strolled through the well-lit streets all went well, but as they entered the dimly lit area the girl, who had heard all about the Dusseldorf monster, became apprehensive. She tried to get rid of her escort and they started to argue.

Just as the argument was becoming more heated, a

man appeared and inquired if everything was all right. The young escort left and an unsuspecting Maria accepted an invitation of something to eat at her new friend's apartment. He took her to a one-room flat in Mettmannerstrasse, where she had a ham sandwich and a glass of milk. Her new friend offered to take her to the women's hotel. Once in an isolated district, Kurten tried to rape her. Maria fought her attacker. As she was about to lose consciousness, Kurten asked her if she knew his address, so that if she ever needed help she would be able to find his flat. Maria said no and in so doing saved her life. He let her go.

Next day, accompanied by the police, Maria identified the flat. While she was pointing out the flat to the police, Kurten strolled up the stairs, walked by the police and Maria, went in his flat and closed the door.

The police arrested their cool suspect. Remember, at this point in time he was suspected of attacking Maria only. Almost immediately, as if to get a great load off his shoulders, Kurten confessed, "I am the Monster of Dusseldorf."

Kurten's trial was the most sensational ever held in Germany up to the time of the Nuremberg war crimes trial. To ensure his security he was placed in a cage. Kurten was exactly the opposite of what one might envision a monster to look like. He was a slight, pleasant-appearing, middle-aged man. He had a remarkable memory, and could give names and dates of his crimes going back years. He liked to describe them all in detail.

Kurten admitted to 68 major crimes, not including those of theft and assault. Officially he was charged with a total of nine murders and seven attempted murders.

Several top psychiatrists declared Kurten to be sane. All agreed he was the most perverted human being they had every examined.

The jury deliberated only an hour and a half before finding Kurten guilty.

On July 21, 1931, Peter Kurten, the Monster of Dusseldorf, was executed.

Danny La Plante

It would be a blessing if murder and its vile ramifications would respect the Christmas season, but such is not the case. In December, when decent citizens enjoy the spirit of giving and goodwill, there are those among us who prey on their fellow human beings with scant regard for the holy season.

The community of Townsend, Massachusetts, is tucked away about 90 km northwest of Boston close to the New Hampshire border. If ever there was a peaceful rural American town, well removed from violent crime, it was Townsend. The 7,000 individuals who lived and worked there did so with a degree of confidence that violence was something to be read about in the Boston newspapers. The God-fearing folks of Townsend were concerned with church affairs, local politics and good old-fashioned gossip. That is, until December 1987, when Townsend lost its innocence.

Lawyer Andrew Gustafson drove through the crisp late winter afternoon toward his Cape Cod style home. It had been an ordinary day at the office. As he drew closer, he anticipated the children's usual enthusiastic greeting. William, five, and Abigail, seven, were the apples of Andrew's eye. He considered himself fortunate to have such a fine family. Of course, there was Priscilla, his 33-year-old wife, who took good care of all three of her charges. Anyone who was acquainted with Andrew knew he worshipped his wife. Yes, that day in December 1987, Andrew Gustafson was looking forward to arriving home to his family.

The house was in darkness. Funny thing for this time in the evening, he thought to himself.

Andrew walked into a scene which no husband and father should ever have to witness. No one responded to his shouts. He made his way to the bedroom, where he gazed in horror and disbelief at Priscilla's body lying on the bedroom floor. She had been shot in the head. Dazed, Andrew dreaded what might have befallen his children. His worst fears were realized. First, in one bathtub and then in another, he came across the bodies of the two children he had anticipated playing with only a few short moments earlier.

Police were at the scene in minutes. State and federal authorities were called in to assist town police in tracking down the triple murderer. Detectives went about establishing the time of death. They learned that William and Priscilla had been alive and well at 1 p.m. when Priscilla had picked up William at his babysitter's. Abigail had been driven home from the Spalding Memorial School, getting off her school bus at 3:30 p.m. Because Andrew had reported the murders at 5:20 p.m., it was theorized that Abigail's murder took place between 3:30 p.m. and 5:20 p.m., while William and Priscilla could have been murdered any time after 1 p.m.

An autopsy revealed that Priscilla had been raped, although she was clothed in a shirt and slacks when found. She had been shot with a .22-calibre weapon. The two children had been strangled and placed in the water-filled bathtubs after death. For some unknown reason, the killer had opened a bottle of beer but had left it unconsumed on the kitchen table.

In Townsend, most of the citizens know each other. Among them were the usual share of bad seeds. One young man who had been in jail years before was questioned and released. Another had robbed a convenience store a year before the murders. He too was questioned and exonerated. Most folks figured the perpetrator of such a crime had to be a stranger. Police picked up the few drifters who had stopped over in Townsend, but all proved to have alibis.

Probably the most notorious young man in town was 17-year-old Danny La Plante. On one side of the ledger, Danny was an average student at St. Bernard High School. He was a star on the school track team and on the football squad. But Danny was a loner and had been in trouble of one kind or another most of his life.

A year earlier, Danny, who lived on Elm St. close to the Gustafson residence, had entered his girlfriend's home in nearby Pepperell, wearing a mask. He had chased the four occupants of the house from room to room. When he tired of the game, he had smeared mayonnaise and ketchup over the walls. That little caper cost Danny a few weeks in a state department of youth services facility. Now, Danny La Plante, because of his reputation, was the prime suspect in a far more serious crime than the wild spree in his girlfriend's house.

Word of the police suspicions spread throughout the community. Danny's relatives were questioned. His brother-in-law stated that on the fateful day, Danny had attended a birthday party for his six-year-old niece. He had played extensively with the child earlier that afternoon. It was inconceivable for anyone who had been at the party to believe that Danny could have been capable of leaving such an event and of immediately murdering three people.

Investigating officers had no concrete evidence against Danny, but decided to bring him in for questioning. Directly after his interrogation, Danny fled from the police station and ran into an extensive wooded area between his home and the Gustafsons'. His guilty actions precipitated a manhunt the likes of which the good folks of Townsend had never seen before. As the search party proceeded through the woods, they found various items discarded by the suspect. The first item was a torn pillow case. Close by were two spent .22-calibre casings. Further on, they came across a yellow glove.

Eventually, the investigators arrived at the La Plante home. A search of the residence uncovered a .22-calibre casing, which eventually proved to have been fired from the same weapon which took the life of Priscilla Gustafson. A match to the yellow glove picked up in the woods was also found.

While the La Plante home was being searched, desperate Danny broke into a home in Pepperell, kidnapped the female occupant and took off in her Volkswagen van. The terrified woman managed to escape unharmed. Minutes later, Danny was stopped and taken into custody. Back at the scene of the abduction, he had opened a bottle of wine but had not consumed any of its contents.

In reconstructing the crimes, investigating detectives believed that William was the first to be murdered so that he would not be a witness to the rape and murder of his mother. After the rape, Priscilla was allowed to dress. She hurriedly put on a shirt and slacks before being shot. It was Abigail's misfortune to return home from school before Danny left. She met the same fate as her little brother.

In October 1988, Danny La Plante stood trial for the three murders. He was found guilty and received three life sentences to run consecutively. In passing sentence, the presiding judge stipulated that he never be set free. Today, Danny La Plante is serving his sentence at Concord State Prison.

Edward Leonski

In 1942, the citizens of Melbourne, Australia had every reason to believe the seemingly invincible Japanese army would invade their country. Thousands of Allied servicemen were stationed in Australia. Life had taken on a nervous, superficial, carefree attitude.

On May 9, Mrs. Pauline Thompson, the estranged wife of a Melbourne police officer, was found strangled in front of her rooming house on Spring St. A post mortem indicated that tremendous pressure had been applied to Mrs. Thompson's neck by someone with unusually strong hands. Although the victim had not been sexually interfered with, her clothing had been torn to shreds. Mrs. Thompson's handbag was found a short distance away. Her attacker had obviously taken the few pounds the bag contained before tossing it away.

What concerned police was the similarity between Mrs. Thompson's murder and that of Ivy Violet McLeod, which had taken place six days previously. Mrs. McLeod, a 40-year-old domestic, was found in a doorway about three miles from her home. Her neck had the same grotesque indentations as those found on Mrs. Thompson. Although she hadn't been raped, she too had had her clothes ripped into shreds. Both women had been killed where their bodies were found.

Despite the imminent threat of a Japanese invasion, the citizens of Melbourne were well aware that a monster was in their midst. Nine days later, the maniac struck again.

Miss Gladys Lillian Hosking, 41, was employed as a secretary at Melbourne University. Her body was discovered by a gardener in Royal Park on the morning of May 19, 1942. As in the case of the previous victims, Miss Hosking had been viciously mangled by someone intent on something beyond cutting off her air supply.

Because of the threat of invasion, an air raid trench had been dug in the park. Distinctive yellow mud had been excavated from the trench. Miss Hosking's body lay face down in this mud. She hadn't been sexually attacked, but her clothing was torn into tiny strips. Miss Hosking's gloves, shoes, handbag and umbrella were scattered within a 10-yard radius of her body.

Three women had been murdered in strikingly similar circumstances within 15 days. All had been accosted relatively close to their homes. It was obvious that they were not well acquainted with their attacker. He killed on the streets with little regard for his own safety. In the case of Miss Hosking, police surmised that she too had been attacked on the street and had been dragged into the park.

Royal Park was located near Camp Pell, at the time an American Army installation. Investigating officers, who at this point had come up with little to lead them to the killer, decided it was possible that the murderer could be an American soldier. Sure enough, they found a guard who remembered a soldier returning to the camp late on the night of Miss Hosking's death. The guard remembered him because he was covered with yellow mud. When casually questioned by the guard, the soldier said he had fallen over a mound of mud while taking a shortcut through the park.

Homicide officers W. Mooney and F. Adam visited Camp Pell. They slowly walked down rows of canvas tents. When they came to tent number 29, they stopped. There, on the ground at the entrance to the tent, was evidence of yellow mud. Inside the tent, the officers found more of the tell-tale mud adhering to a metal bed. The officers left the camp, taking mud samples with them. Later their suspicions were verified when laboratory analysis proved that the mud taken from in front of the tent and the bed matched perfectly with mud samples from the freshly dug trench in Royal Park.

The two detectives returned to Camp Pell to interrogate the occupants of tent 29. Before doing so, they required clearance from the company commander. He surprised the officers by telling them that he had already received a complaint concerning one of the men in tent 29.

Private First Class Edward Joseph Leonski was continually returning to the camp intoxicated, causing a disturbance in the tent, babbling incoherently, sleeping fitfully and waking up in the middle of the night screaming. Once he had inquired of his buddies whether they had ever heard of Dr. Jekyll and Mr. Hyde. During the day, he pored over details of the murders which appeared in the newspapers.

The detectives were incredulous that Leonski's tentmates hadn't complained sooner. The soldiers explained that Leonski was such a likeable guy when sober, it was very difficult to suspect him of hurting a fly, let alone being a vicious murderer.

When Mooney and Adam finally came face to face with their quarry, they knew what the soldiers had meant. Private First Class Eddie Leonski was a well-built, tall blond 24-year-old with a cherubic face. He was a pleasant, good-natured guy, well liked by everyone. He did, however, have the reputation of turning into a real troublemaker when under the influence of alcohol. The guard who had stopped the soldier covered with yellow mud on the night of Miss Hosking's murder picked Eddie out of a lineup of 12 uniformed men.

The police investigated Leonski's background. Born in New York, Eddie had taken up weightlifting while still a teenager. He had a reputation for having extremely strong hands. Eddie was an honor student who played the piano and sang in the choir. The more police delved into his history, the more he resembled an enlistment poster. Eddie exemplified the all-American boy.

Eddie's father had died while he was still a youngster, but his mother had managed to make ends meet and raised him to be a fine upstanding citizen. Or so she thought. In reality, Eddie was overly devoted to his mother. His accomplishments were for her only. His setbacks affected him because he had let his mother down. When Eddie was called into the army, he cried at the thought of being separated from his mother.

Once in Australia, Eddie began to drink heavily. While under the influence, he would become belligerent and, according to his army buddies, he would undergo a strange transformation. His voice would change dramatically, becoming soft and high-pitched, very much resembling a female voice.

Eddie started off by picking up girls in Australia. He didn't do anything to them. He just liked to drink with them and listen to them talk. He drank at every opportunity, was often absent without leave, and in general was a poor soldier. His army record was in direct contrast to his exemplary behavior in civilian life.

Eddie himself knew something terrible was happening to him. Once, he pleaded with a guard, "Please put me in the guardhouse and keep me there. I'm too dangerous to run around loose."

Slowly Eddie gravitated from just talking to girls to trying to strangle them. He would release his grip before they lost consciousness. Eddie later explained that he didn't really want to kill the girls. Their voices reminded him of his mother. He only wanted to remove their voices. These girls had reported his attacks to the police, but in each case the attack had taken place in the dark and they were not able to provide useful descriptions.

Eddie couldn't explain why he became a murderer. He didn't know any of his victims, but he had struck up a conversation with each of them before clasping his hands around their throats. After killing Mrs. McLeod he knew he had to kill in order to possess the voices of his victims. Eddie couldn't explain his compulsion to rip his victims' clothing. He did say that when he read about his crimes in the newspapers he would cry. Yet, knowing what would happen when he drank, he never hesitated to go on a bender whenever the opportunity presented itself.

Eddie told the authorities of meeting Miss Hosking on the street. He asked her for directions back to camp. She was obliging and walked away with him. As the hapless woman talked, Eddie knew he had to possess her voice. Without warning, he clutched her throat and, as his victim went limp, he dragged her into Royal Park. It was there that he stumbled and fell on the excavated mounds of yellow mud.

Eddie was examined by psychiatrists. They all agreed that he was full of unnatural feelings for his mother and was undoubtedly a fetishist. However, in the strict legal sense, he was found to be sane.

Eddie was tried by a U.S. military court, found guilty and sentenced to death. Just prior to his execution, he sang a song in his cell. He sang in a soft, clear female voice.

Edward Joseph Leonski was hanged for his crimes on November 9, 1942.

Bobby Joe Long

Bobby Joe Long felt all his problems were caused by his accident, but he had other problems as well.

Bobby Joe was born in Tampa, Florida into a poverty-stricken family. His mother divorced his father when he was only two years old. Louella Long brought up her son to the best of her ability, maintaining a single room in a motel. She made her living as a waitress. Louella worked nights. Bobby Joe attended school during the day. Sometimes Louella entertained men in the motel room which was her home.

At age 11, Bobby Joe experienced the strangest phenomenon. He started to grow breasts. The boy was shattered. The breasts became so large that other boys teased him. He attempted to hide his deformity, but as time passed it was impossible. Louella had seen the same strange growth in male members of her family before and knew what to do. Although she could ill afford it, she took her son to a doctor, who surgically removed the breasts.

Bobby Joe met Cindy Jean Guthrie when he was 14 years old. He dated her for seven years before they married. Cindy's outstanding feature was her startling resemblance to Louella.

Bobby Joe enlisted in the U.S. army. He was already an electrician and took courses to expand his knowledge in preparation for the day he would reenter civilian life. Unfortunately, six months after his army career began, he met with an accident while driving his motorcycle. Bobby Joe fractured his skull and spent months in hospital before receiving his discharge from the army. He was never the same man after the accident.

The boy Cindy knew as placid and easy going was now an explosive individual who demanded sex several times a day. His work habits were unstable. He drifted from job to job, usually being fired for harassing female employees. By 1980, he was actively trolling for females to relieve his abnormal sexual appetite. Bobby Joe was well aware of his unnatural urges. He even realized that during periods of a full moon his need for sex became unbearable. Yet he seemed helpless to control his desires.

In 1981, Bobby Joe was charged with rape and found guilty. However, he was able to obtain a new trial on the grounds that the girl involved had consented to intercourse. At his second trial, he was acquitted.

While Bobby Joe was hoodwinking the authorities, he was carrying out a series of rapes. He would gain entry into women's homes by scanning classified ads in newspapers. After learning when the woman was home alone, he would pay a visit. A task force was formed to hunt down the man known as the Classified Ad Rapist.

In 1983, Bobby Joe graduated to murder. His first victim was Ngyuen Thi Long, who by coincidence had the same last name as her killer. Ngyuen was a saloon dancer and prostitute, who picked up Bobby Joe on North Nebraska Ave. in North Tampa. He drove outside the city, where he raped and strangled the helpless girl. Next day, Bobby Joe slept for 14 hours. When he awoke, he could hardly remember the incident. He wasn't totally convinced that he had taken a human life until he purchased the local newspaper and read about it on the front page. He had no remorse for the victim or her grieving family. Bobby Joe knew in his heart that he would rape and kill again.

When the urge overcame Bobby Joe, he knew where to hunt for victims. The prostitutes of North Tampa were his prey. Unwittingly, they solicited his business and sped away to their deaths. Although Bobby Joe had no remorse for the prostitutes, he was ashamed of what he was doing. He attempted to put an end to his murderous spree and even thought about suicide, but couldn't get up the nerve to do the trick. After he had killed eight prostitutes, he realized that his fame was spreading.

Bobby Joe was aware that the police were canvassing and cruising along the strip which provided him with his girls. Their efforts seemed childish. He would later state that he could have left North Tampa at any time to avoid capture. By now the rapist/murderer consciously wanted to be apprehended. Cindy had divorced him and remarried. He had nothing to live for and existed only to satisfy his uncontrollable urge to have sex. It had to stop.

After his eighth murder, Bobby Joe spotted a young girl on a bicycle. She had just finished her shift at a doughnut shop and was driving home late at night. Bobby Joe hid in some nearby bushes. As the girl sped by, he pulled her off her bicycle. This girl was different; she was not a prostitute. Bobby Joe was moved and, for the first time in his murderous career, felt some remorse for his captive. He loosely blindfolded the terrified girl.

Bobby Joe drove around for 24 hours talking to the girl, who managed to get brief glimpses of her abductor through the blindfold. Bobby Joe raped his victim, but eventually drove her back to the spot where he had pulled her from the bicycle and set her free. The experienced killer must have known that this young girl would be able to identify him and his vehicle. Was this

Bobby Joe's way of letting himself be apprehended? He has always claimed this to be the case.

Two days later there was a full moon. Despite his wish to be captured, Bobby Joe's need for sex was too strong. He went on the prowl for a female. His ninth and final murder victim was Kim Swan. Bobby Joe came to Kim's aid when he noticed she was having car trouble at the side of the road. Once she was in his car, he attacked her. Although she fought fiercely, she was finally overpowered. Bobby Joe drove the unconscious girl to a secluded area, where he raped and strangled her.

A few days later, the police traced Bobby Joe, mainly from information given to them by the 17-year-old survivor. He was arrested and confessed to all his murders without much prompting.

At Bobby Joe's trial, his lawyers leaned heavily on the head trauma he had suffered years earlier in his motorcycle accident. Despite this factor, Bobby Joe was found guilty and was sentenced to death. Bobby Joe Long presently resides on Death Row in Florida's State Prison.

Kai Metzmann

Whoever coined the phrase that crime doesn't pay never heard of the Metzmann case.

Let's go back to 1987, to the famed German wine country on the eastern slopes of the Palatinate Mountains, to the tiny village of Lambrecht. Among the wealthiest inhabitants of Lambrecht was the Metzmann family.

Willi, the head of the family, was a self-made millionaire. He had started out as a mechanic and ended up owning a prosperous welding equipment company. Willi's wife of 26 years, 48-year-old Renate, worked at her husband's business, as did their 19-year-old son Kai and 25-year-old daughter Silke. They all lived in a luxurious home, complete with expensive cars in the driveway and an extensive riding stable.

The tranquil life of this successful family was shattered forever on the morning of Tuesday, February 24, 1987. On that bitterly cold morning, Kai Metzmann lurched into the village's police station and blurted out, "My folks are all dead!" The boy was near collapse. Officers comforted the lad as best they could before rushing out to the Metzmann residence. Once there, they realized their limitations in handling the first multiple murder ever to take place in their village. They summoned experienced homicide detectives from the closest city.

Inside the Metzmann residence, police found Willi's body in the master bedroom about 12 feet from the bed. On the bed lay the body of his wife Renate. Silke's body was found in the study.

Renate had been shot in the forehead with a 30-

calibre rifle. After death she had been stabbed three times with a sword and eight times with a kitchen knife. She had then been beaten about the head with a rifle butt. Police believed Renate had been shot and attacked while she slept. Willi had been shot six times with the same weapon and stabbed with a sword which had gone directly through his body. Silke had been shot twice in the chest, after which she had received a total of over 40 stab wounds inflicted by knife and sword. The estimated time of death for all three victims was between midnight and two in the morning.

Detectives examining the murder scenes and the entire house found large sums of money and jewelry lying about. Obviously robbery had not been the motive for the triple murder.

Kai told investigators that he had arrived home from a party in Neustadt in the morning and had walked in on the slaughtered remains of his entire family. Detectives were sympathetic, but were taking nothing for granted. They noted the names of the other young people who had attended the same party as Kai.

Within hours, at least a half dozen teenagers told police that Kai and his best friend, Jurgen Lischer, hadn't left the party until 8:30 in the morning. Apparently, the party had been quite a blast, with drugs and liquor available in seemingly unlimited quantities. At least 50 young people had attended. The statements of the partygoers, some of whom didn't know Kai that well, effectively eliminated him as a suspect in his family's murder.

Detectives learned that on the way up the entrepreneurial ladder, Willi Metzmann had stepped on a few toes. Boris Andower, a former competitor in the welding business, held a grudge against Willi. He had gone into bankruptcy some years earlier and had always blamed his rival for the demise of his business, although as far as the police could ascertain, Willi had nothing to do with Boris' business failure. Another man, Karl Bursch, had been a foreman in Boris' firm. When the business closed down, he lost his job. He too blamed Willi for his misfortune. Both men were thoroughly investigated. Although they admitted threatening Willi, they swore they were not involved in the murders.

When Boris' home was searched, police found a 30-calibre rifle with blood on the stock. Boris explained away the blood with the unlikely tale that he had killed a chicken in his garage and no doubt had gotten blood on the stock at that time. The weapon was confiscated and the blood analyzed. Well, son of a gun, the blood on the stock turned out to be chicken blood. In time Boris Andower and Karl Bursch were absolved of all complicity in the crime.

Officials believed that it was quite possible that the murders would never be solved. The motive was a mystery. Nothing had been taken from the home. The two men who might have sought revenge, no matter how unfounded, were innocent of any involvement. The murder weapons — sword, kitchen knife and rifle, had been in the house at the time of the murders and had been carried away by the killers. Police couldn't figure out why they would take away the weapons.

Detectives reconstructed the crime. From the evidence, it appeared that two killers were involved. They either had a key to the house or had picked the lock to one of the doors. All the occupants had been asleep. The killers entered the master bedroom and shot Renate as she slept. Willi jumped out of bed and was brought down as he attempted to advance towards his adversaries.

The intruders must have pounced on the already dead victims with sword, kitchen knife and rifle butt. Silke, in her bedroom down the hall, must have heard the shots. She ran out of her bedroom into the study and locked the door. While she frantically attempted to phone police, her killers broke down the door and shot her dead. When found, she was beside the telephone, which was lying out of its cradle. The killers then left the house, removing all the murder weapons.

The reconstruction was no doubt accurate, but did little to reveal the identity of the killers. More in desperation than for any other reason, investigators decided to recheck Kai Metzmann. After all, he stood to gain his parents' complete fortune.

The young people who had been at the wild party were questioned again. This time, several admitted that by 10 p.m. everyone was so high on drugs that they had no idea if Kai or Jurgen had been at the party between 11:30 p.m. and 2:30 a.m. Originally, they had been asked if the two suspects had left the party. At that time they had truthfully stated that they hadn't seen Kai or Jurgen leave. Now, with their negative statements, police realized that both young men could have left the party, committed the murders and returned to the party without being missed.

Kai was picked up and questioned. His main interest was to confirm that under the German Juvenile Criminal Code, the maximum sentence for murder for a 19-year-old was 10 years imprisonment with the distinct possibility of parole after five years. Once assured of the law, Kai confessed, implicating his friend Jurgen. They had left the party, killed the Metzmann family, and had returned to the party. They were not missed.

The motive was cold, hard cash. Kai was tired of working for his father. He wanted his freedom from family ties and his parents' money in order to live as he saw fit. Jurgen confessed and corroborated Kai's version in every detail. He had agreed to take part in the murders in return for a portion of the inheritance. The two killers led police to the Speyer River, where they had tossed the rifle, sword and knife. All the weapons were recovered.

In January 1988, Kai Metzmann and Jurgen Lischer pleaded guilty to premeditated murder and were sentenced to 10 years juvenile detention. Both have since been paroled. Kai Metzmann, released at the age of 24, is the richest young killer in Germany.

Blanche Taylor Moore

Blanche Kiser was your average pleasant Southern girl, who spoke in that friendly North Carolina drawl that we northerners find so fascinating. Blanche, a minister's daughter, had been raised to follow the word and fear the Lord. She worked as a checkout clerk at Krogers, one of the large grocery chains in the southern U.S.

At 18, Blanche married James Taylor, a local Alamance County man. James, an antique dealer, was 26, but those who knew the couple considered Blanche to be the more mature of the two. The years passed and the Taylors had two daughters.

It is unfortunate to report that as the Taylor marriage approached the 20-year mark, James's health gradually deteriorated. Nothing you could put your finger on, mind you, he just complained of not feeling well. Obviously, his complaints were well founded. On October 2, 1973, he died in his bed. Doctors attributed his death to a massive heart attack.

In times of crisis, you can always tell who your true friends are. Blanche was fortunate in having Ray Reid at her side as she went through the trauma of her husband's death. Blanche and Ray had known each other for years, but only became close when they were co-workers at Krogers, where Ray was manager.

About two years before the death of James, Ray and his wife Linda, who had two sons, were divorced. That was just about the time James began to complain about not feeling well. Blanche had comforted Ray during his divorce. It was only fitting when James died for Ray to be at Blanche's side. They prayed together and they went to bed together, not necessarily in that order.

During moments when the two friends were, shall we say, comforting each other, Blanche let Ray know that she and her daughters were in dire straits financially. James had left a pile of debts. In the following few years, Ray admired Blanche, some say to the extent of $10,000 in loans and outright gifts.

Despite Ray's attention and generosity, Blanche's feelings for him gradually cooled. Oh, she still prayed for his salvation and delivered piping hot dinners to his home, but their gymnastic machinations became fewer and fewer. You see, Blanche had met Reverend Dwight Moore, pastor of the United Church of Christ in nearby Columbia. The reverend was infatuated with Blanche. After all, she displayed those qualities near and dear to his religious heart. She prayed a lot and was forever performing kind acts for those in need.

Blanche's friend Ray Reid took ill around the time that Blanche and Rev. Dwight became an item. Blanche spent a lot of time visiting Ray. When he was in hospital, she saw to it that he had a generous supply of her outstanding rice pudding. Kind, gentle Blanche was popular with the nurses who attended Ray. She brought them sandwiches, which they sometimes ate while Blanche fed Ray his rice pudding.

While in hospital, Ray instructed his two sons that Blanche was to be the executor of his will should anything happen to him. They agreed that the angel of mercy was entitled to one-third of their father's estate.

Blanche was a busy girl. What with visiting Ray, romancing Dwight and attending church regularly, she had scant time to run routine errands. That's why she asked Rev. Dwight to pick up some poisonous Anti-Ant powder down at Ken's Quickie Mart, where she had previously purchased a supply. Nasty ants had infested her home again. Dwight was more than happy to oblige.

As summer gave way to the fall of 1986, Ray's condition worsened dramatically. Doctors agreed that he was close to death and they were right. On October 7, Ray, age 50, went to his great reward.

Medical authorities, who had always been mystified as to the cause of Ray's illness, suggested an autopsy. Blanche, the executor of the deceased's will, would not give her permission, claiming that Ray would not have approved. The pain of losing her dear friend was soothed somewhat by her inheritance of $45,000, one-third of Ray's estate.

During the next few years, Blanche and Dwight were inseparable. In 1989, they married. While they were on their honeymoon, Dwight took ill with severe stomach cramps. The happy couple were forced to return home to North Carolina.

Dwight visited a doctor, who found it difficult to pinpoint the cause of his discomfort, but there was no denying the seriousness of the problem. Dwight was in such extreme pain he was admitted to Memorial Hospital in Chapel Hill. In time, he was transferred to the intensive care unit.

Dwight's condition didn't improve. His body was distorted in agony as he periodically lost consciousness. Blanche was a rock. She ministered to her seriously ill husband day and night, while doctors frantically performed test after test in an attempt to discover the cause of his strange illness. They informed the distraught Blanche that they were helpless and death was imminent.

As the end drew near, attending physicians were

shocked to receive the results of urine tests indicating that their patient had been poisoned by arsenic. In fact, the readings indicated that Dwight had the highest concentration of arsenic ever found in a still-living human.

Doctors questioned Blanche. Had her husband come in contact with arsenic used around their home? Blanche could only tell them that he puttered around the garden. She didn't know whether he used arsenic or not. It was decided to notify police of the strange illness which had befallen the popular pastor.

Investigators questioned Blanche. She could add nothing to what they already knew. They interrogated Dwight in his hospital bed. The pastor was recovering from the brink of death, but it was a slow, painful recovery. He searched his memory of the day when he first had stomach trouble, but could add nothing that would help the investigation. He did casually recall that years earlier a friend of his wife's named Ray Reid had died suddenly. Come to think of it, so had her husband, James Taylor, back in 1973.

Records were checked. Nurses who had attended Ray were interviewed. Blanche's habit of bringing tasty rice pudding to Ray was of particular interest. Blanche was questioned again. Despite the irrefutable fact that she had fed Ray in hospital, she steadfastly professed that she had never brought food to the institution.

On June 13, 1989, Ray Reid's body was exhumed from Pine Hill Cemetery in Burlington. It was laced with arsenic. Three weeks later, James Taylor's body was exhumed.

It too contained large amounts of arsenic.

On July 18, Blanche was arrested and charged with Ray Reid's murder. There was grave suspicion that over the years she had sent others to their deaths, including her own father, Parker Kiser, whose death had been attributed to a heart attack. When his body was exhumed, small amounts of arsenic were found to be present. The same results were obtained when Blanche's former mother-in-law, Isla Taylor, was exhumed.

In the end, Blanche was tried only for the death of Ray Reid. She was found guilty and sentenced to death. Today, Blanche Taylor Moore resides on Death Row in North Carolina Women's Prison. She is a model prisoner and reads the good book several times each day.

Rev. Dwight Moore has obtained a divorce and is now pastor of a small congregation in Virginia. He is trying to start life a new after his narrow escape at the hands of his devoted wife.

Judith & Alvin Neeley

He called her "Lady Sundance." She called him "Nightrider." There were those who called Judith and Alvin Neeley the most sadistic, cold-blooded killers who ever roamed the highways and byways of the United States.

Judith claims she was sexually abused as a child. She ran away from home at the age of 15 to marry Alvin. If ever there was an unholy union, it was the Neeleys. Although Alvin was 26 when he met Judith, many believe she was the dominant personality.

The Neeleys lived by their wits, wandering through Tennessee, Alabama and Georgia, pulling off small thefts and passing bad cheques. In 1980, they attempted to graduate to armed robbery and were quickly apprehended. Alvin spent several months in jail, while Judith was placed in the Youth Development Centre in Rome, Georgia, where she gave birth to twins.

Two years later, Judith and Alvin were free once more. Alvin took a job at a garage and promptly absconded with the company's weekend receipts. With the proceeds of the theft, he purchased a Ford Granada for himself and a Dodge Charger for Judith. Equipped with CB radios and .38-calibre revolvers, they transformed themselves into Lady Sundance and Nightrider. It is difficult to pinpoint when the evil pair made the transition from dangerous punks to sadistic murderers, but transform they did.

In September 1982, Lisa Millican, 13, a ward of the Ethel Harpst Home for neglected children, was taken on a trip to a shopping mall in nearby Rome. Seven girls and six boys made the trip. Once at the mall, they were told to stay in groups and meet at a prearranged location for the return trip home at 8 p.m. Lisa didn't show up. Counsellors and children searched the mall, but Lisa was nowhere to be found. Police were notified.

Hours before she was reported missing, Lisa met a young woman, who struck up a conversation with her. The lady told Lisa that she was new in town and very lonely. Little Lisa, a solitary, lonely child herself, knew just how the lady felt. She accepted a drive in the country in the stranger's Dodge Charger. Once in the car, Judith Neeley's voice crackled over the airwaves, "This is Lady Sundance. Do you read me?" Nightrider read his accomplice only too well.

It is not necessary to detail the horrible fate which befell little Lisa Millican. It is enough to know that she was moved from motel to motel and sexually abused in every way imaginable. Judith was later to state that after a couple of days the little girl complied with every indignity in order to please her tormentors and avoid being killed.

For some diabolical reason known only to the perpetrators themselves, they decided to kill the child by injecting Drano and Liquid Plumber into her veins. Judith later told investigators that the caustic substances were used for no other reason than to satisfy her curiosity. Detective theorized that the killers were trying to give the murder the appearance of an overdose.

Even as killers of a helpless child, Judith and Alvin were inept. Judith couldn't find the youngster's vein. The searing substance was injected intramuscularly. The pain must have been excruciating, but not fatal. Lisa was spirited away to remote Little River Canyon and again injected with cleaning fluid. Judith was disappointed. The child didn't die. She was then dragged to the lip of a 100-foot deep canyon. There, Judith drew her .38 revolver and shot the child in the back. She listened as Lisa Millican's body plunged to the jagged rocks below. Alvin watched from a few feet away.

Judith wanted more than sex, more than murder. She wanted the thrill of the hunt. She called police and told them where they could find the missing Lisa Millican's body. Because of the nature of the terrain, the child's mutilated body was not recovered until the next day.

Police studied the tape recording of the woman who called and told them where to find Lisa's body. They knew they were listening to the voice of a murderer, but no leads to the killer's identity were uncovered until some days after the body was found.

Not far from Rome, a man was shot in the back. The Neeleys had struck again. Twenty-six-year-old John Hancock and his fiancée, Janice Chatman, were strolling down Shorter St. in Rome. A Dodge Charger with Tennessee plates pulled up beside the young couple. The driver explained that she had just arrived in the area and was very lonely. If they wanted a ride into the countryside, they were welcome to hop in. John and Janice had nothing better to do. They were happy to accept. Once they were inside the car, Lady Sundance told them that a friend of hers would join them with a cooler of beer. In minutes, Nightrider appeared in his Ford Granada. The two automobiles pulled into a secluded wooded lane.

Judith placed her .38-calibre pistol directly between John Hancock's eyes. She then marched him into the woods. Without warning, Hancock heard the loud report of the gun going off. At the same time, he felt a searing pain in his back. John fell to the ground, feigning death, but was conscious and well aware that the slightest movement meant a second shot and most probably death. Alvin Neeley called into the woods for his wife. Judith left the fallen Hancock where he lay. The pair sped in their vehicles with the terrified Janice Chatman.

A few minutes later, John Hancock was able to stagger to the road and wave down a passing motorist. In hospital, police played the tape of the woman who had called in the whereabouts of Lisa Millican's body. John believed his abductor's voice and the voice on the tape were one and the same. The hunt was on for the two vehicles, but the identities of Lady Sundance and Nightrider were still unknown.

The connecting information came from the Youth Development Centre in Rome, where Judith Neeley had once been confined. Someone had called the home and threatened to kill members of the staff in retaliation for abuses received while the caller had lived there. The recipient of the call listened to the taped call from Lisa Millican's killer. It was his opinion that the same woman had made both calls.

Detectives began the dogged work of checking every girl who had been released from the institution in the previous two years. By the process of elimination, they came up with six suspects. John Hancock was shown the six photographs. He picked out Judith Neeley's photo as the woman who had shot him.

The identification was too late for Janice Chatman. She had been taken to a motel immediately after John Hancock was shot. She was handcuffed naked to a bed and sexually abused all night. Early in the morning, Judith and Alvin drove their hapless victim to a lonely area of Chattanooga County and shot her in the head and back.

The wanton pair found themselves short of money. Reverting to their old method of raising money fast, they decided to pass a few worthless cheques in Murfreesboro, Tenn. They were caught within hours and quickly identified as the suspected murderers of little Lisa Millican and the abductors of Janice Chatman. Alvin couldn't wait to ingratiate himself with police. He drew maps indicating where Janice Chatman's body could be found. Alvin's maps were authentic. Janice's body was speedily recovered.

Eventually, Alvin Neeley pleaded guilty to the murder of Janice Chatman. He received one life sentence for aggravated assault and a second life sentence for murder. He is presently serving these sentences in a Georgia prison.

Judith Neeley was charged with the murder of Lisa Millican. She was found guilty and sentenced to death. While in jail, Judith gave birth to her third child.

Today, Judith Neeley is one of only two women under sentence of death in the State of Alabama. She is presently on Death Row in the Julia Tutiwiller Correctional Institute in Wetumpka, Ala. The assistant warden of the institution, Mrs. Shirlie Lobmiller, informs me, "Judith has adjusted well to the institution while her sentence is being appealed."

In compliance with a state law, her cell is checked every 30 minutes night and day. Judith has access to TV and enjoys soap operas and religious programs. Each morning, at 6:30 a.m., she is moved to a shower by a guard, but is allowed her privacy in the shower for five to seven minutes. Her mornings are spent in handicrafts. Lunch is served from 10:30 to 11:00, after which Judith takes a nap. She keeps herself clean and well-groomed, although she is compelled to wear a plain white dress.

After supper Judith watches TV. Lights are automatically turned off at 10:00 p.m. except for a solitary safety bulb, which casts a dim glow while the prisoner sleeps. Mrs. Lobmiller points out that Judith has led this enforced Spartan existence for close to 12 years. She adds, "You would never think Judith is the same person who committed the horrible crimes attributed to her."

Lisa Millican and Janice Chatman are not here to voice their opinions.

Dale Nelson

Manson, Bundy, Gacy, Dahmer — the names are synonymous with horrific acts perpetrated by evil men. Their exploits have been recounted in books, on TV and in movies. Yet one of Canada's most terrifying tales of wanton murder has gone relatively unnoticed by the country's media. The unspeakable deeds of Dale Nelson took place during the course of one night in Creston Valley, a rather isolated area in southeastern British Columbia.

Dale was in his early 30s back in 1970 when the crimes took place. A logger by profession, he lived with his wife, Annette, and their three children in a modest house along Corn Creek Rd. Dale was a good husband and a kind, caring father, except when he drank with his logging buddies in Creston. On those occasions, he would become aggressive, rowdy and unpredictable. Earlier that same year, Dale had gone into a deep depression and had made an unsuccessful attempt to take his own life. He underwent a psychiatric examination, after which he was returned to his family.

Dale's main hobby was hunting. He was an expert marksman in an area where hunting is the chief diversion from the back-breaking labor of the logging and farming industries. Everyone in the area knew Dale. Many were related to him. Sure, he had his moods and drank a bit, but there was nothing really wrong with Dale Nelson. When he was right, there was no finer fellow in the whole valley.

On September 4, 1970, Dale drove his blue Chevy into town. He picked up a six-pack of beer and a bottle of vodka at the liquor store and proceeded to the

Kootenay Hotel, where he was well known. No one noticed anything unusual about Dale's behavior. He downed eight beers and chatted with friends, mostly about the upcoming hunting season.

After leaving the bar, Dale drove over to Maureen McKay's home to pick up his 7-mm bolt-action rifle, which he had previously loaned to her. He then made his way to Creston and purchased ammo for his rifle, as well as a further supply of booze from the liquor store. Even though he had been drinking on and off all day, Dale was in surprising control of his faculties. He strolled into Creston's King George Hotel and consumed another half dozen beers. Around 10:30 p.m., he was invited to one of the hotel rooms, where he and two friends drank more liquor.

The various people who crossed Dale's path that day had no way of knowing they would later be witnesses at a sensational murder trial. Clerks, drinking buddies and casual friends all thought Dale was in a good mood. He displayed no hint of what was to follow.

It was now past midnight. Ironically, the hunting season had opened moments earlier. Dale drove to the home of Shirley and Alex Wasyk. He knew that Alex was not at home, but had no way of knowing that one of the Wasyk children, Laurie, had accompanied her father. That left Shirley at home with daughters Debbie, 12, Charlene, eight, and Tracey, seven.

Debbie was alone in her bedroom when Dale Nelson came calling. She recognized his voice. After all, Dale was her cousin and often took her hunting. Suddenly, Debbie heard her mother scream, "No, Dale, don't!" The cry was followed by silence. Debbie sneaked out of her room to get a better view. She saw Dale lead Charlene into Tracey's bedroom, where her sister lay asleep. Debbie kept quiet and sneaked into her mother's room. She gasped when she saw her mother lying on the bed with her hands tied behind her back. A fire extinguisher lay close by. Trembling with fear, Debbie untied her mother's hands. When she heard Tracey scream, she picked up the fire extinguisher and dragged it to her room. She threw the extinguisher through the window and jumped out, just as she heard Dale at the bedroom door. Debbie ran to Maureen McKay's and hysterically blurted out her tale of terror. Maureen called the RCMP detachment in Creston.

The Mounties arrived at the Wasyk home to find that Shirley and Tracey had both been murdered. Shirley had been savagely beaten to death with the fire extinguisher. Tracey had been stabbed repeatedly. Charlene had been taken from the house, but had been set free. Dale's Chevy was still parked beside the house.

Fearing for the lives of Mrs. Nelson and other potential victims, the Mounties drove to the Nelson home and evacuated Annette and her children. In all, they were away from the Wasyk home for a total of 15 minutes. When they returned, they were stunned to find that Tracey's body was missing, along with Dale's Chevy. Obviously, he had been hiding outside in the deep brush watching as the RCMP officers drove away.

Officers realized they were dealing with a man who had just taken two lives for no apparent reason. He was armed with a rifle, was a crack shot and was driving in pitch darkness through the countryside with Tracey's body.

Ray Phipps, 42, and his common-law wife, Isabelle St. Amand, 27, lived a few kilometres down the road in little more than a shack. Three of the children, Paul, 10, Cathy, eight, and Brian, seven, were Isabelle's by a previous marriage. Eighteen-month-old Roy was the child of Ray and Isabelle. It was Isabelle who called the RCMP detachment in West Creston. Among other disjointed phrases she whispered, "There's a man here with a gun!" The RCMP rushed to the Phipps home. They were too late.

Ray and Isabelle Phipps had both been shot in the head. The baby, Roy, had been shot as he lay in his crib. Paul and Brian had also been shot in the head. Eight-year-old Cathy was nowhere to be found, which the led the Mounties to surmise that Dale, who had taken seven lives in a few hours, had driven away with the little girl in his Chevy.

As dawn broke, Mounties from several neighboring detachments poured into Creston Valley. Systematic spot checks of houses in the area were conducted by the Mounties, who had no idea where Dale would strike next.

The following afternoon, Dale's vehicle was spotted from the air by the pilot of a Piper Cub engaged in the search. The unoccupied car was stuck in a ditch. Investigators found a bloodstained hammer on the front seat. The woods surrounding the Chevy bore grisly results. Parts of Tracey's body were discovered scattered throughout the immediate area.

Darkness fell on the valley with the monster still at large. Next day, the search intensified. Men stayed home from work. Rifles were taken down from racks. The hunting season was officially open, but the quarry on everyone's mind was Dale Nelson.

Late in the afternoon, Dale was located in the woods close to his own home. He offered no resistance. The question on everyone's mind was the fate of Cathy St. Amand. Without hesitation, Dale informed his captors that the girl was dead and pointed out the location of her body on a map. The RCMP found the child's body in the exact spot indicated by Dale.

From the time of his arrest, Dale underwent a series of psychiatric examinations. When he stood trial for the murders of Tracey Wasyk and Cathy St. Amand, there was only one question to be decided: Was Dale Nelson sane or insane? He had admitted committing all eight murders, but could give no reason other than his intoxication.

The B.C. jury found Dale sane and guilty. He was sentenced to life imprisonment.

Twenty-five years have elapsed since the madman ran amok through the peaceful countryside. Dale Merle Nelson has spent every one of those years in a B.C. prison. As you read this, he is still incarcerated. Should he ever be paroled, he will immediately be charged with the remaining six murders.

Alferd Packer

To normal folk the practice of cannibalism is down-
right disgusting. After all, the consumption of a fellow
human is not compatible with pleasant dining nor does
it do anything for one's digestive system.

Despite the repulsive nature of cannibalism, the subject does hold a certain fascination. Usually it is associ-
ated with another crime, such as murder. Rarely do we
humans kill each other for the sole purpose of a good
nourishing meal. All of which brings us to the subject
of Alferd G. Packer.

In the fall of 1873, Alferd, together with 19 inexperienced prospectors, trudged from Salt Lake City deep
into Colorado's San Juan Mountains searching for
gold. Alferd had some knowledge of the area, but his
fellow travellers were strangers to each other and to
the region.

The party had no success in their quest for the elusive yellow metal. For weeks they searched until, with
little left in the way of supplies, they stumbled, half
starved, into the Indian camp of Chief Ouray. The
chief not only fed the ragtag group, but provided
them with enough food to continue their prospecting
venture.

A problem arose. Ten of the men wanted to give up
the hunt for gold and return to Salt Lake City. Their
close brush with death had given them their fill of the
prospecting game. After many arguments, these 10
men decided to return to Salt Lake City.

Alferd, who had headed the faction wanting to continue prospecting, became the unofficial leader of the
party. He led the remaining men to Los Pinos and

beyond, figuring that the rumors of gold strikes up the Gunnison River would at last bring riches to himself and his group. After trudging along the river for weeks, supplies grew dangerously low. Four men elected to return to Los Pinos and on to Denver. Alferd and the remaining five men left the river bank for the treacherous mountains. Their names are worthy of mention, mainly because no one ever saw Swan, Bell, Miller, Noon and Humphrey alive again.

In February, Alferd made his way out of the frigid cold back to Los Pinos. He looked terrible and was practically in rags. Someone thrust a bottle of whisky into his gnarled fingers. Alferd greedily consumed huge gulps from the flask. When he was offered food, Alferd said that he wasn't that hungry; the booze would do just fine, thank you.

Alferd had a story to tell. He said that he had become ill and that his five companions had left him in the mountains to die. Instead of dying, he had recovered and miraculously had made his way to Los Pinos. He figured that the lure of gold had affected the good judgment of his companions. No doubt they had starved to death in the unforgiving mountains.

Alferd stayed at Los Pinos recuperating for 10 days. He had an abundance of money which allowed him to stay well oiled most of the time. In due course, fit as a fiddle, he left and made his way to Saguache. Word of his remarkable feat had preceded him, along with the nasty rumor that he had a lot of money for a man who had started out broke. Then there was the unmentionable insinuation that he was extremely well nourished for a man who had spent so many weeks in the wilderness.

On April 2, 1874, two of Chief Ouray's men arrived

in camp with the distressing news that they had found strips of frozen meat from white human beings in the snow just outside the camp. When faced with the gruesome evidence, Alferd broke down and confessed. He claimed that supplies had run out. The men were desperate. One day, when he returned to the group after collecting firewood, he found that Swan had been killed by a blow to the head. The four remaining men were in the process of cooking portions of his body and dividing up the $2,000 removed from the dead man's pockets.

Assorted parts of Swan lasted only a few days. The men eyed each other suspiciously. Little intrigues and cliques developed. Who would be the next to go? Answer — Miller. When he wasn't looking, one of the men split his head open with a hatchet. In time, Humphrey and Noon were killed, roasted and eaten as well. Alferd claimed that he and Bell agreed that they wouldn't attack each other, but would remain together even if it meant starving to death. Despite the agreement, Bell went out of his mind and attempted to club Alferd with the butt of his rifle. Alferd overpowered his adversary and killed him with his trusty hatchet.

Our boy wasn't telling the absolute truth. We know that for a fact, because early in June artist John A. Randolph, while traipsing through the mountains doing sketches for Harper's Magazine, came across the bodies of the five men. Noon, Humphreys, Swan and Bell had been shot in the back of their heads. Miller's body, sans head, was found some distance from the others. The head was found nearby and showed evidence of having been hacked with a hatchet. Now for the bad part. Strips of flesh had been removed from the chest areas of each body.

Shortly after the bodies were discovered, Alferd escaped from custody. For nine years he led an exemplary life in Salt Lake City under the name of John Schwartze. It's quite possible he would have remained at large forever had he not had the misfortune to run into one of the original members of his ill-fated prospecting trip on the streets of Salt Lake City.

Alferd was immediately arrested and brought to trial on April 3, 1883. He claimed that he had killed only Bell and that was done in self-defence. Part of his statement is startling: "When I came to Los Pinos, I threw away the strips of flesh I had left and I confess I did so reluctantly, as I had grown fond of human flesh."

No one believed Alferd's story and he was found guilty on five counts of murder. His lawyers managed to obtain a new trial on a technicality. This time he was more fortunate, being convicted of five counts of manslaughter. In 1885, 12 years after the murders, Alferd was sentenced to a total of 40 years imprisonment. He served 16 years in prison before being paroled in 1901. Alferd died of natural causes in Denver on April 24, 1907.

You may be interested to know that Alferd's name will live on. Students at the University of Colorado in Boulder have named their cafeteria The Alferd G. Packer Grill. They commemorate his dubious deeds each spring with an Alferd G. Packer Day. One of the major events on that special day is the students' raw meat eating contest.

Jesse Pomeroy

I am often asked if wanton mass murder is a recent phenomenon. Are the Mansons, Sutcliffes and Olsons the products of modern society? The truth is, the strange mental processes which motivate these modern-day monsters have always been with us.

Probably the most reprehensible mass murderer of the nineteenth century was the American teenager, Jesse Pomeroy.

Jesse's family owned a retail store in Boston and was relatively well off. The Pomeroys knew they had a troubled youngster from the very beginning. When he was only nine, Jesse displayed an aggressive attitude towards other children and took delight in making life miserable for neighborhood dogs and cats.

A brooding, introverted youngster, Jesse was cursed with grotesque features. One of his eyes was covered with a white film, the result of a cataract. There was an unsightly twist to his upper lip which gave him the appearance of wearing a perpetual snarl. Altogether, Jesse was a repulsive-looking character who, because of his innate meanness, was shunned by other youngsters.

In 1881, when Jesse was 14, several children between the ages of seven and ten were reported missing in Boston. A short time later their bodies were discovered in fields and garbage dumps. Other hapless victims were found nailed to the doorways of buildings on dark, deserted streets. Some were discovered tied to posts.

In all, the murders of 27 young boys and girls were attributed to the unknown killer. A wave of hysteria and shock, similar to that which was to envelop

Atlanta, Georgia, a hundred years later, swept through Boston. Despite the concentrated efforts of the police, no clue to the identity of the murderer was immediately uncovered.

Twelve-year-old Albert Pratt's father had hired an armed bodyguard to accompany his son home from school. This precaution had received some publicity and eventually came to the attention of the killer.

Mr. Pratt received an unsigned letter in the mail telling him that his son would be the next to die. A few days after this letter was delivered Harry Pomeroy, Jesse's younger brother, knocked on the door of Albert Pratt's classroom and told teacher William Barnes that Albert's father was outside and wanted to see his son. Mr. Barnes excused Albert from the classroom. Two days later Albert's mutilated body was found in a field outside the city.

Questioned by police, Harry Pomeroy would only say that a tall man in a blue suit had requested that he pass along the message. The next strange incident to take place in a case fraught with the unbelievable occurred when one potential victim escaped the clutches of the monster.

Nine-year-old Willie Barton was playing near a field when a big boy grabbed him and tried to take off his clothes. Willie wrenched free of the bigger boy's grasp and ran away.

Because Harry Pomeroy was already connected with the case, police thought that young Willie might be able to identify his assailant at Harry's school. Willie shrieked in horror when he spotted not Harry, but Jesse Pomeroy. The white eye, snarling lip, and coarse features couldn't be missed.

Instead of denying his guilt, Jesse readily confessed

to all the murders. He seemed to relish the spotlight, was defiant, and swore, "I shan't be hanged. I'll fool you all again!"

At his trial, Jesse discussed his case intelligently with lawyers and the judge. At other times he swore he would kill all those who testified against him, as well as the members of the jury.

Jesse was found guilty, but insane. Unbelievably, one year later he was released from an asylum as cured. His release didn't go unnoticed by the general public. A great many petitions were forwarded to Governor Groves of Massachusetts demanding that Jesse be kept in jail. Both the governor and the presiding judge at Jesse's trial were convinced that he was cured.

A year passed. Jesse stayed close to home. There was a real fear that relatives of his victims might take matters into their own hands and kill him.

Eventually, other matters captured the public's interest. Soon Jesse Pomeroy was out of the spotlight, but not for long. One day his parents left him in charge of their store. A little girl, Alice Curran, entered the Pomeroys' store and was never seen again.

Police naturally questioned Jesse, but he vehemently denied having had anything to do with the disappearance, claiming that he was being harassed because of his past. Other children disappeared. Fields and marshes were searched, but no bodies were found.

At the rear of Pomeroys' store there was a large refuse dump. That summer neighbors claimed that an offensive odor was emanating from the refuse. The city ordered Mr. Pomeroy to remove the dump. Buried in the refuse, authorities uncovered the bodies of twelve children. As the bodies were removed Jesse watched in the yard, smiling. He was enjoying the sight.

Such a furor accompanied this second group of killings that Governor Groves, who had authorized Jesse's release, was forced to resign.

Once more Jesse confessed in detail to all the murders. He was his cocky, defiant self and swore he would seek vengeance on all who were against him.

Jesse was tried and found guilty of murder in the first degree. While a mob outside the courthouse shouted, "Lynch him!" Jesse was sentenced to death by hanging. However, there were those who thought that Jesse must certainly be insane and should not hang. They worked frantically to save him. Finally his sentence was commuted to solitary confinement for life.

Jesse Pomeroy entered prison at the age of 17 and immediately began planning to escape. It wasn't an easy task. He was watched constantly while in solitary confinement. Cunning Jesse was a model prisoner, conforming to all the rules, and spending much of his time reading. Soon he was receiving small privileges.

His mother visited him and tried to help her wicked son to escape. Once she brought him a large meat pie for Thanksgiving. At the last moment guards found some small tools baked in the pie. On another occasion Jesse complained of back trouble and asked permission to have his mother bring him an armchair. Guards found tools and hacksaws hidden in the stuffing of the chair. After this last incident Mrs. Pomeroy was not allowed to bring her son gifts.

Jesse continued to try. His next scheme took three years. He found out that the prison was heated by gas, and that a gas pipe ran directly behind his cell wall. Jesse decided to get through the wall in some way, tap the gas line, and fill his cell with gas. He would then light a match and blow the place up. He didn't seem to

232

care if he blew himself up in the process.

Jesse talked his keepers into providing him with a few simple tools, ostensibly to work on inventing a pencil sharpener. Every night for three years Jesse scraped at the cement which held his granite block cell together. The scrapings were then kneaded into his bread, which he ate.

Finally, he broke through and made a hole in the pipe, allowing the gas to fill his cell. He had secreted away one match months before. He lit the match. The whole area exploded. Two prisoners in adjoining cells were killed. Jesse was blown through the cell door. He was found alive, but badly injured.

Jesse recovered. This time he was watched day and night in a special escape-proof cell in Charleston Prison. It was as close to living in hell as you get on earth. Years passed, Jesse was forgotten. Many assumed he had died.

In 1924, an old man, sick, frail, but still defiant, was transferred from prison to Bridgewater State Farm. Jesse Pomeroy, the "White-Eyed Boy Murderer of Boston" had served forty years in solitary confinement. Special security was provided at Bridgewater to prevent Jesse from escaping. He remained there until the day he died.

Michael Ross

As I drove down the main street of Jewett City, Connecticut, Al Schumanski was busy at his Amoco Gas station pumping air into the rear tire of a little boy's bicycle. Hendel's Furniture Store didn't have a single customer despite the big mattress sale signs in their front window. Clair LaPointe sold gas and cigarettes at Chucky's Country store.

"Visited Toronto years ago," Al Schumanski told me. "Is the Spaghetti Factory still there? Great place. Haven't been back for years." The little boy pedalled away toward the town square where East Main and North Main intersect. It's dry and hot in the David Hale Fanning Park where three large stones list the names of every soldier in the vicinity who served in World Wars I and II and the Korean War. There is no memorial for those who served in Vietnam.

This is small town New England, the heart and soul of the U.S. The tiny Connecticut towns are reminiscent of Norman Rockwell paintings: Danielson, Brooklyn, Canterbury, Plainfield, Jewett City, Lisbon, Griswold, Preston. They run into each other, similar, neat, sun drenched, off the beaten path. No real need to lock a door at night. Most neighbors have known each other for a lifetime. Violence and its ugly ramifications belong in Boston and New York, not in these pleasant, quaint towns.

Police Chief Thurston Fields knows pretty well every one of Jewett City's 4000 inhabitants. His five-man police force keeps the peace with the aid of two patrol cars. Chief Fields assures me, "There has never been a murder in Jewett City in the 11 years I've been chief and I can't remember one before that."

On January 5, 1982, the small community of Brooklyn, Conn. was shocked when Tammy Williams, 17, disappeared. Hundreds of acres of brush and swamp in the area along Route 6 were searched. Tracking dogs were used. Five hundred volunteers searched the rough terrain. No trace of Tammy was found.

On June 15, 1982, Debbie Taylor and her husband James of Jewett City ran out of gas near Danielson. Debbie walked down the highway looking for a service station, while James walked in the opposite direction. Debbie never returned. Next day she was reported missing. Four and a half months later, Debbie's body was found in a Canterbury cornfield. Her skull had been crushed.

No doubt a sex-crazed stranger had lured Debbie into his car. It was horrible. It was shocking. But after all, it was an isolated incident.

Over a year passed. Most people forgot about Debbie Taylor's fate. Most forgot about the missing Tammy Williams, but not Tammy's father. He frequented flea markets, bazaars and other public gatherings, inquiring about his missing daughter. He never turned up a clue.

On November 16, 1983, Robin Stavinsky disappeared off the streets of Norwich. The attractive high school student and state discus champion had a date that day, but never kept it. A week later a jogger found her body in a wooded area on the outskirts of Norwich on Thames Hospital property. Robin had been strangled to death.

Two girls murdered and one missing in two years. Were they unrelated or were the murders the work of one deranged individual? Rumors spread throughout the Connecticut towns.

Leslie Shelly, 14, and April Brunais, 15, were last seen walking on the streets of Jewett City. When they failed to return to their respective homes on April 22, 1984, they were thought to be runaways. The two friends had run away once before for one day. This time they apparently left for good.

Seven weeks later Wendy Baribeault, 17, left her Lisbon home on Round Hill Court to make a purchase at Chucky's Country Store. She left a message for her parents telling them where she was going.

Police Chief Fields and I measured off the distance between Wendy's home and the Country Store. It is exactly 1.6 miles. Somewhere in that short distance Wendy Baribeault disappeared. Wendy was immediately reported missing. A massive search of the area uncovered her body two days later. She had been sexually attacked.

The killer's luck had run out when he murdered Wendy Baribeault. This time an alert citizen informed police that she had seen Wendy walking along the road. A man in a blue 1983 Toyota seemed to be following her. Police checked over 2,000 vehicles with the State Department of Motor Vehicles. By elimination they came up with Michael Ross, 24, a man who had attacked a woman in Ohio years before.

At that time Ross pretended to run out of gas in front of a house he had picked at random. He asked to use the telephone. Once inside, he attacked the lone woman occupant. Ross had picked the wrong woman. She was an off-duty police officer who was an expert in ju jitsu. He managed to get away, but was arrested a short time later.

Michael Ross was arraigned in Ohio, but allowed to return to his Brooklyn, Conn. home when his parents posted a $1,000 bond. He received psychological evaluation for two months before being brought back to Ohio, where he served four and half months in jail. He was released on December 22, 1982 to spend Christmas with his parents in Connecticut.

Michael Ross was arrested and charged with the murder of Wendy Baribeault. Connecticut detectives are reluctant to discuss details, but the fact remains that almost immediately after Ross' arrest, they recovered the bodies of Tammy Williams, Leslie Shelley and April Brunais in woods beside local roads. Ross has been charged with felony murder in the deaths of all six girls. Felony murder carries the death sentence in Connecticut.

Born in Brooklyn, Michael Ross lived most of his life in eastern Connecticut. In 1977 he graduated as an honors student from nearby Killingly High School. His teachers remember him as a keen student, who was quiet and well-behaved. In 1981 he graduated from Cornell University with a major in agricultural economics.

He lived in Jewett City in a large green and white house at 158 North Main St. His girlfriend, Debbie Wallace, divorced mother of three children, lived there with him. She refused to believe that Michael could be responsible for the brutal murders of six women. Neighbors also find it difficult to believe that the polite, well-dressed, friendly young man could be a killer.

While living in Jewett City, Ross was employed with the Prudential Insurance Co. of America as a district agent and registered representative. An official of the insurance company has stated that of the 26,000 agents employed across the U.S. by the company, nothing like Michael Ross has ever happened before.

The hamlet of Brooklyn, Conn., population 900, was

incorporated in 1796. A large statue of Major General Israel Putnam, a hero of the War of Independence, adorns its main thoroughfare. A little further up the road Michael Ross' family owns and operates one of the largest businesses in town, a poultry and egg factory.

It is here that Michael grew up, an unobtrusive boy who worked hard at his father's business. His parents refuse to discuss their son since his arrest. Some of the townspeople can't believe that their town may have spawned a serial killer.

Carol Kovacs, an employee of the New England Centre for Contemporary Art, remembers well hearing the devastating news that an acquaintance had been arrested for the alleged murder of six girls. Carol knew Tammy Williams, one of the victims. She intersperses her emotions with such words as "unbelievable," "dumbfounded," and "shocked" when discussing the arrest of Michael Ross.

Connecticut police inquired about Michael Ross' activities in other locations. While he was attending Cornell University in Ithaca, New York, 25-year-old Vietnamese student Drung Ngoc Tu was murdered. Her body was found at the bottom of a gorge. Miss Tu was majoring in agricultural economics and lived one block from the Alpha Zeta fraternity house. Michael Ross lived at the fraternity house at the time of her murder.

But Ross' connection with Miss Tu was dropped when he was found guilty of murdering Tammy Williams and Debbie Taylor. For these murders he was sentenced to life imprisonment.

On July 6, 1987 Michael Ross was found guilty of the murders of Robin Stavinsky, Leslie Shelley, April Brunais and Wendy Baribeault. He has been sentenced to death in Connecticut's electric chair.

Ramon Salcido

Ramon Salcido was born in Los Mochis, Mexico, but as he grew up his heart was in glamorous California to the north. While still a teenager, Ramon dreamed of getting into the U.S., making a fortune and returning to Mexico as a millionaire. It wasn't that he didn't have a good life in his native country. His parents were upper middle class and were more than willing to provide their son with every advantage.

In 1980, Ramon smuggled himself across the border into California and made his way to the wine country near Fresco, where he quickly gained employment with one of the many vineyards in the area. Ramon was an attractive young man with a steady job, but it bothered him that he was an illegal immigrant.

To correct this situation, Ramon married a local girl, obtained his green card and became a legal resident of the U.S. The couple had one child, a daughter, but the marriage didn't work out and Ramon split. He travelled to the famed Napa/Sonoma wine country, where he again had no difficulty catching on with one of the local vineyards.

One day, quite by chance, in Santa Rosa, Ramon met Angela Richards. To say Angela was attractive would be an understatement. The 19-year-old was a beautiful young girl, certainly the most beautiful creature Ramon had ever met. It didn't matter that he couldn't speak a word of English and she couldn't speak a word of Spanish; there was an electricity between the two young people. But there were problems. Angela's parents were very strict. She had never been on a date before meeting Ramon. In order to see her lover, it was necessary for Angela to climb out of her bedroom window at night while the family slept. Angela and Ramon made love in the back seat of Ramon's old Ford LTD.

When Angela became pregnant, there was no way out but to inform her parents. Furious at their daughter's predicament, and distasteful as Ramon appeared to be, they insisted that the couple marry. An uneasy peace prevailed between Ramon and his in-laws. Inwardly, the Richards didn't like Ramon and he burned inside at their reluctance to accept him as a true member of the family.

As the years passed, the Salcidos had three daughters. Ramon was steadily employed at a winery, while Angela augmented the family income by working as a seamstress. Perhaps life would have unfolded peacefully in its normal way had not other factors come into play. Ramon had never told Angela that he had been married and, more importantly, that he had never been divorced from his first wife.

In 1989, Ramon's first wife was successful in locating him. She obtained a court order forcing him to pay her $511 a month, as well as $5,807 to the Social Service Department of Fresno County to repay sums turned over by that agency to her. Angela was devastated. As if this wasn't enough, she had other reasons not to be enthralled with her husband. Angela's exceptional beauty had recently come to the attention of two modelling agencies, who seriously felt she might have a lucrative career in television commercials. Ramon wouldn't hear of his wife straying from their home. He became unreasonably jealous, often following her when she went grocery shopping.

By March 1989, Ramon was under extreme pressure,

all of it his own doing. He constantly argued and fought with his wife, truly believing that every man she met was a bona fide threat to their marriage. On the night of April 13, Ramon visited his favorite bar. As he gulped beer and wine, he grew despondent. Life held no hope, only disgrace and failure. Ramon drove home to his duplex on Baines Ave. in Boyes Hot Springs. Angela wasn't in, but the three girls lay peacefully asleep in their beds.

Ramon loaded the children, Sofia, 4, Carmina, 3, and Teresa, 2, into his LTD. He drove to a landfill site at the edge of town and there committed one of the most gruesome murders ever perpetrated. He slit the children's throats and tossed them over an embankment. Sofia and Teresa bled to death where they came to rest. Carmina landed on her head and was rendered unconscious.

Ramon drove to his in-laws' home in nearby Cotati. Marion Richards must have put up a courageous struggle, but was no match for the powerful Ramon. He viciously cut her throat. Angela's two sisters, 12-year-old Ruth and eight-year-old Maria, met the same fate. At work, Bob Richards had no way of knowing that his son-in-law had entered his home and killed his wife and two daughters.

Ramon wasn't through. When he returned to his own home, Angela was there, unaware of the havoc and death her husband had meted out that night. There is evidence that Angela raced from room to room in an attempt to escape his intense rage. There would be no escape. She was beaten and then shot to death.

The deranged man's mind turned to those men whom he believed were attracted to his wife. He drove to the Grand Cru vineyards, where he met one of his imagined adversaries, 35-year-old Tracy Toovey, just inside the vineyard gates. Toovey was attempting to get out of his old Volkswagen Carmen Ghia when he was mowed down by six well-aimed bullets in the face from Ramon's .22 revolver.

It was exactly 8:18 on the morning of April 14 when police were called to the scene of a shooting. Ken Butti, a foreman at the Grand Cru winery, had been shot in the shoulder. Ken informed police that Ramon Salcido had driven up to his home in his old LTD. When Ken got up to greet him, he was amazed to see Ramon aiming a .22 at him. Ramon fired and wounded him in the shoulder. Ken's wife, who was standing nearby, screamed. Ramon fired at her, but the gun either misfired or was empty. Ken had no idea why Ramon, whom he knew well, had shot him. He told police that at one time Ramon had been a valued employee at Grand Cru, but in recent months his work had deteriorated. Rumor had it that Ramon was experiencing financial and marital difficulties.

The hunt was on for Ramon Salcido. Although investigators were unaware of the other crimes Ramon had committed during the preceding hours, they realized they were after a man with a gun who had wounded one man and, only by luck, had missed wounding or killing Mrs. Butti.

Within hours, police came across the body of Tracy Toovey.

Other officers were dispatched to Ramon's home, where they found Angela's bullet-riddled body. Great concern was felt for the three Salcido children, who were nowhere to be found. That same morning, officers learned of the animosity between Ramon and his in-laws. Detectives drove to the Richards' home, where they found a body in each of three rooms.

On Saturday, over three days after the murder spree began, a young man walking along the edge of a quarry bordering a county dump came across the bodies of two little girls lying on their backs. He ran to the quarry supervisor's office and summoned police. Meanwhile, the young man and the supervisor returned to the crime scene. They were amazed to find a third little girl, Carmina Salcido, in a sitting position, staring straight ahead. She was alive. Carmina couldn't answer the men's questions. She simply stared into space, sitting there in her blood encrusted nightgown. Within minutes, she was being rushed to hospital.

A massive manhunt, both in United States and Mexico, was on for Ramon Salcido, now charged with seven murders and three attempted murders. The wanted man made his way to his hometown in Mexico, where his own relatives turned him in to the authorities. He was immediately returned to the U.S.

Ramon was tried in Redwood City, Calif. He was found guilty of six counts of first-degree murder, one count of second-degree murder and two counts of attempted murder. In the courtroom, when the death sentence was passed, sat Bob Richards. In one night of horror his son-in-law had murdered his wife, his three daughters and two of his three grandchildren.

Little Carmina Salcido underwent a tracheostomy and had a tube inserted into her windpipe to ease her breathing until her neck wound healed. She was unable to talk for some time, but her voice has since returned and she has long since been released from hospital. Bob Richards says that his granddaughter has received over 15,000 cards and letters from well wishers all over the world.

Lydia Sherman

I drove through the lush Connecticut countryside towards the small town of Derby. It is difficult to imagine that this peaceful community tucked away on the side of a hill along the Housatonic River was once the home of one of the most prolific female mass murderers in the history of the U.S. It was here that Lydia Sherman ended her career of dispensing arsenic with a degree of abandonment rarely experienced before or since.

Lydia's infamous history can be traced back to 1847, when she married a policeman, Edward Struck, in New York City. The marriage was to last for seventeen years, during which Lydia gave birth to six handsome children: Lydia, Anne Eliza, William, George, Edward, and Mary Ann.

After such a lengthy period of marital bliss, an incident occurred on the streets of New York that was to have far reaching effects on the Struck family. Edward was abruptly dismissed from the Metropolitan Police Force. Evidently there was some question concerning Struck's reaction under pressure. It was reported that he hurriedly left the scene of a disturbance, leaving a citizen to disarm a madman in a saloon.

Lydia was not only furious — she was embarrassed and ashamed. She began making excuses for her husband. He was ill, he was insane — anything that came to mind.

Meanwhile, Lydia had to face the practical problem of feeding her children. Lydia obtained a position as a nurse to Dr. L.A. Rodenstein. It was while employed with Dr. Rodenstein that Lydia first became acquainted with arsenic and its lethal qualities.

One glorious day in May 1864, Lydia dropped into a Harlem drug store and purchased a quantity of arsenic. She explained to the druggist that her apartment was "alive with rats." What better way to rid herself of the wee beasties than a good dose of arsenic? The deadly powder cost her ten cents.

That night Lydia cooked up a batch of warm oatmeal for Edward. It didn't agree with him at all. Within hours he was confined to bed. Lydia was concerned. She nursed him all night, attempting to relieve his agony with assorted medicines. She even endeavored to bolster his strength with more oatmeal, but Edward had lost his appetite.

In the morning Edward was in such bad shape that Lydia called in a neighboring physician, Dr. N. Hustead. At this point in Lydia's saga it is rather strange that no one wondered why she did didn't summon her employer, Dr. Rodenstein, but at the time no one gave it a second thought.

At any rate, it was too late for Edward. He died in agony before Dr. Hustead arrived at his bedside. Lydia was overcome with grief at her loss. The good doctor could scarcely stand the way she carried on. She suggested that "consumption" carried poor Edward away." Dr. Hustead agreed, and signed the death certificate accordingly.

Once Lydia got the hang of the poisoning business, there was no stopping her. In the following months she proceeded to annihilate all six of her own children. July 5 seems to have been a red-letter day — on that day she killed three of her offspring.

By the time the second anniversary of Edward's demise rolled around, the entire family was dead and buried. Lydia was clever enough to employ various doctors, all of whom attributed the rash of deaths to natural causes.

Only one man was suspicious. Reverend Mr. Payson of the Harlem Presbyterian Church, who had watched Lydia, the eldest Struck daughter, die in agony, couldn't get certain evil thoughts out of his mind. Several days after young Lydia's death he passed his suspicions along to the district attorney's office. The D.A. failed to act.

Through an acquaintance, Lydia secured a position in Stratford, Connecticut, as nurse and housekeeper to a Mrs. Curtiss. There seems little doubt that Mrs. Curtiss was ripe for one of Lydia's little white powders, but the old lady proved to be a crusty, intelligent New Englander who wouldn't be bamboozled. Lydia let it be known around Stratford that she was available for employment elsewhere if the opportunity presented itself.

Eight uneventful months passed. One day, while grocery shopping in John Fairchild's store, Lydia was told by Mr. Fairchild that an old gentleman named Dennis Hurlbut of Corum, Connecticut had just lost his wife and was looking for a housekeeper. When Lydia learned that Hurlbut was over seventy-five years old and was reputed to be wealthy, she required no further encouragement.

Lydia dashed over to Corum, now known as Shelton. Harlbut, who was approaching senility, expected an old lady with whom to argue away his remaining years. The old dog was smitten the moment he laid eyes on attractive, trim, 44-year-old Lydia.

Within a week Hurlbut proposed. The odd couple married on November 22, 1868. Lydia played the industrious housekeeper and loving wife to the hilt. Three months after the knot was tied, Hurlbut made his will.

Eleven months later Lydia, complete in widow's garb, buried her second husband. Old Hurlbut's demise left Lydia a wealthy woman by 1870 standards. She became the sole owner of her late husband's farm, as well as cash amounting to $10,000.

Today, 125 years since the murder, you can still find the record of the unsuspecting Hurlbut's death in the registry of births, deaths, and marriages, at the Shelton Town Hall. Under cause of death is the ominous notation — arsenic poisoning.

Lydia always seemed to be in the right place at the right time when it came to members of the opposite sex. This time, Mr. William Thomas, who delivered the mail to Lydia's farm, told the brand new widow that a man named Nelson Sherman of Derby had just lost his wife and was left with four children. He was in dire need of a housekeeper. Lydia indicated that she was interested, even though her true love, old Hurlbut, was scarcely two months removed from this mortal coil.

A meeting was arranged. Nelson Sherman, who held down a good job with a Derby tack manufacturer, was delighted at the prospect of having good-looking Lydia as his housekeeper, and who knows, maybe even much more.

He explained to Lydia that he had an infant son and three other children at home. Besides his offspring, he was stuck with his deceased wife's mother, Mrs. Mary Jones. His mother-in-law simply didn't get along with his children, and things were going from bad to worse. His 14-year-old daughter Ada and Mrs. Jones were at each other's throats constantly. Horatio, 18, Nattie, four, and Frank, the nine-month-old baby, rounded out the household.

In the ensuing months Nelson wooed the widow Hurlbut. This time, with old Hurlbut's coin rattling in her pockets, Lydia was in no particular rush to wed. However, when she felt the time was right, she once more let herself be led to the altar.

On September 2, 1870, Lydia became Mrs. Nelson Sherman. Things did not proceed smoothly from the very first day. The mother-in-law proved to be an ornery old woman, who relished arguing with young Ada. Baby Frank was a handful. Slowly it dawned on Lydia that by marrying Nelson Sherman she had bitten off more than she could chew.

One day, completely frustrated at the direction of events were taking in his household, Nelson blurted out that he wished baby Frank were dead. Then his dear old mother-in-law would have no further reason for staying on.

The cool waters of the Housatonic River flowed gently past the Shermans' white house the day Lydia heard this very practical suggestion. Her ears perked up. A twinkle came to her eye. Did someone suggest a death in the family might be beneficial?

Lydia strained to hear. Yes, she was positive — there were rats scurrying about in the attic. She must fetch some arsenic and get rid of the nasty little devils.

Quick as a wink, Frank became ill. He simply couldn't hold anything in his stomach. Small wonder. Lydia had laced the baby's milk with arsenic. To put it in her own words, "I was full of trouble, and not knowing what to do, I put some arsenic in his milk."

Mother-in-law Mary Jones grew alarmed and sent for

Dr. A. Beardsley, the family physician who lived a few doors away from the Shermans. Dr. Beardsley arrived at the house in the morning, took one look at Frank, and declared that the child was suffering from colic. The doctor gave the sick child several medicines. By late afternoon the baby appeared to be recovering slowly. Lydia put a stop to all that. When the doctor left, she gave little Frank some of her own medicine. Frank was dead by 11 o'clock that night.

Around this time it is quite possible that Nelson Sherman had some inkling that he had married a monster. Always a man who liked his whisky, Nelson took to the bottle with a vengeance. Rarely did he show up at the tack factory where he was employed. In fact, at this juncture in his life, Nelson was pretty well in the sauce all the time. He had good reason.

During the holiday season of 1870 a heavy snowfall descended on the peaceful little village of Derby. Sleighs pulled by proud horses, gaily decorated with Christmas bells, dashed through the centre of the town. No one was aware that in their tranquil community dwelt a mass murderer who poisoned without feeling or remorse. Lydia had by now chalked up nine victims.

That Christmas, Nelson's daughter Ada was busy helping the Rev. Morton decorate the tree down at the Congregational Church. Unaccountably, Ada became so ill that Rev. Morton sent her home. Lydia felt that Ada had partaken of too much candy, but Rev. Morton thought the matter much more serious.

He was so concerned that he showed up at the Sherman residence later that afternoon with Dr. Beardsley, the same doctor who had unsuccessfully treated Ada's brother Frank. Dr. Beardsley prescribed brandy for his patient. Ada lived through the night.

Lydia was later to state, "I felt so bad I was tempted to do as I had done before. I had some arsenic in the house and I mixed some in her tea and give it to her twice. She died the next morning."

After the death of his second child, Nelson Sherman stayed drunk all the time. Things were not going well for Lydia, who was financing Nelson's drunken sprees in New Haven. But to every cloud there is a silver lining. Nelson's mother-in-law moved out.

Lydia's joy at seeing Mary Jones depart was diluted by Nelson's unquenchable thirst. Now a confirmed drunk, he no longer shared her bed. In short, he became an absolute bore.

One fine day in April, Lydia hitched up her wagon and together with five-year-old Nattie, drove over to the village of Birmingham. She pulled in front of the Birmingham Drug Store and walked inside with Nattie. Mr. Peck, the proprietor, waited on Lydia, who stated, "We are overrun with rats. What is best to kill them?"

Mr. Peck suggested several patent poisons, but in the end added that, "Arsenic is cheaper and just as good." Lydia chose arsenic.

When Lydia returned home Nelson was away in New Haven, dissipating $300 he had received from selling the family piano. Lydia waited for her husband's return for several days before dispatching Horatio, the eldest son, to bring his father back to Derby. After much saloon searching, Horatio located his father and brought him back.

Nelson immediately had an attack of stomach cramps. Lydia was up to her old tricks. "I had about a pint of brandy in the house, and I put some arsenic in it. That night he drank some of the brandy, and the next morning he was very sick."

For the next few days Nelson continued to suffer. Dr. Beardsley was called in. He attributed Nelson's trouble to his excessive drinking. The patient grew weaker. Dr. Beardsley brought in a colleague, Dr. Pinny, but Nelson continued to deteriorate. Nelson lasted a week before expiring.

It was now all too much for Dr. Beardsley. He had been the attending physician at three Sherman deaths. Despite the grieving wife, despite the alcoholic husband, something was wrong. All three deaths had been accompanied by similar symptoms — dry mouth, nausea, vomiting, stomach pain, faintness, and great thirst, all symptoms compatible with arsenic poisoning.

Dr. Beardsley actually was bold enough to ask Lydia if she had given her husband arsenic. Lydia was aghast. Heavens no, she replied. The concerned doctor then asked for permission to perform an autopsy. Lydia consented.

On Saturday, the day after Nelson's death, his liver and stomach were rattling along the New Haven railroad, on the way to Yale University to be examined. The next day the bodies of Ada and Frank Sherman, as well as Dennis Hurlbut, were exhumed. Their vital organs were sent to Yale as well.

On Monday, before the results of the tests for arsenic were returned to Derby, Lydia took off for New Brunswick, New Jersey, where detectives took her into custody. She was returned to Derby, and later transferred to New Haven, to stand trial for the murder of Nelson Sherman. Meanwhile, doctors had examined the vital organs of Nelson, Ada, and Frank Sherman, as well as those of Dennis Hurlbut. All were laced with arsenic.

Lydia Sherman's trial for murder began on April 16, 1872. Throughout the several months of her incarceration at Derby, she steadfastly maintained her innocence. Her case captured the imagination of the entire country. It was a rare day that curious onlookers and reporters didn't hover about the Derby jail, hoping for a glimpse of the "Birmingham Borgia."

Lydia's trial lasted ten days and concluded with her being found guilty of murder in the second degree and being sentenced to life imprisonment. While in jail awaiting her lawyer's attempts to obtain a new trial, Lydia dramatically confessed in detail to killing six of her own children, her three husbands, and the two Sherman children. In all, eleven murders.

Despite her admissions, she did not give detailed motives for her horrible crimes. Students of the Sherman case believe Lydia did away with Dennis Hurlbut, her second husband, to gain his wealth. In her confession, she mentioned that she killed several of the children so they would be "better off."

Lydia was imprisoned in the Connecticut State Prison for five and a half years, until her death on May 16, 1878.

Charles Starkweather

Wanton murder is impossible to anticipate. There is very little defence against it. The difference between a traffic light turning red or green can place an innocent victim in the sight of a deranged sniper. You can cross the paths of desperate men during the commission of a robbery through no fault of your own.

When innocent people become the victims of such a murderer, the public has a natural abhorrence to the crime. We can all relate to being in the wrong place at the wrong time.

On Tuesday, January 27, 1958, Charlie Starkweather, 19, visited the home of his 14-year-old girlfriend, Caril Fugate. It was a blustery grey day in Lincoln, Nebraska. Charlie had brought along his .22 rifle. He and Caril's stepfather, Marion Bartlett, had a date to go hunting. As soon as Charlie entered the house, Caril's mother, Velda, started telling Charlie that she didn't want him around the house any more. A heated argument erupted and Velda slapped Charlie in the face. Charlie retaliated by slapping his girlfriend's mother.

Finally, Mr. Bartlett couldn't take any more. He came at Charlie. Without any more provocation than that, Charlie Starkweather raised his .22 and calmly shot Marion Bartlett in the head. Mrs. Bartlett grabbed a knife and advanced towards Charlie. The rifle was raised a second time and Charlie shot her, again with a bullet to the head. Two-and-a-half-year-old Betty Jean Bartlett started to cry. Starkweather beat her to death with the butt of his rifle.

The house became silent. Everyone but Caril and Charlie was dead. Charlie carried Mr. Bartlett's body out to a chicken coop at the rear of the house. He dragged Mrs. Bartlett's body to an outhouse. Little Betty Jean was placed in a cardboard box and put beside her mother. Charlie cleaned the blood off the floor, and unbelievably, he and Caril settled down to watching television for a few hours. Then Charlie went out to use a phone. He called Mr. Bartlett's employer and told him that Bartlett had the flu and wouldn't be in to work for a few days. Upon returning to the house he had intercourse with Caril. Later, he was to state that he had sex with Caril every day and twice on Sunday.

The young couple stayed on in the house. In the normal course of events, people started to arrive at the front door. Caril didn't answer some callers and they went away. The more persistent were told through the door that everyone had the flu and the doctor had ordered the house placed under quarantine. For six days the two teenagers stayed in the house after the killings. Finally Caril's elderly grandmother, sensing that something was wrong, went to the police, who investigated and discovered the three bodies. Caril and Charlie had left just before the police arrived. Starkweather took Bartlett's .410 shotgun with him.

They hadn't travelled far when Charlie's car got stuck near August Meyers' farm. Charlie, who knew Meyers, walked up to the house and asked for help in getting his car out of a ditch. The farmer went into the house for his overcoat. When he came back out, according to Charlie, he had a gun. Without hesitation, Starkweather shot him in the head. They got the car out of the ditch and drove away, but it wasn't long before they were stuck again. This time young Robert Jensen and his girlfriend, Carol King, stopped to see if they could help in any way. Charlie and Caril pulled their guns on the surprised pair. They had the terrified couple drive to a deserted school a few miles from Bennet, Nebraska. Starkweather led the pair to a storm cellar, shot young Jensen in the head, raped and stabbed Carol King, and shot her in the head as well.

That night Starkweather and Fugate spent the night in the Jensen car. The next day they walked into the home of wealthy Laver Ward in Lincoln, Nebraska. A maid opened the door to the young couple. It was to be her last day of life. Mrs. Ward came downstairs in her nightclothes. Later, on some pretext, she got permission from Starkweather to go upstairs to dress. Charlie waited for her for 40 minutes, and then went upstairs to investigate. He claimed later that Mrs. Ward was waiting for him with a rifle. He overpowered her and stabbed her to death in minutes.

At 6:30 in the evening Mr. Ward arrived home. He immediately sized up the situation and instinctively knew his only chance was to attack Starkweather. He lunged at Charlie with an electric iron. Starkweather shot him in the head, and as he spun around, he was again shot in the back. The maid was taken upstairs, tied and gagged. She was found dead of suffocation.

Charlie and Caril left the house and headed for Wyoming. They decided to change cars about 10 miles outside of Douglas, Wyoming. They hailed a passing motorist, salesman Merle Collison. In order to gain possession of his car Charlie shot him nine times.

Then Charlie's luck ran out.

As soon as he killed Collison, another motorist stopped, thinking the two vehicles were having difficulties. The driver, Joe Sprinkle, got out of his car. Charlie levelled a revolver at him and said, "Raise your hands, help me release the emergency brake or I'll kill you."

Out of the corner of his eye Sprinkle saw the body of Merle Collison lying on the floor of the car. He lunged for the rifle and wrestled it away from Charlie. Later he was to state that he knew instinctively that to lose this tug of war meant death. Unarmed, Charlie dashed for his car. Strictly by coincidence, Deputy Sheriff Bill Romer drove up. Caril, who had been in the dead man's car, ran to the deputy. Starkweather roared away in Collison's vehicle. The sheriff used his radio and a car driven by Douglas Police Chief Robert Ainslie took up the chase. He fired some shots at the fleeing vehicle. One bullet went through the rear window of Starkweather's car. Charlie pulled up and dashed out of the car screaming that he was bleeding. A sliver of glass from the broken window had nicked his ear.

Immediately after his capture Charlie Starkweather started to talk. He confessed to one other murder that had taken place seven weeks before his murderous spree began. It involved a gas station robbery where the owner was taken into the woods and shot to death. In all, 11 people fell to the deadly impulses of Starkweather, the last 10 in the space of two weeks.

From the beginning Charlie insisted that Caril was a hostage and had nothing to do with the actual killings. Caril also professed to be terrified of Charlie, and thought she would become a victim at any time during the killing orgy. Later Charlie, who made seven different confessions, changed his story and implicated his girlfriend, stating that she was a willing lover and accomplice.

When they placed Charlie in the electric chair on June 25, 1959, his last request was to task the guards to tighten the leather straps holding his chest and arms.

Caril's main defence was based on the fact that she was a hostage. The prosecution attorney pointed out the many times she was armed or alone and could have run away during the deadly two weeks.

In the end, she received a sentence of life imprisonment. Imprisoned at the age of 14, Caril spent more than half her life in prison. She was twice denied parole. However, she had her sentence of life imprisonment commuted. Caril has since been granted parole.

Howard Stewart

Howard Stewart couldn't stand the thought of his wife Brenda sleeping with another man. It didn't matter that he and Brenda were separated. In fact, folks around Corsicana, Texas, never could fathom why Brenda married Howard in the first place.

To say that 37-year-old Howard was not well liked around town would be an understatement. The man wore a perpetual scowl and had the reputation of blowing his cool at the least provocation.

In the summer of 1987, Howard shaved his head and outfitted himself with military camouflage clothing and combat boots. He became something of a character around Corsicana, a town of 30,000 solid Texans.

Folks shook their heads when he took to wearing a .22 automatic with a 50-bullet clip strapped to his leg. About the only living creatures Howard acted civilly towards were his two pet bulldogs. Behind his back, people called him Rambo.

In hindsight, Howard Stewart was a bomb waiting to explode. When he lost his job at Hulcher Services Inc., he had time to think. He had a lot to think about. First there was Brenda and her new boyfriend, Edward Persons.

The thought of her making love to that stranger drove him mad. Then there was Dennis Wade, his former supervisor who had fired him. It wasn't fair for a man to lose his job and his wife. Howard was relegated to living alone with his two bulldogs. No, it wasn't fair.

On September 9, Howard Stewart decided he had to get away from Corsicana to pull himself together. He boarded a bus and spent a week with relatives in

Lebanon, Missouri. The change of scenery didn't help. A rage burned within Howard, a rage that could not be extinguished. Slowly, he donned his camouflage garb, taking special care to strap his .22 automatic to his leg. He told his relatives that he was hitchhiking back to Corsicana.

George Brewer, 43, and his wife Carol, 36, left their mobile home in their white Chevy van. It was their misfortune to pick up Howard Stewart who was hitchhiking back to Texas. Both George and Carol were shot in the head by Howard. The double murder first came to the attention of the authorities when the Brewers' abandoned van was found by a sheriff's deputy. The interior of the vehicle was drenched in blood. A search of the area uncovered George's body, but Carol was nowhere to be found.

Almost simultaneously with the discovery of George's body, police received a missing person's report filed by Mrs. Steve Vestal. Her husband had been scheduled to meet her at the church in nearby Phillipsburg for choir practice. When Steve failed to show up, his wife grew worried and called police.

The few days in September 1987 were fast becoming the busiest and strangest in the history of peaceful Laclede County, Missouri. Instead of locking up a few locals for being inebriated, police found themselves with one murder, possibly a second one, and a third person missing. The activity didn't abate.

Volunteers searched for Carol Brewer's body. A man in a truck spotted some clothing in a ditch about a mile and a half from where her husband's body had been recovered. What he thought was clothing turned out to be Carol's body. She too had been shot in the head.

Ten miles down the road in Lebanon, a woman noticed blood dripping from a truck onto the pavement of a parking lot. She peered into the vehicle. Slumped on the floor of the truck was the body of Steve Vestal, a bullet hole through his head.

Police were stymied. Ballistic checks on the .22 calibre slugs indicated that all three victims had been shot with the same weapon. A bloody shoeprint found beside George Brewer's body matched one found on Steve Vestal's jacket, but an investigation into the backgrounds of the victims indicated that the Brewers had not been acquainted with Steve Vestal. Money and jewelry had not been taken from any of the victims. Who would kill three individuals without any apparent motive?

Authorities had no idea of the existence of Howard Stewart. He had managed to hitchhike back to Texas without casting any suspicion on himself. Back in Corsicana, Howard told a friend that he had wasted three people in Missouri. The friend laughed. What could you expect from a guy who dressed like Rambo?

Howard Stewart wasn't finished killing. A week after his murderous spree in Missouri, he woke up in a rage and struck out at what he may have loved most of all. He shot his two bulldogs and let the bodies lie in his van where they had fallen.

Howard drove to the location of his former employment, Hulcher Services Inc. By chance, the first man he met was Dennis Wade, the very man who had fired him weeks earlier. In front of a witness, he poured ten slugs into Wade and left the premises without uttering a word.

Howard drove across town and walked into the Seventh Avenue Steak House where his estranged wife

Brenda worked as a waitress. He fired three shots into the ceiling before the assistant manager told him his wife wasn't scheduled to report for work until three that afternoon. As if his entrance had been of no importance, Howard thanked the man for the information and calmly walked out of the restaurant.

The assistant manager firmly believed that Brenda's life was in danger. He phoned Brenda and told her that he believed Howard was on his way to her house with nothing good on his mind. Then he called police. Brenda took the warning seriously, but felt that she could handle Howard. She was wrong.

Within minutes, Howard was storming through Brenda's house. Edward Persons was in bed when Howard entered, guns blazing. Edward was shot dead where he lay. Brenda raced to the bathroom and locked the door.

Howard sprayed the door with bullets and knocked it in. He found Brenda cowering with fear in a corner. Without hesitation, Howard fired and Brenda died instantly.

No doubt Howard heard the police sirens approaching. As they drew near, he placed his .22 automatic to his temple and pulled the trigger.

The killing was over. Six innocent individuals had been murdered and the man who dressed like Rambo had taken his own life.

Mary Beth Tinning

Can a woman murder eight of her nine children over a period of 14 years and go undetected? That's what the 70,000 citizens of the factory city of Schenectady, N.Y. are asking themselves.

Mary Beth Tinning, 44, was born in the area back in the war years when the local General Electric plants employed 45,000 workers churning out strategic war materials. That large figure has steadily declined, and today 12,000 are gainfully employed at G.E., still the largest industry by far in Schenectady. The town, adjacent to Albany, has seen better days.

Joe Tinning worked at General Electric as a systems analyst. He and Mary Beth had moved frequently over the years. No one gave it much thought. The area around Albany, the state capital, is surrounded by villages and towns. It is difficult to ascertain where one stops and the next one begins. There was one thing different about the Tinnings. They suffered tragic misfortune with their children — all nine of them.

On January 3, 1972, the Tinnings' new baby Jennifer, died while still in hospital. She was eight days old. Jennifer is the only Tinning death not considered to be suspicious. Seventeen days later, on January 20, two-year-old Joseph died. Understandably, the Tinnings were devastated. But there was more to come. On March 2, 1972, four-year-old Barbara died.

What a horrible experience for any family to endure. In two months less a day all three Tinning children were dead. Their deaths were attributed to natural causes. Those who knew the Tinnings offered their sympathy. It happens. There was little anyone could do.

Nine months later, Mary Beth gave birth to a son, Timothy. On December 10, 1973, 14 days after his birth, Timothy died. The cause of death noted on the death certificate is SIDS (Sudden Infant Death Syndrome). In its purest sense, SIDS is not a cause of death. It really means that the cause of death is unknown.

With Timothy's death occurring so soon after being taken home from hospital, rumors spread among the Tinnings' few acquaintances. Was it possible that there was something wrong with the Tinnings' genes, some imperfection which caused their offspring to die suddenly?

Just under two years after this tragedy, five-month-old Nathan died. When Nathan died on September 2, 1975, various individuals in official capacities, such as doctors and social service workers, became somewhat suspicious. However, it must be pointed out that the same doctors and social workers were not necessarily involved in all the deaths. Autopsies were performed on all the Tinning children. The results were always the same. Death was attributed to natural causes.

Dr. Robert Sullivan, the Schenectady County Medical Examiner, admitted that when Nathan died, he was aware of the earlier deaths. Nathan's death was thoroughly investigated, but no evidence of foul play was found. Dr. Sullivan revealed, "The parents were doing nothing wrong. They were initiating examinations into the deaths of the children."

Joe Tinning had a responsible position at the G.E. plant. He is an avid bowler. Over the years, Mary Beth often worked as a waitress to supplement the family's income. Sometimes she served as a volunteer ambulance driver. There was absolutely nothing to distinguish the Tinnings from their neighbors.

Absolutely nothing except the inexplicable deaths of their children.

After Nathan's death, three and half years passed before Mary Beth gave birth to another child, a daughter, Mary Frances. The beat continued. Mary Frances died at age three and a half months.

Ten months later, Mary Beth had a little boy, Jonathan. He died three months later, on March 24, 1980. That same year, the Tinnings adopted a son, Michael. He died a year after Jonathan, on March 2, 1981.

Michael's death put an end to the theory that some kind of black genetic evil was at work causing the strange deaths of the Tinning children. After all, he was adopted. An autopsy was performed. The official cause of death was listed as viral pneumonia. Now, suspicions ran rampant. Although there was no proof of any wrongdoing, pediatricians and social workers advised police that should any further Tinning children die, a forensic pathologist should be called in immediately.

Eight children were dead. It seems unbelievable that, despite an extensive investigation into some of the deaths, nothing more than dark suspicions were cast in Mrs. Tinning's direction. The bodies of Timothy and Nathan were exhumed, but nothing new was found.

Over three years passed. Mary Beth became pregnant for the eighth time. She gave birth to Tami Lynn, who died four months later, on December 20, 1985. This ninth death initiated a massive investigation. I have been unable to unearth just what, if anything, investigating officers uncovered. Evidently, a tip concerning Tami's death came from someone attached to the Schenectady County Social Services Department's

Child Protective Unit.

On February 4, 1986, Mary Beth was picked up by detectives and taken to the nearby State Police Headquarters at Loudonville. Under intensive questioning, which lasted a total of 10 hours, Mary Beth admitted killing three of her children: Timothy, Nathan and Tami.

She was duly arrested, lodged in jail and charged with two counts of second degree murder concerning Tami's death. More specifically, she was charged with one count of "having intentionally caused her daughter's death by smothering her with a pillow," and in the other count, "with showing depraved indifference to human life by engaging in conduct which caused Tami Lynne's death."

Joe Tinning was not suspected of the crimes.

The maximum penalty for second degree murder in New York state is life imprisonment. The minimum penalty is from 15 to 25 years.

On March 19, after spending a month and a half in jail, Mary Beth Tinning was released on $100,000 bail. She immediately instituted court proceedings to have her confession deemed inadmissible evidence at her impending murder trial.

Mary Beth professed that her constitutional rights had been violated when the confessions were obtained. The suppression hearing into this charge was concluded in April. As a result, the details of what was said on the night Mary Beth confessed to detectives, can now be made public.

The first statement, given in narrative from, describes how Mary Beth smothered Timothy, Nathan and Tami, "With a pillow, because I'm not a good mother. I'm not a good mother because of the other children." She also said, "I did not do anything to Jennifer, Joseph, Barbara, Michael, Mary Frances or Jonathan."

In a second question and answer session with detectives, Mary Beth gave more details of Tami's death. She arrived home that night, five days before Christmas in 1985, at about 8:35 p.m., after being out shopping with a friend. Her mother-in-law and father-in-law had been babysitting four-month-old Tami. They, as well as her friend, left at about 9:30 pm. Mary Beth sat in a recliner chair with Tami on her lap. After a while she put the baby to bed.

Mary Beth related, "I tried to give her a bottle, but she didn't want it. She fussed and cried for about a half hour. She finally went to sleep. I then went to bed." Joe came home at 11 p.m. They chatted for a few moments.

"I was about to doze off when Tami woke up and started to cry. I got up and went to the crib and tried to do something with her to get her to stop crying. I finally used the pillow from my bed and put it over head. I did it until she stopped crying." Mary Beth went on, "When I finally lifted the pillow off Tami, she wasn't moving. I put the pillow on the couch and then screamed for Joe and he woke up and I told Joe Tami wasn't breathing."

It was this chilling recital that Mary Beth attempted to suppress. However, a county court judge ruled that her statements would be admissible at her upcoming murder trial. He also ruled that they had been given willingly and voluntarily.

On July 19, 1987, Mary Beth Tinning was found guilty of second degree murder in the case of her infant daughter Tami. She faces a sentence of 25 years to life imprisonment.

266

Jean-Baptiste Troppmann

We are inclined to think multiple murder is a modern phenomenon. Such is not the case. Let's go back in time to 1869, when one of the most despicable killers ever to grace the pages of criminal history made his appearance in Paris, France.

Jean-Baptiste Troppmann was born in the small town of Cernay in Alsace. His father was a mechanic and moderately successful inventor. Jean dropped out of school at age 14 to labor in his father's workshop. When one of his father's inventions was sold to a factory in the Parisian suburb of Pantin, it was necessary for Jean to move to the big city. When a second machine was sold to a firm in Roubaix, young Jean was sent there.

At age 19, Jean met Jean Kinck, a man more than twice his age. To Jean, his new friend oozed success. Kinck owned three homes in Roubaix, a small factory and a pleasant summer home. In addition, his happy marriage to wife Hortense had produced six children: Gustave, 15; Emile, 13; Henri, 10; Achille, 8; Alfred, 6; and Marie, 2.

The very first day Kinck met Jean, he brought him home to meet his family. Thereafter, a close relationship existed between the two men. Despite the difference in their ages, they seemed to enjoy each other's company immensely. Seldom did a day pass that they weren't seen together chatting over an aperitif in a neighborhood cafe. Jean was constantly talking about schemes that would make them both rich. Kinck enjoyed the conversations, but dismissed the ideas as being too far-fetched. Unknown to Kinck, his friend, now in his twenties, had already made up his mind to kill him for his money.

Eventually, Jean came up with a scheme which fascinated Kinck. He claimed he had been put in touch with a gang of coin counterfeiters operating out of a deserted house in Alsace. They were going to disband their business, which had made them wealthy. Jean had offered them 5,000 francs to take over their operation. Kinck's mouth watered. This time he felt Jean's scheme was foolproof. Count him in.

Jean travelled to Bollwiller equipped with a bottle of prussic acid. Kinck joined him there. The two friends set out for the home of Jean's parents in Cernay. Jean arrived alone. He was greeted warmly by his parents, who had no idea their son had poisoned his friend on the way to their home. Jean appeared to be very prosperous. He even had an expensive watch.

Next day, Jean dashed off a note to Mme Kinck. Unfortunately, her husband was unable to write. He had a slight injury to his writing hand and was dictating this note to Jean. In essence, the letter explained their business deal was proceeding famously. Kinck requested that his wife forward 5,500 francs to him in care of the post office in Guebwiller. The moment Hortense received her instructions, she went to the bank, procured the money and posted it as requested.

Jean showed up at the post office, but the stubborn postmaster refused to release the letter because Jean didn't have the proper documentation to accept the mail of Jean Kinck. Jean wrote Hortense in Roubaix, again under the guise of Kinck, advising her that since he was now nowhere near Guebwiller, would she please dispatch Gustave with the proper documentation so Jean could pick up the money at the post office.

Gustave left immediately without the all-important letter, but with his mother's promise that she would send it along as soon as she received it from the bank. Furthermore, Kinck instructed Hortense to meet him in Paris with all the children.

The cunning Troppmann went to Paris and checked in at the Railroad Hotel. Hortense waited a few days until she received the necessary documentation, which she sent along to Gustave, but Gustave had lost his patience and had left for Paris to meet his family. Troppmann met him at the station. The boy dashed off a telegram to his mother, advising her all was well. Then he went off with Jean Troppmann.

In September 1869, Gustave Kinck was stabbed and beaten to death. Jean buried him in a shallow grave near Pantin. Having murdered both father and son, Jean found himself in a complicated scenario of letters, instructions and bogus schemes designed to part the Kinck family from their worldly goods. So far, all his machinations had netted him only a few francs and a gold watch from Jean Kinck's pockets.

Undaunted, Jean sent off a further missive to Mme Kinck, again posing as her husband. He beseeched her to carry with her all pertinent documentation pertaining to their homes, cottage and business. With their friend Jean Troppmann's assistance, they were about to embark on a new and successful life. Hortense, who was pregnant, bundled up the children and headed for Paris. Once there, she went to the Railroad Hotel and inquired if Jean Kinck was registered. Of course Troppmann had registered under her husband's name. Hortense was disappointed to learn from Troppmann that her husband and her son Gustave were at Pantin, but not to worry, he would take them there without delay.

And so the strange journey by horse-drawn enclosed cab began. Inside, Hortense and her five children were together with a human monster in the form of Jean Troppmann. At a deserted spot known as Quatre Chemins, Jean motioned the cabbie to pull up. Jean, Hortense and two of her children started off into the darkness. The three boys stayed in the cab. They chatted with the driver. Twenty-five minutes later, Jean returned alone. He told the boys they were staying in a house down the way and instructed the cabbie to return to Paris.

There, in the fields near Pantin, this most diabolical of killers had dug a grave, into which he had placed the bodies of Hortense and the two children. Within a half hour the remaining Kinck children were murdered and buried in the same grave. At last, Jean Troppmann had the birth certificate and ownership documentation belonging to Jean Kinck. He would immediately start selling his victim's worldly goods. Soon he would sail for America and no one would be the wiser.

Next day, a laborer named Langlois spotted fresh blood on a mound of earth, as well as a handkerchief sticking out of the ground. He called police and, within hours of the foul deed, Jean Troppmann's great plans were in the process of crumbling. Gendarmes uncovered the bodies of Hortense and her five children. All had been brutally stabbed and strangled.

At the scene, police recovered a broken kitchen knife, a pick and a spade, all stained with blood. The proprietor of the hotel where Hortense had stayed with her children gave police a description of the man who had registered as Jean Kinck, the woman's husband. Where was Hortense's husband? We all know he and his eldest son were dead and buried, but the police had no idea the Jean Kinck they were looking for was in reality Jean Troppmann.

It was left to a gendarme in Le Havre to sight Troppmann in a cabaret. The officer asked Jean to accompany him to a police station. While crossing a dock, Jean bolted and fell off the dock into the harbor, hitting his head on the way down. Once back on dry land, it wasn't long before Jean was identified as the man who had posed as Jean Kinck. A few days later, Gustave Kinck's body was uncovered a few yards from those of the rest of the family. Jean Kinck's body was found in Alsace.

Arrogant, defiant Jean stood trial for the murder of the entire Kinck family. The cab driver, the clerks who sold the implements of murder and the postmaster at Guebwiller left little doubt that Jean was the killer. He was found guilty and sentenced to death.

On January 19, 1870, Jean-Baptiste Troppmann's head fell into a basket of bran after Dr. Guillotine's infernal machine had done its job.

Dorothea Waddingham

Dorothea Nancy Waddingham despised working on the family farm located about six miles north of Nottingham, England. She was thrilled when, at age 23, she secured a job at the Burton-on-Trent Workhouse Infirmary. It was here that she obtained her nursing experience, although she never did become a registered nurse. Nurse Waddingham, as she came to be known, was destined to go down in criminal history as one of England's most notorious female killers.

After two years working at the infirmary, Dorothea met Thomas Leech. In 1925, they married. Tommy wasn't that great a catch. He was more than twice Dorothea's age, didn't have two coins to rub together and was sickly. Dorothea spent most of her time working and looking after her husband. During the course of their marriage, Tommy was well enough to sire three children; Edwin, Alan and Mary.

After eight years of this less than ideal existence, Tommy introduced his wife to a friend, Ronald Sullivan. A short time later, generous Tommy invited Ron to move in with him and his family. Tommy didn't care that his wife was planning to make a nursing home out of their modest dwelling on Haydn Rd. in Nottingham. He did co-operate in his own fashion by dying of natural causes. Ron Sullivan stayed on with Dorothea and the kids. Soon after Tommy's demise, Dorothea and her menagerie relocated to 32 Devon Dr., where she went about attempting to build up a nursing home business.

One fine day in 1935, an official of the County Nursing Association called at the house on Devon Dr.

Miss Blagg was constantly looking for adequate accommodation for the chronically ill. She approached Dorothea about two prospective clients — elderly Mrs. Baguley and her daughter, Ada. Mrs. Baguley was a feeble 90-year-old. Ada, 50, suffered from paralysis sclerosis and was grossly overweight. Both women had reached the stage in their lives where they couldn't look after themselves. Miss Blagg struck a deal with Nurse Waddingham and the pair moved into her nursing home. They accepted the arrangement on a trial basis for a month, stipulating that they would stay on if the accommodations and medical attention met their standards.

Three weeks later, Ada and her mother informed Miss Blagg that they were more than pleased with the home and planned to remain there. Several acquaintances visited in the following months and found both women cheerful and content. One touch of sadness befell the home when the only other patient, a Mrs. Kemp, died. In her final days her doctor prescribed morphia tablets, which were to play a large part in events to follow.

Life went on. Nurse Waddingham soon realized that the Baguleys required much more care than she had anticipated, although they were pleasant and obviously happy living at her home. Ada was not without funds. She often stated that these funds were a guarantee that she and her mother would not have to end their days in what was then called a poorhouse. The few thousand pounds and some property had been left to her dear mother. A cousin, Fred Gilbert, was executor and trustee of their wills.

Fred held a very special place in Ada's heart. Some 20 years earlier, they had been engaged to marry. The

273

onset of Ada's illness postponed the wedding until finally, with the spreading of her disease, both knew they would never marry. Fred remained a close friend of Ada's and visited her often.

Some four months after Ada and her mother moved into the nursing home, Ada made a new will, leaving her entire estate to Nurse Waddingham in exchange for accommodation for herself and her mother for the rest of their lives. Ada's lawyer attempted to talk her out of such a will, pointing out that if anything unforeseen happened to Nurse Waddingham, she might find herself and her mother in a precarious position. Ada insisted, but did allow her lawyer to add Ron Sullivan to the will as an equal recipient of her estate.

Six days after this document was signed, Mrs. Baguley died and was buried at Caunton Church. All the participants in our drama attended the sad affair. Fred Gilbert guided Ada's wheelchair into the churchyard. When it was over, Ada returned to the nursing home. Months passed. Ada's good friends in the area continued to visit her at the home. On September 10, 1935, an old friend spent some time with Ada in the garden. The next day, around 9 a.m., Ron Sullivan called for medical assistance. Dr. Manfield arrived after 12 a.m. to find Ada dead. He attributed death to cerebral hemmorhage due to cardiovascular degeneration. Ada's body was scheduled to be cremated according to her wishes.

The first suspicion regarding Ada's death was raised when a crematorium official received a note allegedly written in advance by the deceased. It read: "It is my last wish that my relatives not know of my death." The unusual request prompted Dr. Cyril Banks, Medical Officer of Health for Nottingham, to institute an investigation into Ada's death.

A post-mortem examination was conducted. The results indicated that Dr. Manfield's stated cause of death had been wrong. Ada had died from morphine poisoning. It was found in her stomach, spleen, kidneys, liver and heart. There was no doubt Ada had been poisoned and grave suspicion that Mrs. Baguley might also have been poisoned. Her body was exhumed. Once again, morphine was evident.

The day after this last distasteful fact was made public, Fred Gilbert committed suicide. It is believed Fred had become depressed at the untimely deaths and may have felt had he married Ada, both mother and daughter would still be alive.

Once the conditions of Ada's will became known, Nurse Waddingham was immediately suspected of double murder. She was arrested and stood trial for murder. Prosecution attorneys leaned heavily on the fact that morphine tablets were in the home after Mrs. Kemp died. Doctors testified that at no time had they prescribed morphine for Ada or her mother.

Dorothea Waddingham was found guilty of murder. She was hanged on April 16, 1936 at Winson Green Prison in Birmingham.

George Kent Wallace

Some criminals never reveal the reasons for their perverse and violent actions. Quite possibly they don't know the deep-seated trigger mechanism which activates their aberrant behavior. Such a criminal was George Kent Wallace.

The series of strange murders began on the evening of February 17, 1987, when 15-year-old Bill Domer was sent to the grocery store by his parents to purchase snacks. The Fort Smith, Arkansas lad never returned home. Five days later, his body was found by small boys playing near a pond adjacent to Leard Cemetery, just yards over the state line in Oklahoma. Bill's fully clothed body was lying face down in seven inches of water. He had been shot twice in the back. Despite the best efforts of the police, months and years passed without any concrete clues being uncovered which would lead to the killer.

Four years later, on November 11, 1990, Mark McLaughlin, 14, left his home in nearby Van Buren to pick up a loaf of bread at the neighborhood grocery store. He was last seen riding his bicycle towards the store. Next morning, a fisherman found Mark's body in the same pond where Bill Domer had been found years earlier. Like Bill, Mark had been shot in the back. He also had bruises on his buttocks, which pathologists felt were the result of a beating.

Only 12 days after the tragic death of Mark McLaughlin, another boy, Alonzo Cadeiz, attended a basketball game at Westark Community College in Fort Smith. After the game, friends saw him riding away on his bicycle. Alonzo was never seen alive again.

Two weeks passed. Authorities were frantically attempting to get a handle on the individual who was preying on Fort Smith boys when Chris Ferguson, 18, another Westark Community College student, finished his work at a grocery store in Van Buren. Chris jumped in his pickup and was about to drive away when a four-door 1981 Chevrolet pulled up behind him. A well-dressed man approached Chris and flashed ID indicating he was a police officer. The man in the dark blue suit asked for Chris' driver's licence before ordering him to get out of his vehicle and lock the doors. Chris complied.

The officer placed handcuffs on Chris' wrists and fastened leg irons around his ankles. He then led Chris into his Chevrolet. Chris studied the interior of the vehicle, noting there was no police radio or anything else to identify the car as a police vehicle. As they drove along, he grew suspicious. When he asked why he was being treated in this manner, the man told him he was a strong suspect in a grocery store robbery in Booneville.

The Chevy pulled off the road. The well-dressed man climbed into the back seat, pulled down Chris' pants and inflicted a severe beating to his buttocks with a stick, which Chris thought might have been a broom handle. Chris, who stood five-feet, two-inches tall and weighed barely 120 pounds, cringed in pain. Finally, his assailant tired and pulled up Chris' pants. He forced the hapless youth to walk ahead of him through the woods. Chris was well aware of the two younger boys who had been murdered. He was sure this man was no police officer, but the mad killer the police were seeking. As they trudged through the woods, the strain proved to be too much. Chris whirled and shouted, "Are you going to shoot me?" The man opened his suit coat, indicating he wasn't carrying a gun. His captive was ordered to keep walking.

Without warning, Chris felt the poker-hot sting of a knife being plunged into his back over and over again. Instinctively he felt the best thing he could do was play dead. He fell to the ground, attempted to hold his breath and let his body go limp. Chris' attacker undid his handcuffs and leg irons before trying to remove his pants. Chris decided to act. He jumped to his feet and ran for his life. The man ran after the terrified teenager, but Chris made it to the parked Chevrolet, praying the key would be in the ignition. As luck would have it, the key was there. Chris roared away, leaning on the horn all the way to attract attention. He stopped at the first house, where the occupants called police.

Chris was rushed to hospital. He had been stabbed five times in the back and once in the arm. Although he had lost a lot of blood, he survived. Meanwhile, police had no difficulty picking up George Kent Wallace trudging along the highway.

Wallace, a part-time truck driver, also ran a mail-order business in Fort Smith. Since arriving in the community, he had served a year in jail for forging bogus figures on credit cards used by his mail-order customers. Wallace also had a prison record before settling in Fort Smith. Back in 1966, he had been convicted of abducting a police officer. For this offence, he was sentenced to 15 years imprisonment, but was released after serving nine years.

Shortly after his release, Wallace was convicted of kidnapping and assault with a deadly weapon. For this infraction, he received a sentence of eight to 10 years, but was paroled after serving only three years. Significantly, the kidnapping charges for which

Wallace was convicted involved the paddling of his victims across their buttocks.

In addition, Arkansas authorities learned that Wallace had been suspected but never charged in the abduction and murder of two young boys in the Winston-Salem area. These two homicides were still unsolved.

The dates of all the attacks and murders coincided with dates when Wallace was not in prison. All the paraphernalia used during Chris Ferguson's ordeal was recovered. Police were able to locate handcuffs, leg irons, flashlights and the ID Wallace had used to pose as a police officer.

On December 20, 1990, with George Wallace safely behind bars, the body of Alonzo Cadeiz was discovered in a nearby gas well drilling pond. Alonzo had been stabbed in the back and beaten across the buttocks.

Wallace was charged with attempted first-degree murder and kidnapping in the Chris Ferguson case. He confessed to this crime and also the murders of Bill Domer and Mark McLaughlin, relating in detail the abduction, beating and murder of both boys. He refused to discuss his own youth or how he had developed the weird perversion of spanking young boys and then killing them.

A myriad of charges were eventually brought against Wallace. He received a 60-year sentence for the abduction and attempted murder of Chris Ferguson. For the Domer and McLaughlin murders, Wallace was sentenced to death. Because these bodies were found across the Oklahoma State line, George Kent Wallace currently resides with 125 other inmates on Death Row in McAlester, Oklahoma.

Chris Ferguson, by escaping the clutches of this madman, is believed to have saved many lives. He has received several civic rewards for his actions.

David Wood

Authorities were sure they knew the identity of the rapist killer, but couldn't quite prove it.

Marjorie Knox, 14, of Chaparrel, New Mexico, shouted over her shoulder to her parents that she was going to the convenience store at the corner of her Byrum St. home to purchase a soft drink. That was on September 14, 1987. Marjorie never made it to the store and has never been seen since.

Six months later, on March 7, 1988, Melissa Alaniz, 13, of nearby El Paso, Texas, told her mother she would be back in time for dinner. She was going out to play with some other kids down the street. Melissa has never been seen again.

The heat of summer descended on the dry desert country just north of the Mexican border. It was quite possible that there was no connection between the disappearances of the two girls, although a parent of each girl was employed with Rockwell International, the giant aerospace company.

The terror which came with the knowledge that a serial killer could be in their midst accelerated on June 2, when Desiree Wheatley, 15, went missing. Desiree left her parents El Paso apartment to purchase an ice cream. She never returned. An investigation into her disappearance uncovered the fact that the young girl had chatted with some friends on the street after she left home. One youngster saw her talking to a man who had pulled up in a pickup truck. When she looked again, both the truck and Desiree were gone.

Panic spread throughout the area, when only three days after Desiree's disappearance, Karen Baker, 20, simply vanished off the streets of El Paso as she walked to visit a friend.

Whoever was plucking girls off the streets sped up the frequency of the abductions. The third girl to disappear that June was Cheryl Vasquez-Dismukes, 19, who didn't return after leaving her apartment to purchase a pack of cigarettes.

The citizens of El Paso and surrounding communities were terrified. They purchased weapons and locks, although there was no evidence that the killer had ever entered a home to abduct a victim. Detectives knew precious little about the man, who seemed to operate like a phantom in broad daylight. They felt he might be driving a pickup truck and he could have black hair. It was theorized that because the victims had not cried out, they might have been acquainted with the abductor.

The reign of terror continued. Maria Casio, 24, who had travelled from Addison, Texas to visit friends in El Paso, disappeared after she left her friends' home. A month later, two water company employees came across her body in a shallow grave in the desert at the edge of the city.

Police were quickly at the scene, searching the area for clues. Instead of clues, they found another body, that of Karen Baker, 20, who had been missing since the previous June. Both women had been strangled to death. From their partially nude bodies and the position of their clothing, it was ascertained that they had been raped before being killed.

Two weeks later, hikers, aware of the rash of disappearances, came across a patch of disturbed earth which looked suspiciously like a grave. They brushed away the earth, revealing the body of Desiree

Wheatley, the little girl who had left her parents' home to buy an ice cream. Near Desiree's body, police uncovered the body of yet another victim, Angelica Frausto, 17, who had been reported missing on September 6.

An investigation into the backgrounds of the victims uncovered several connecting links between the girls. Some of the girls had attended the same high school. Three of the victims' parents were employed at Rockwell International and two of the girls, Wheatley and Knox, had known each other. Police felt that the connecting links could be nothing more than coincidence. Unable to overlook any possibility, this tangent of the investigation was vigorously pursued.

Police received the first break in the case when two rather unsavory women came forward with their stories. Both had been previously charged with prostitution and drug-related crimes. They felt compelled to tell their stories for the good of the community, although they realized, because of their records, that they might not be believed. One woman, whose name has not been made public, told of getting into a pickup truck on an El Paso street. The driver pulled out a knife and drove into the desert, making his intentions clear to the terrified prostitute. Convinced that she would be killed, the woman jumped from the moving vehicle. She was unhurt, except for cuts and bruises, and managed to hitchhike back to El Paso.

Next day she told her best friend of her ordeal. As she did so, her friend confessed that she too had experienced a similar incident. A man picked her up and pulled out a gun. He drove her into the desert, threw her a shovel and ordered her to start digging. She was convinced she was digging her own grave, when both she and her abductor heard strangers approaching. The man ordered her back into the truck and drove into the city, where he raped her. Then, inexplicably, he let her go.

Both women said they were reluctant to tell their stories, but felt they might be the only ones who could identify the serial killer suspect. The description they gave police fit a known sex criminal, 30-year-old David Wood. Wood had once been convicted of raping a 13-year-old girl and later, a 19-year-old. For those crimes, he received two 20 year sentences, but was paroled in January 1987, after serving seven years in prison. He was released eight months before the rash of disappearances in El Paso.

Wood was placed in a police lineup. Both women positively identified him as the man who had abducted them. Wood was charged with kidnapping and rape. He claimed that he was totally innocent and was not the serial killer.

Police had little to directly tie Wood to the series of murders. He claimed, "I am a lover, not a killer." Wood has been tried for the abduction of the two prostitutes and the rape of one of them and has been found guilty of sexual assault. The Texas jury took only 40 minutes to reach their verdict.

David Wood has been sentenced to 50 years imprisonment, the maximum sentence allowed by law. With his arrest and incarceration, the rash of murders in and around El Paso came to an abrupt end.

Graham Young

As I drove into the peaceful village of Bovingdon, it was early in the morning. The fog was lifting from the rolling English countryside. I couldn't help but think of Graham Young driving up to work over these very same roads, his mind contemplating how much antimony he would administer to his fellow employees. Would Diana Smart get enough to send her home for a few days? Would Peter Buck be back today? If so, it just might be his turn for a dose.

But the Graham Young story doesn't start in this quaint English village. It begins in Honeyport Lane Maternity Hospital, North London, on September 7, 1947; for that was the day Graham was born.

Molly Young didn't have an easy pregnancy. She had pleurisy while carrying Graham, and although her new son grew to be a healthy baby, it was discovered that Molly had contracted tuberculosis. She died two days before Christmas when Graham was three months old.

Fred Young, a machine setter by trade, was beside himself with grief at the loss of his wife. He decided to keep his little family as close to him as possible without the benefit of a mother. Fred had one other child, a daughter, Winnifred, who was eight-years-old at the time of her mother's death. Winnie and her father went to live with Fred's mother at Links Rd., while Graham moved in with an aunt and uncle at 768 North Circular Rd. in the Neasdon section of North London. The two addresses were not that far apart, and the little family managed to get together each weekend.

Three years later, Fred Young met another lady named Molly. At the age of 33, Fred calculated that he could still have a chance for a happy and contented life with a new wife and his two children. He married Molly, purchased the house at 768 North Circular Rd., and moved in with Winnie and three-year-old Graham.

As Graham grew up it was noted that he wasn't a joiner. He read incessantly. Other than playing with his sister and a cousin, he kept pretty much to himself. Throughout his early years in school, he was considered to be well above average in his studies. His stepmother, Molly, doted on Graham, who appeared to return her love with genuine affection.

At the age of nine, Graham Young was experimenting with varnish and nail polish. He was not doing anything malicious with these substances, but experimenting with them to ascertain the qualities inherent in various products. For a nine-year-old child, many would think this advanced element of curiosity in Graham's makeup to be a very admirable trait. When Molly found acid and ether in Graham's room, she rightly felt that her son's interest had become abnormal for a child his age. Upon being questioned, Graham told his mother that he had found the substances in garbage thrown out by the local drugstore. Later she found books on witchcraft and the Nazi party in Graham's room.

By the time Graham was 12, his teachers believed that he had an outstanding future in the field of chemistry. Unknown to them, he was poisoning rats and performing autopsies on their bodies. His family was continually amazed at his advanced knowledge of chemicals. They could show Graham a detergent or waxing agent and he would rhyme off the chemicals which made up the product and what interaction was involved to make the substances perform as advertised.

At the age of 13, Graham knew the exact quantities of various poisons which could prove to be fatal. He also knew the effects of administering small quantities of certain poisons over a prolonged period of time. In fact, Graham was now an expert on the subject of poison. While everyone thought him a quiet little boy, no one knew the extent of his weird obsession.

In April 1961, Graham gave a cock-and-bull story to the chemist in his neighborhood, and managed to purchase 25 grams of antimony. He signed the poison book with the fictitious name M.E. Evans, and gave a phony address. Out of his allowance received from his father, and with money from odd jobs performed at a local cafe, Graham continued to purchase quantities of antimony.

His closest school chum, Chris Williams, remembers that Graham often showed him a vial of poison. Chris thought it was a great joke, somewhat akin to the country boy showing his pet frog to his buddies.

Once the boys had a falling out, as little boys often do. A few days later Chris had severe stomach pains. He had to leave school for the day. All through the spring and summer of 1961, Chris suffered from severe stomach pains which were often accompanied by vomiting. Later he realized that his discomfort always followed those occasions when he and Graham skipped school together. On those days Graham was in the habit of sharing his sandwiches with Chris.

Chris' stomach pains and headaches became so bad that he was forced to visit his family doctor, Dr. Lancelot Wills. The doctor couldn't find anything specifically wrong with Chris, but thought his headaches were migraines.

One day, while cleaning Graham's room, Molly found a bottle of antimony. She had no idea what it was, but clearly understood the skull and crossbones on the label. She told Fred of her discovery. They both faced Graham and forbade him to have such dangerous substances in the house. Molly then went around to the chemist shop named on the bottle, and, in no uncertain terms, told the chemist never to sell Graham any dangerous materials. Unknown to his parents, Graham merely changed chemists.

It wasn't long after this incident that Molly Young began suffering from an upset stomach. She felt weak and lethargic. She often discussed her illness with Graham. It was his custom to have tea with his mother every day after school. Finally, Molly became so ill, she was taken to hospital, where she made a speedy recovery. Her illness was thought to be an ulcer. Poison was never suspected.

It is interesting to note that once antimony has passed through the body, no trace can be detected. Molly's recovery was to be temporary.

One day Winnie, now an attractive 22-year-old girl with a steady boyfriend, collapsed outside a cinema. She, too, was having periodic spells of abdominal pain accompanied by vomiting. This most recent attack set Winnie thinking. Why hadn't it occurred to her before? Her kid brother with his silly chemistry experiments. No doubt he had used the family dishes to perform the experiments. Some toxic substance might have adhered to a cup, causing Molly and her to become ill. She decided to speak to her father.

Fred Young didn't believe that Graham would bring poison into the house after being told to keep the terrible stuff away. Nevertheless, Fred gave Graham a real tongue lashing.

Soon Fred came down with a severe case of cramps. He never complained much, because at the same time his wife Molly became seriously ill. This time she had a complete new set of symptoms. She woke up on Easter Saturday, 1962, with a sensation of pins and needles in her hands and feet. Graham was concerned and solicitous towards his stepmother. It was decided to rush Molly to the hospital.

Once in the hospital Molly said to one of the doctors, "I hope you're not going to be long about this, because I've got my husband's dinner to get." Within minutes of making this frivolous remark, Molly Young, aged 38, was dead. For about a year, Graham had been feeding Molly antimony and observing the results. On the evening before Molly died, Graham had laced a trifle with twenty grains of thallium. It was this massive dose which caused her death. Graham probably didn't know it, but he had just become the first person in England ever to commit murder by the administration of deadly, tasteless, odorless thallium.

A post mortem failed to reveal the true cause of death. The following Thursday, Molly was cremated. Graham Young, at the age of 14, had committed the perfect murder. When mourners gathered at the family residence to pay their respects, Graham doctored a sandwich with a small quantity of antimony. One of his mother's relatives became violently ill. Graham was just having a little fun.

A few days after his wife's funeral, Fred Young suffered a series of stomach pains accompanied by violent bouts of vomiting. Finally his daughter Winnie forced him to see their family physician, Dr. Wills. The doctor could find no reason for the illness, but was startled when, at the conclusion of the examination, Fred collapsed on the office floor. He was rushed to Willisden General Hospital, where Molly had died less than two weeks before.

After spending two days in hospital, often comforted by his son who visited him constantly, Fred Young began to feel better. Graham seemed to enjoy himself around the hospital, amazing doctors by his knowledge of things medical. Fred was taken home, but in a few days his pains became so severe that Winnie rushed her father back to the hospital.

That same night doctors were surprised when extensive tests confirmed that Fred was suffering from antimony poisoning.

We must pause here to keep in mind that Graham was a quiet, studious youngster of 14. It was difficult for his family to accept the facts as we are able to do from the benefit of hindsight. Graham's father was the first to actually believe that his son had been administering poison to the entire family for more than a year. Doctors told him that one more dose of antimony would have proven fatal. Fred Young recovered, but has a permanently damaged liver as a result of his son's handiwork. He also lives today with the realization that Graham was responsible for his stepmother's death.

While Fred Young lingered in hospital with his dark suspicions, direct action came from another source. Graham's chemistry teacher, Mr. Hughes, heard of Mr. Young being rushed to hospital so soon after his wife's death. Lately, Mr. Hughes had wondered about Graham's lack of interest in his chemistry experiments. It appeared that the boy was obsessed with experiments using poisons, and recording data derived from his experiments in a notebook. Mr. Hughes decided to stay late at school and search Graham's desk. He found several bottles of poison.

Recalling Chris Williams' illness, Mr. Hughes felt the whole thing was just too much. He contacted the headmaster of the school and together they went to see Dr. Wills. The three men exchanged notes and, for the first time, the magnitude of Graham's poisonous endeavors came to light.

They arranged for a psychiatrist, posing as a guidance counsellor, to consult with Graham. Graham loved to display his knowledge of pharmacology and had a learned discussion with the psychiatrist, who was amazed at the lad's understanding of the subject. He went straight to the police with his suspicions.

Next day, Detective Inspector Edward Crabbe searched Graham's room. He found quantities of antimony, thallium, digitalis, iodine, atropine, and barium chloride. When Graham was searched, police found a vial of antimony, as well as two bottles of thallium, in his shirt. Later he referred to the vial of antimony as his little friend. Taken to jail the following morning, Graham revealed his entire career as a poisoner to the police.

Graham Young was unique. Obviously his age alone set him apart from most killers, but, above all, the fact that he lacked any motive made his crimes different. He did not dislike the people he poisoned. They were given poison specifically because they were close at hand and could be observed. Graham was experimenting, much as a scientist does with guinea pigs.

On July 5, 1962, Graham was tried in London's Old Bailey, one of the youngest ever to appear in the famous old court. He was charged with poisoning his father, his sister, and his schoolchum, Chris Williams. The charge of murdering his stepmother was not pressed. Her ashes were scattered, and it was believed nothing could be gained by bringing further charges against such a young boy.

Dr. Christopher Fysh, a psychiatrist attached to the Ashford Remand Centre, where Graham had been housed awaiting his trial, told of his conclusions after having extensive conversations with Graham. He quoted Graham as telling him, "I am missing my antimony. I am missing the power it gives me." The doctor elaborated on Graham's knowledge of drugs, and stated that on several occasions Graham had corrected him in minor areas when the properties of various drugs were discussed. Dr. Fysh suggested that Graham was obsessed with the sense of power his poisons gave him. In the doctor's opinion, given the chance, Graham would continue to experiment on humans. Dr. Fysh thought Graham should be confined to a maximum security hospital. As a result, he was sentenced to Broadmoor for a period of 15 years.

In July 1962, the gates of the ominous old brick structure closed behind 14-year-old Graham Young. He was one of the youngest patients ever to be admitted, but not the youngest. That distinction belonged to Bill Giles, who died there at the age of 87. He had been convicted of setting fire to a hayrick at the age of 10 in 1885. Giles had spent 77 years in Broadmoor, and coincidentally died three months before Graham was admitted.

About a month after Graham arrived at Broadmoor, an incident occurred which, all things considered, gives one room for thought.

John Berridge was a 23-year-old patient who had

killed his parents. Quite suddenly one day he went into convulsions, collapsed and died. A post mortem revealed that his death was due to cyanide poisoning. The inquiry which followed established that no cyanide was kept at Broadmoor. However, the investigation also revealed that laurel bushes, from which an expert could extract cyanide, grew adjacent to the institution.

Several patients immediately confessed to poisoning Berridge. Among those confessing was Graham Young. He was the only one who could explain in detail the process involved in extracting cyanide from laurel bushes. The authorities chose not to believe any of the confessions. They leaned towards the theory that somehow the poison was smuggled into the institution. The Berridge case remains unsolved to this day.

At first Graham Young, the lad from the reputable suburb of North London, had difficulty adjusting to the maximum security institution. But as the years went by, he seemed to respond to psychiatric treatment. Dr. Edgar Udwin held high hopes for a complete recovery and early release for his young patient.

Meanwhile, Graham's family regarded his poisonous ways as mental illness. His sister Winnie, cousins, aunts, and uncles all felt that Graham had been sick and was now on the road to recovery. His father Fred had a difficult time accepting this live and let live view. He could forgive Graham for almost everything, but he could never forget that his own son had studied and apparently enjoyed the death of his poor wife Molly.

After consulting with Winnie, it was decided by Dr. Udwin that Graham be released for one week in November 1970. During the eight years of Graham's incarceration at Broadmoor, Winnie had married and was now the mother of a baby girl. She and her husband decided, in conjunction with Dr. Udwin, that no precautions against poison be taken during the week of Graham's visit.

Winnie now lived in a fashionable suburb of Hemel Hempstead, a city of 85,000, located about 30 miles north of London. Graham visited for the week, and the experiment was a huge success. With his doctor's consent and his family's urging, he visited at Christmas time for another week and was a delight to have in the house.

On February 4, 1971, 23-year-old Graham was released from Broadmoor. He was sent directly to Slough to the government resettlement centre for 13 weeks, training as a stockboy and shipper.

Nearing the completion of his course, on April 24, 1971, Graham performed two tasks which were to have far reaching effects. He applied for a job as a storekeeper at John Hadland Photographic Instrumentation Ltd., Bovingdon, Hertfordshire. Then he went to the centre of London, walked into a drugstore, and purchased 25 grams of antimony.

It was a stroke of luck when Graham's application for employment was accepted at Hadland's in Bovingdon, a quaint rural village only three miles from Hemel Hempstead.

Graham would have the steadying influence of a member of his family, but would still live and work in an independent environment. He took a room at 20 Maynards Rd. in Hemel Hempstead. His landlord, Mohammed Saddiq, a native of Pakistan, had no idea a murderer and former inmate of Broadmoor was his new roomer. At the time Mr. Saddiq didn't speak one word of English.

Seven years later, when I knocked on the door of 29 Maynards Rd., Mr. Saddiq well remembered his infamous tenant. He led me up the stairs to the room Graham had occupied. He pointed out the windowsill where Graham had stocked enough poison to kill scores of people. There, in a corner, was the bed under which Graham kept his diary of death. Mr. Saddiq assured me that his star roomer never ate at his home, nor had he ever entered his kitchen. Seven years before, Mr. Saddiq had considered himself fortunate to have such a quiet, well behaved roomer in his home.

I drove the three miles to the village of Bovingdon, and met with a director of Hadland's, Terry Johnson. Mr. Johnson explained how Graham Young became an employee of the firm. Young answered an advertisement and was granted an interview. He was highly recommended by the training school, having just completed a course in storekeeping, the exact position the firm was attempting to fill.

He accounted for the previous nine years by telling Mr. Foster of Hadland's that he'd had a nervous breakdown upon the death of his mother, but was now completely cured. Before hiring Graham, Mr. Foster checked out his story.

The government training centre got in touch with Dr. Udwin, the psychiatrist who was instrumental in securing Graham's release from Broadmoor. He obligingly sent along a letter confirming that Young was normal and competent in every way. At no time was Hadland's informed that Young had been a patient at Broadmoor, or that he had been convicted of being a poisoner.

On May 10, 1971, Graham went to work. He became assistant storekeeper at a salary of £24 a week.

The one hundred employees at Hadland's are a friendly, cheerful group. Mr. Johnson, who showed me the premises, was called Terry by everyone we met. Hadland's exports expensive industrial photographic equipment all over the world. The firm received some measure of satisfaction from its mention in Guinness Book of World Records. They have produced a camera which takes 600 million pictures a second.

The men in the storeroom welcomed Graham in his new position. Within days he had gained the reputation of being a bit quiet, but certainly a nice enough bloke. His boss, Bob Egle, was 59 years old and looking forward to retirement. Bob had been married 39 years. He found out that his new assistant loved to hear of his wartime experiences, especially his evacuation from Dunkirk.

Fred Biggs was 60 and a senior employee in the Works in Progress Department. The two older men liked Graham Young.

Jethro Batt worked side-by-side with Graham in the stores. Each day after work Jethro would give Graham a lift the three miles back to Hemel Hempstead.

Twice a day May Bartlett wheeled a tea wagon down the long hall to the stores area. Members of the staff would then fetch their tea from the wagon. That is, before Graham came to work at Hadland's. Soon it became customary for Graham to pick up the tea from the wagon and distribute it to his fellow employees in the stores.

About a month after Graham started working at Hadland's, his boss Bob Egle became ill. He took a few days off work, but the pains in his stomach persisted. On June 18, he and his wife took a week's vacation at Great Yarmouth. The time off seemed to work wonders.

Bob appeared so much better when he returned.

Two days before Bob was due back, Graham had travelled to London and purchased 25 grams of thallium. Within 24 hours of stating that he was feeling just great again after his vacation, Bob Egle took terribly ill at work. He went home, complaining of numbness in his fingers. Later he began to stagger. By morning the weight of the sheets on his bed caused him excruciating pain.

On successive days Bob Egle was transferred from West Herts Hospital in Hemel Hempstead to the intensive care unit at St. Albans City Hospital. He lingered in great pain for eight days before dying.

Back at Hadland's, everyone was concerned about the well-liked boss of the stores passing away so suddenly. None seemed to take it any harder than the new man, Graham Young.

A post mortem was performed on Bob Egle. Death was attributed to bronco-pneumonia in conjunction with polyneuritis. The following Monday, several members of the staff indicated a desire to attend Egle's funeral. It was decided that the managing director, Mr. Geoffrey Foster, would attend representing management, while Graham Young would represent the staff. The two men travelled together to the funeral. Foster remembers being surprised at Young's intimate knowledge of the medical diagnosis surrounding Egle's death.

Diana Smart, a fill-in employee in the stores section at Hadland's, didn't feel well all that summer. Nothing severe, but she was in enough discomfort to force her to go home several days during that July and August.

In September, Peter Buck, the import export manager, noticed that he always felt queasy after tea time. A few weeks later Diana Smart's attacks became more severe. Around this time Jethro Batt also became ill. One day he accepted a cup of tea from Graham and then gave him a lift to Hemel Hempstead. Next day Batt couldn't raise himself out of bed. Pains racked his stomach and chest. In the ensuing days his hair began to fall out in large tufts. He suffered hallucinations and became so distressed that he wanted to kill himself. Batt was admitted to hospital. Unknown to him or his doctors, the fact that he was removed from Graham Young and his poisonous ways saved his life. He gradually recovered.

In the meantime, David Tilson experienced violent stomach pains accompanied by vomiting. He was rushed to St. Albans Hospital, where he too started to lose his hair. After a short while, he began to recover and was discharged.

It seems that everyone at Hadland's had taken ill. By now the death of Bob Egle had the entire staff on edge. Could the outbreak of the strange undiagnosed illness be the same thing that killed Bob?

On a weekend early in November, the stores department at Hadland's was sorely understaffed. Bob Egle was dead. Both Tilson and Batt were off sick. Fred Biggs and his wife came in on a weekend to help Graham Young catch up. Graham made tea that Saturday for Biggs. Next morning Fred could hardly move. He would never return to work. Twenty days later Fred Biggs was dead.

By now, as one can well imagine, rumors were running rampant through the Hadland's plant. For some time previous to the current outbreak of sickness in the area, a virus had on occasion swept through Bovingdon, causing stomach complaints. These outbreaks were often blamed on the Bovingdon Bug.

To quell the rumors and suspicions of the employees, the management of Hadland's decided to call in Dr. Robert Hynd, Medical Officer of Health for the Hemel Hempstead area. Dr. Hynd inspected the plant and could find no cause for the wave of illness. Despite the doctor's statement that the cause of the illness didn't originate in the plant, rumors still persisted. They ranged from toxic chemicals being used in the manufacturing processes to medieval curses. After Fred Biggs died, some men even considered leaving Hadland's.

Management took another stab at coming up with the solution to the riddle. They called in the local general practitioner, Dr. Iain Anderson, to have an informal, morale-boosting chat with the employees.

Everyone had gathered in the cafeteria to hear Dr. Anderson. He explained that the authorities had ruled out radiation. They also checked out thallium, which was sometimes used in the manufacture of index lenses such as those manufactured at Hadland's. However, Hadland's did not keep thallium on the premises, so this agent had been dismissed as a possible cause of the sickness. The doctor leaned heavily toward a particularly strong strain of the Bovingdon Bug as being at the bottom of all the trouble. He assured the employees that the authorities were doing everything possible to isolate the cause of the dreadful sickness.

At the conclusion of his talk, the doctor inquired if there were any questions. Dr. Anderson was amazed when one employee, Graham Young, posed complicated questions regarding heavy metal poisoning and its effects. The doctor had a hard time getting the young man to sit down. The meeting was hastily brought to a close.

Dr. Anderson later made it a point to find Young and

pursue the subject of poison. Again, he was dumbfounded at Young's detailed knowledge. Who was Graham Young, anyhow? Dr. Anderson and the chairman of the board, John Hadland, discussed the matter. Hadland called in the authorities, who checked Young's record at Scotland Yard. It revealed that he had been released just six months earlier from Broadmoor, where he had been sentenced for poisoning.

In Graham's room at 29 Maynards Rd., police uncovered his diary, detailing the dates and quantities of poison he had administered to Hadland employees. Graham Young had been playing God. He chose that some should die, while others should live. All were observed during their illness.

Young confessed to all his crimes, and to this day has never shown any remorse for the suffering he caused. All tests and examinations have indicated that he has above average intelligence, and is, in the legal sense, perfectly sane.

Young received several sentences of life imprisonment for his crimes. His victims, some of whom still live and work in the Hemel Hempstead area, want to forget Graham Young.

As I prepared to leave the Hadland's plant with its airy, cheery atmosphere, I asked director Terry Johnson, who had lived through the terror which was Graham Young, how in a sentence he would describe what went on there.

He answered without hesitation: "It was unbelievable."

more thrilling crime from

MAX HAINES

the collected works of max haines

Volumes 1, II and III

Each of Max Haines' popular collector's anthologies brings together over 150 tales of murder and mayhem in a single sensational edition, comprised of tales from his *True Crime Stories* books. Join Max as he recounts crimes both famous and little known, including scurrilous scams, fabulous frauds, raucous robberies and macabre murders.

Max Haines' twice-weekly "Crime Flashback" column made its first appearance in the Toronto Sun in 1972 and has since covered over 1500 cases of infamous murders, crimes and assorted scams. The column is now syndicated in 40 newspapers across Canada, and across the globe.

from PENGUIN BOOKS

MAX HAINES

Multiple Murderers

Volume 1

Helter Skelter. Silence of the Lambs. Natural
Born Killers. What is our fascination with mass
murderers? In this intriguing volume, crime
guru Max Haines collects an array of accounts of
the world's most notorious multiple murderers.
Some of the names will be immediately familiar
— the Boston Strangler, Son of Sam, and the
Reverend Jim Jones — while other, less publicized
villains committed their horrendous deeds in an
array of foreign locales. Told in the inimitable style
of Canada's master of mayhem, this is a fiendish
collection of repeat killers from throughout
the annals of history.

A PENGUIN BOOK

paging Doctor Death...

MAX HAINES

Doctors Who Kill

This anthology of true crime recollections is comprised
of over forty tales of murdering MDs from around the
world — men and women who have abused their
trusted positions to take lives instead of save them.
Max returns to the scene of some of the most notorious
murders perpetuated by doctors over the past 150 years.
Doctors who killed for love or money; doctors who
disposed of inconvenient wives and lovers; doctors who
poisoned their way into the annals of crime. Written
with the wit and attention to fascinating detail that
have become the hallmarks of Max Haines' popular
crime anthologies, this unsettling new volume takes a
chilling look at some of the most dangerous members
of the noble profession — doctors who kill.

A PENGUIN BOOK

stranger than fiction!

MAX HAINES

True Crime Stories

Volumes 1, II, III, IV, V

"Short, snappy and well-written, Haines's
stories will especially appeal to fans of such
TV programs as *A Current Affair, Hard Copy,
Unsolved Mysteries* and *Inside Edition*."
— *Ottawa Citizen*

What was the true story of the chilling Atlanta child
murders? Of the facts behind the movie Mississippi
Burning? Of Charles Manson's reign of terror? Return to
the scene of the crime as Max leads us through the most
remarkable criminal investigations of our time. With help
from a cast of blunderers, bigamists, serial killers and
cannibals, Max does it again, in five collections of
sometimes obscure, always fascinating tales of
misconduct and murder, sure to make you shiver.

PENGUIN BOOKS